John Gill

Systems of Education

A history and criticism of the principles, methods, organization, and moral

discipline advocated by eminent educationists

John Gill

Systems of Education
A history and criticism of the principles, methods, organization, and moral discipline advocated by eminent educationists

ISBN/EAN: 9783337312084

Printed in Europe, USA, Canada, Australia, Japan

Cover: Foto ©ninafisch / pixelio.de

More available books at **www.hansebooks.com**

SYSTEMS OF EDUCATION:

A History and Criticism

OF THE

PRINCIPLES, METHODS, ORGANIZATION, AND
MORAL DISCIPLINE ADVOCATED BY
EMINENT EDUCATIONISTS.

BY

JOHN GILL,

PROFESSOR OF EDUCATION, NORMAL COLLEGE, CHELTENHAM
ENGLAND. AUTHOR OF "INTRODUCTORY TEXT-BOOK
TO SCHOOL EDUCATION," ETC.

BOSTON
D. C. HEATH & CO., PUBLISHERS
1889

PREFACE

TO

FOURTEENTH EDITION.

THE Notes to the present Edition have been revised throughout, and a few passages unnoticed in former editions have been explained. The references to Keightley's Mythology have been replaced by short notes, which will be found to contain what is necessary for the understanding of the text. Where more information is required, the Classical Dictionary may be consulted.

April, 1878.

PREFACE.

IN the year 1852, the Syllabus for Students in Training Colleges, issued by the Committee of Council on Education, required that they should be instructed in the Systems of Education that had been in use in this country. It thus became the Author's duty, in that and following years, to explore the field, and to give lectures in the course thus opened out to him. Gradually his course shaped itself into the form in which it is presented in this volume. At the request of the Bishop of Tasmania, then Principal of the Training Colleges, Cheltenham, some of these lectures appeared at intervals in the Papers for the Schoolmaster. The whole course is now offered in a more permanent form, at the request of many of the Author's former pupils. But another consideration has had weight. School Education has to become a Science. One means to this end is to gather and examine what has been done by those who have been engaged therein, and whose position or success has given them a right to be heard. Nor these alone. Others have been employed, if not *in* it, yet about it. School education, at its present standpoint, is the result of many agencies, individual, social, and national, and these have been very varied, and often antagonistic. It has been a growth, to which the philosopher, the politician, the doctrinaire, and the amateur have contributed, as well as the actual workers in schools. With these—excluding those whose object has been mercenary—it has been a course of efforts, schemes, mistakes, and failures, but sometimes of partial successes, all of which have yielded something to the fabric as it now stands. The Author's hope is that the sketch here feebly attempted may stimulate those just starting in their profession, ever to work with the purpose of ultimately placing their art on a scientific basis.

One word as to the form. In few cases are the words of the educational writers or workers used. Having but a very limited time, not one hour weekly, in which to present the salient points of each system, he found he could better do this, without quotation. But he has never consciously altered or coloured any one's views. In this plan he was confirmed by finding how successfully it had been followed in the *Schoolmaster*, published by the Society for the Diffusion of Useful Knowledge; to which book and to its other publications, the writer gratefully acknowledges his indebtedness.

February 28, 1876.

CONTENTS.

CHAPTER I.
GRAMMAR SCHOOLS.

PIONEERS—English taught in schools—John Cornewaile—Increase of schools—Influence of Chaucer—Revival of learning—Colet—Wolsey's instructions to masters—First English grammar.

ROGER ASCHAM—His education—Origin of the Schoolmaster—Discipline in relation to learning—Marks of a good scholar — Chiding — Correction of mistakes — Corporal punishment—Quick and hard wits—Competent teachers—Learning to be intelligent—Thoroughness—Examples before rules—Nothing to unlearn.

COMENIUS—Monitorial principle—Intuitive faculties—Pictorial teaching—Picturing-out.

JOHN MILTON—Spirit of the educator—Influence on the nation's life—No formal routine—Pestalozzian principle anticipated—Baconian method.—Course of study—Motives to be employed.

JOHN LOCKE—Incidents in life—Physical education—Moral culture—Its Place in a system of education—Its nature—Necessity of knowing childhood—Difference in children—Early impressions—Means of moral training—Authority—Shame—Opposed to corporal punishment—Obstinacy—Rewards—Natural consequences—Skilful teaching—Learning made pleasant—*Saturday Review* quoted—Pleasant books—Method of penmanship—Grammar—Composition—French.

VICESIMUS KNOX—Opposed to Locke—Advantages of classical culture—Bias of scholar—Easy methods suspicious—Culture of memory—Early reading—Latin basis of school discipline—Greek and French—English composition—Geography. . . . . . Pp. 1—47

CONTENTS.

CHAPTER II.
The Common School.

EDGEWORTHS—Influence of their writings—Kindergarten anticipated—Early learning—Objections to alphabetic teaching—Phonic method suggested—Spelling should follow reading—Arithmetic by objects—Power of attention—Short lessons—When to end teaching—Connection in teaching—Difficulty of language—Personal motive—Selection of books—History, how taught—Place of poetry—Moral discipline—Natural consequences—Submission—Commands and prohibitions.

PESTALOZZI—Incidents in life—Books on education—Become a schoolmaster—Qualification—Experiments and failures—Leading principles—Opposed to common practices—Socratic development—Was the old method utterly bad?—Ideas before words—Child an active agent—Object lessons—Simple to complex—Graduation of exercises—Harmonious development—Absurdities in his practices—Moral and religious training—How develop religious feeling.

Pp. 48—75

CHAPTER III.
Infants' Schools.

OBERLIN—School at Lanark—School at Westminster.

WILDERSPIN—The gaudy cap and its lesson—Qualifications for his work—His enthusiasm—His enterprise—Principles—Follow nature—Physical culture—Characteristics of childhood—Moral education—Moral truths and principles—Moral constitution—Playground—Cultivation of intelligence—The Senses—How to think rather than what—Object lessons—Lessons in number—Ball frame—Pictures.

MAYOS—Expounders of Pestalozzianism—Pestalozzian principles—Education should be religious—Should be moral—Should be organic—Action parent of power—Liberty—Harmonious development—Progressive.

HOME AND COLONIAL SCHOOL SOCIETY—Primary object in infant culture—Infants' schools are too often hot-beds—Aim of this Society—Huge gallery banished—Sectional division of school—Development and intuition—Hand, head and heart—Religious training—Its mode—First ideas of God—Graduated instruction—Scripture prints—Moral culture—Based on religious truth—Springs of action—Systematic culture of the feelings—Conscience—Training rather than teaching—Power of example—School discipline—Authority—Punishments—Treatment of obstinate children—Rewards and praise—Cultivation of intelligence—The senses—Object lessons—Lessons on animals—Colour and form—Size and weight—Number.

KINDERGARTEN SYSTEM—Fröbel—Observes children—Their characteristics — Gifts — Forms — Inventions— Activity—Taste—Number—Reading. . . . Pp. 76—161

CHAPTER IV.

THE ELEMENTARY SCHOOL.

DR. ANDREW BELL—Origin of monitorial system—Province of the school—Religion and morality—Relation to future callings—Attention and exertion—Means of securing—Home exercises—Principles and methods—Something to do—Definite and thorough work—Repetition—Reading—Writing—Organization of school—Subordinate officers—Large classes—Arrangements of room—School keeping—Supervision—Paidometer—Discipline—Prevention better than cure—Personal improvement—Emulation—Place-taking—Treatment of offences—Punishment—objections to corporal punishment.

JOSEPH LANCASTER—Devotedness to education—Moral training based on religious instruction—Periods of school life—Graduation of lessons—Reading—Arithmetic—Organization distinct classes for arithmetic—classes and drafts—Teaching staff—Discipline—Influence of master—Public opinion in school—Fellenberg's practice—Offices of trust—Training of the will — Emotions of self-love of distinction—Class emulation.

INTELLECTUAL SYSTEM—Culture of intelligence—Knowledge of child mind—No royal road to learning—Qualifications of

teachers—Disciplined mind—Apt to teach—Methods—Interrogation—Explanation—Exposition of reading lesson.
STOW'S TRAINING SYSTEM—Origin and progress—Infant school—David Caughie—Establishment of first normal college training and teaching—Function of the school—Religious and moral training—Bible lessons—Telling not training—Currie on doing—Locke on training—Action teaches—Condition of moral training—Knowledge of aptitudes—Development of tastes—Freedom from restraint—Fear prevents confidence—Temptations not removed—Uncovered school room—Moral review—Sympathy of numbers—Public opinion—Long on school opinion—Reid on school boy's influence—Currie on sympathy of numbers—Intellectual culture—Leading principle—Master to teach—Necessity of learning—Nothing told that can be discovered—Understanding, then memory—Not reasons for everything—Logical faculty—Outlines first—Picturing out—Words—Scenes—Bible lessons—Training out—Mistakes and absurdities—Induction—Collective lessons
Pp. 162—262

CHAPTER V.
AMATEURS AND HELPERS.

Present interest in education—Brougham's efforts—Central Society.

THOMAS WYSE—Knowledge of mind—Education must be religious that it may be moral—How teach the Bible—Intelligent training—The senses first—All the faculties—Method should be eclectic.

HORACE GRANT—Interest in education—Special qualifications—Inductive labour—Principles—*Saturday Review* on arithmetic.

EDUCATION DEPARTMENT—Shuttleworth—Principles of method—Found's Battersea college—Professor Moseley—Religious training—Moral discipline—Training of teachers—Oral lessons—Tripartite organization—Grade schools—Tremenheere—Oral lessons—Education of the whole nature—Knowledge of mind—Poetry—Reading lesson. . Pp. 263—304

SYSTEMS OF EDUCATION.

CHAPTER I.

Grammar Schools.

Section I.—Pioneers.

The reign of Edward III. witnessed, after a struggle of three centuries, the triumph of English in the schools, as well as in social life and the courts of law. Schools had been chiefly those connected with cathedrals and monasteries, some of the latter class having been founded before the Conquest. These were intended chiefly for the training of ecclesiastics. But there were other than these, found in towns and villages, which were open to the laity. Of these were those held probably in the chamber over the porch of the church, *parvise*. The serjeant in the Canterbury Tales had been at *parvise*. In these schools Latin and French were taught, and were the medium through which other things were acquired. John Cornewaile appears to have been the first to break through custom and prejudice, by introducing into the school the reading of the mother tongue. It spread, so that in the course of a generation "In all the grammar schools of England children learneth French and construeth and learneth in English." The Visions and Creed of Piers Ploughman (Langlande), the tracts and Bible of Wycliffe, and the burst of song in Chaucer came to stimulate and reward this movement. Other schools under private persons, that is, not connected with the religious houses sprang up, due greatly to Wycliffe and those who abetted him. The movement was countenanced by Wykeham, to whom it has been attributed, that his school at Winchester was designed to rescue the early training of youth from the hands of the monks. The increase of these schools seems to have alarmed the ecclesiastical bodies. They opposing Lollardry, obtained a law making it illegal to send children for tuition to private persons. But the impetus had been given, and though for a century after Chaucer no great English writer appeared, yet it is evident that the learning of English spread more and more, until literature was no longer the possession of a class, but had begun to be the heritage of the people. This is shown by the literature in demand; compendiums of the scientific and historic knowledge of the day; the common-place dramas, mysteries, and poems, and the rhyming chronicles. It is also shown by the extent of the demand. It was beyond precedent, so that few occupations were so thriving as the scriveners. It is also shown in the demand of some of the clergy of London in 1477, for leave to open schools in their respective churches. But the strongest proof of all is in the success that attended William Caxton, and his noble efforts, by translation and printing, to meet the ever increasing demand.

The revival of learning in Florence, due greatly to

the Greek scholars, who had fled there, on the taking of Constantinople by the Turks; and due also to the influence of the Medici; and the spread of this revival in Europe was another element in the upward movement. Grocyn, Linacre, and somewhat later Colet, having studied in Florence, returned to kindle the fire in Oxford, and to adopt means to promote the new learning.

The reformation, in one of its phases a collateral result of the revival of learning, brought into the homes of the people the light of sacred truth, with its necessary result, intellectual awakening; and placed within their reach the Bible in English.

It was a necessary consequence of the revival of learning that schools and colleges increased. During the latter years of Henry VIII. more grammar schools were founded than during the three preceding centuries. In the reign of Edward and Elizabeth the good work went on, until a system of schools was established for the middle-classes, which bore noble fruit in the next generations. It was natural that this revival and progress should draw attention to school methods and practices, which should issue in efforts for their improvement. Dean Colet led the way in both movements, by the establishment of his school at St. Paul's, placing it under the charge of Lilly, and by reforming the matter of study and the mode of instruction. Fifteen years later, Wolsey wrote to the masters of the school he had founded at Ipswich a letter of instruction as to the methods to be pursued, gathered probably from the writings of Erasmus, and the practice on the Continent. The main points of this letter, separated from the detail of daily work in each class are, to be careful in first teaching, to suit the matter to the capacity, not to force to learning by blows or harsh threats, to make learning a game rather than a task, to explain, illustrate and arrange, to commend, and to exact correctness in speech at play as well as in school.

But this revival was not confined to classical learning. In the reign of Elizabeth, there burst into leaf, the tree of English literature, with a vigour, a life, and a growth, which have never since departed from it. With this there came the demand for such culture in schools, as would put this literature into the hands of England's children. The first attempt was the humble unpretentious English Grammar, of the head master of St. Paul's school, Alexander Gill.

Section II.—Roger Ascham.

Roger Ascham may be considered the father of school method. For though his "Scholemaster" deals necessarily with classical learning, yet it contains principles which are applicable to all school subjects. His book was not that of an amateur, but of one who had, for the age, fair experience and success in the work of tuition. Born in 1515, he entered, at the age of fifteen, St. John's College, Cambridge, just when the Greek revival under Cheke was drawing many to that University. Ascham's progress was rapid, and the bent of his mind was shown by his teaching, while yet a boy, other boys the Greek he had so quickly acquired, with the design too of facilitating his own acquisition and use of it. He became early distinguished as a scholar, obtained his bachelor's degree at the age of nineteen, and was elected a Fellow of his College a month later. He employed himself as tutor and lecturer, and many of his scholars afterwards rose to great distinction. Ascham was not only proficient in classical learning, he had skill in music, and was one of the few that excelled in penmanship. This influenced his fortunes. About 1544, he was appointed by Henry VIII. to teach penmanship to Edward and Elizabeth, and somewhat later he became Greek tutor to that princess. Subsequently he was Latin secretary to Edward VI., an office which was continued to him by the good offices of Gardiner under Mary, and which he retained under Elizabeth. With this queen he also read classics daily, until his death in 1568.

The origin of Ascham's book gives the key to its matter. In 1563, Sir William Cecil tells in Ascham's presence of boys that had run away from Eton for fear of a beating. He also expressed an opinion that masters often punish nature rather than the fault of the scholar; and drove from learning those they had in charge. This gave rise to a discussion, whether learning was better promoted by love alluring, or beating driving to it. Ascham expressed himself against punishments, and in favour of methods that would render punishment unnecessary. His work is in two books. Book I.—"Teaching the bringing up of Youth." Book II.—"The ready way to the Latin tongue. The former book, to which we confine ourselves, treats of discipline and method.

Ascham is at pains to distinguish between the discipline which is to promote progress in learning with the love of it, and the discipline which has to form the manners, root out vice, and promote growth in virtue. In this latter sphere, he thinks there may be reasonable severity, but he thinks that such discipline does not belong to the schoolmaster. This opinion has not altogether died out, there being schools now, where masters think their only responsibility rests in their pupils' progress in learning. Still, even in Ascham's day, there were those who held that the school had a higher function in education. "In such places," he urges, "the discipline to promote learning should not be of the same kind as that which has to form the character and reform the manners." Referring to the discipline amongst the Ancients he observes:—"The schoolmaster taught him learning with all gentleness; the governor corrected his manners with much sharpness, the father held the stern of his whole obedience. And so he that used to teach did not commonly use to beat, but remitted that over to another man's charge. But what shall we say, when now in our days the schoolmaster is used both for preceptor in learning, and *pædagogus* in manners? Surely, I would he should not confound their offices, but discreetly use the duty of both, so that neither ill touches should be left unpunished, nor gentleness in teaching anywise omitted. And he shall well do both, if wisely he do appoint diversity of time, and separate place for either purpose." Here is a very important distinction shadowed forth, involving a very great principle, and indicating a noble practice. Nothing should be done in discipline that will tend to confound moral distinctions in the mind of the young; or, that will make them think that a false quantity is on the same footing as a lie. This distinction too is important, when weighing arguments on corporal punishment; for it must be evident that such as may establish the propriety, expediency, or necessity of it in the one case, may be utterly worthless in the other.

Quoting from Plato the marks of a good scholar in the judgment of Socrates, he sets forth these as the objects of discipline. Secure to him a good "memory, quick to receive, sure to keep, and ready to deliver; a love of learning; a desire to labour; a will to take pains; willingness to be taught by any one; and not to be ashamed to ask questions."

To attain these objects, "*never chide hastily.*" Look well to your ground and consider what will be its effect on the pupil. "Hasty chiding dulls the wit and discourages diligence." "Why are you angry, sir? Indeed I am doing as well as I can,"—was a reply that elicited from Arnold, "I was never so ashamed in my life." "*Monish gently.*" Faults have to be pointed out, but it should be in a way "that shall make him both willing to amend, and glad to go forward in love and hope of learning." Hence monition should be mixed with encouragement. Love is a better spur than fear, gentleness is better than bullying, soft words are better than stinging ones. "For whatsoever the mind doth learn unwillingly from fear, the same it doth gladly forget without care." In further illustration he compares children learning to ride, and learning their book. "Schoolmasters by fear do beat into them the hatred of learning; and wise riders, by gentle allurements, do breed up in them the love of riding. They find fear and bondage in schools, they feel liberty and freedom in stables." Meeting an obvious objection that riding is a pastime and therefore easy to children, while learning is labour and wearisome, he rejoins, "Beat a child if he dance not well, and cherish him though he learn not well, ye shall have him unwilling to go to dance, and glad to go to his book," for "the mind of a child is like the newest wax, able to receive the best and fairest printing," hence a child's likings or dislikings are due to his educators.

Correction of mistakes or faults should not degrade, nor discourage, but stimulate. In doing this necessary work, there must not be a frown, nor the fault put down to wilfulness. "Cicero would have used such a word, or put it in such a place." Here he exhibits knowledge of human nature. An illustration is at hand in the "Daily News" of the autumn of 1872. Its correspondent attended the field manœuvres of the English army, and a few days later he was performing a similar duty with the German army in the neighbourhood of Berlin. "If an officer in the former case made a mistake he was soundly rated in the presence of the staff; but in the case of the German, the General said 'Had I been charged with such a movement, I would have conducted it so and so.' Here the self respect of the officer was considered, who, beside, would on a similar occasion try to do the thing as his distinguished general would have done it."

Beating should never be employed to promote learning. Generally it breaks rather than bends, mars rather than mends. It tends to associate such disagreeable things with learning as to make children detest, rather than love it, drive from it, rather than allure to it. *It often leads to tyranny.* Beaters often allow ill humour at other things to find vent on the pupil. Indulging the practice of inflicting pain for faults not of a moral nature, has a tendency to harden the master, and to render him insensible to the claims of justice. *It is often unjust.* As Cecil said, it more frequently punishes nature than corrects faults ; for the slow, and dull, and heavy get the beating, while the quick and easy getters obtain the praise. Pain is thus inflicted for natural qualities, instead of being reserved for moral offences.

There should be discrimination between quick and hard wits. Quick wits are apt to take, unapt to keep, easily got and quickly gone, soon hot and soon cold. They are like sharp-edged tools, which enter easily but do not penetrate to a great depth, because their edges are soon turned. Hence few quick wits are ever profound ; but exception is to be made here for the excellently gifted. But as a matter of fact, the quick at school seldom turn out well as men ; they live obscurely and die unknown. The remedy is a judicious system of repetition which will make their learning thorough. Hard wits are the hope of the school, and ultimately do society and the commonwealth most service. Here is encouragement. Hard wits are those who find it hard to learn, and who are hard to teach. He compares them to hard woods and hard stones in the hands of the engraver and sculptor. The tool makes scarcely any impression ; it requires much toil and much skill to trace a line or to chisel a feature, but the work is lasting. Lapse of time and the action of the elements destroy it not. It realizes "I work for eternity." Now your hard wits are just such. Hard to get, hard to lose, sure to keep. He compares them also to tools which enter with difficulty, but penetrate deeply. Here is probably the reason of their slowness, they are not satisfied like the quick with being superficial. They are not like the butterfly, here and there, but like the bee, staying at a flower till it has gathered all it contains.

The principles for conducting instruction found in Ascham are few but pregnant. His first care would be to provide a competent instructor. But, alas! "men look for a cunning man for their horse, but not for their children." They show this in the salaries they give. "Two hundred crowns to the one, two hundred shillings to the other." They reap accordingly —"tame, well-ordered horses, wild children. They get more pleasure from their horses than comfort from their children."

Ascham requires that the master shall teach as well as the pupil learn, and in order thereto. The pupil should *understand*. The master is to spare no pains to make him carry away the sense. He requires as a test and as a means that the child shall do by himself what he had before done with his tutor. It is only through teaching that learning is profitable. "Learning without teaching makes lubbers,—always learning, never profiting." He draws a comparison between what children learn from books, and what they obtain by the use of their senses and by experience. The one is practical and valuable, the other stale and profitless. Learning without intelligence is simply, "on the tongue and lip, to be spit out when occasion needeth; that which is understood ascends to the brain, is assimilated, and becomes fruitful."

Learning must be thorough as well as intelligent. These things satisfy the mind of the pupil and clear his path. "They give pleasure to children, pleasure excites love, love provokes labour, and labour effects its purpose." Thoroughness requires that there should be order in his work and repetition. "Let the master read unto him the Epistles of Cicero. First let him teach the child cheerfully and plainly the cause and matter of the letter; then let him construe it into English so oft as the child may easily carry away the understanding of it; lastly, parse it over perfectly. This done thus, let the child by and by both construe and parse it over again, so that it may appear that the child doubteth in nothing that his master taught him before. After this the child must take a paper book, and sitting in some place where no man shall prompt him, by himself, let him translate into English his former lesson. Then, showing it to his master, let the master take from him his Latin book, and pausing an hour at least, then let the child translate his own English into Latin again in another paper book. The master must compare it with Tully's book, and lay them both together."

In order to thoroughness and subsequent progress, there should be cultivation at first only of a small area. He recommends that a good but easy and short book should be selected, and this so completely worked and mastered as to be equally at command with the mother tongue. This advice, necessary then, is tenfold more so now. How wide the area of human research at present! How vast the domain of knowledge already won! How persistent the devotee to each special subject, that his shall enter into the curriculum of the school! How dogmatic the doctrinaire, that the subjects in school shall be many, and that their limits shall not be circumscribed! And with what results? Let the disclosures in connection with the Civil Service examinations, and the system of enfeebling cram, give the reply. No! the hint of Ascham should be the rule in school—" a small area well cultivated." This only will give thorough knowledge, strength of mind, and sound education.

"Heedful mending of faults" is necessary both to intelligence and thoroughness. Correction of mistakes is oftentimes the best instruction. We get a clearer insight. "A child learns more from two faults than from four things rightly hit."

Examples before rules, and rules deduced from examples, are two important principles which are indicated by Ascham. Speaking of Latin, he would have the learner become familiar with the language, and for himself discover its syntax, rather than the common practice of giving him the rule and leaving him to apply it. These two invaluable principles are but now bearing fruit in school matters, so persistent is bad method, and so difficult to overcome the inertia that prevents thought. But our author has no sympathy with idleness, nor with any master who adopts what seems the easier method of tasks, instead of one that makes constant demand on his own mental power

The practice of a boy being set to do things at such a time, or in such a way, that he learns many things that he has afterwards to unlearn, comes under animadversion. Thus are often produced faults that no later care can cure. His instance is taken from setting boys to Latin composition before they had sufficient knowledge and skill in the language. The rule condemns the too frequent practice of giving for correction false syntax, false speech, and false spelling; and the permitting of practices in learning, and in reading, writing, and arithmetic, which afterwards prove hindrances to progress.

Section III.—*Comenius.*—*Milton.*

John Amos Comenius was born at Comna in 1592. His parents were Moravians, and he himself became a pastor in that community. Forced by the burning of Fulneck, in the religious war, to leave that town, he became rector of a school at Lesna, in Poland. Here he began his career as an educational reformer. In 1631 he published his "Janua Linguarum," and other works followed. Of these the "Janua" and the "Orbis" were translated into most European and into some of the Oriental languages. Having thus become known he was sought for by several Governments to put their systems of public instruction on a better basis. For this purpose he was invited to England, and remained here from 1638 to 1642, when the outbreak of the civil war caused him to leave. In 1638 he published in London an edition of his "Janua Linguarum," in Latin, English, and French,—"The Gate of Tongues Unlocked and Opened." In this and his other books there are many valuable suggestions for the improvements of method of instruction.

Acting on the hint of Quintilian, that the new learner is the best teacher, he employed pupils to instruct less advanced pupils, thus anticipating, as had been done with Ascham at Cambridge, the monitorial plan of mutual instruction. His "Gate of Tongues" and his "Orbis" unfold a plan of aiding the acquisition of languages by calling into exercise the perceptive and intuitive faculties. For this purpose he would have the matter of the lessons such as would address itself to the senses, or would be easily understood; as natural history, trades and professions, and science. He also introduced pictorial illustration into his books and teaching. This practice instantly became popular; Dr. Doddridge informing us that it was the common method in his childhood, for mothers thus to teach their little ones. A still further advance is the recommendation, when things and pictures fail, to employ graphic description, or "picturing out." It is curious to note the use by Comenius, of a term, for the supposed invention of which Stow received some hard criticism.

It is evident that these practices of Comenius contain the germs of things afterwards associated with the names of Pestalozzi and Stow. It also may be safely assumed that many methods that are now in extensive use, were then not unknown to earnest teachers, for it is hard to believe that any one ever was a real teacher who did not employ rational methods.

JOHN MILTON was induced by a friend to write a

small tract on what he calls "one of the greatest and noblest designs, the reforming of education." This tract appeared a few years subsequently to the departure of Comenius, to whom the author evidently refers, when, not denying his obligations to the Ancients, he asserts no inclination to search "Modern Januas and Didactics." Milton's scheme was not that of a mere theorist, but of one who himself had been engaged in tuition. His own education had been carefully conducted, being already an accomplished scholar, when, at the age of fifteen, he entered St. Paul's School.

The opening proposition, whether intended so by Milton or not, admirably sets forth the spirit in which the work of education should be carried on. "The only purpose which should act as a motive in the pursuit of any object worthy to be remembered or imitated is the love of God and of mankind!" This excludes mercenary motives. Not that a man should not be paid for his labours, and that in proportion to its value to the commonwealth, and to the skill and ability it requires; but to attain the highest results in education, results not to be appraised by a money value, a man must be animated by a far higher consideration than the amount of money it secures.

Living in stirring times, in which many were making sacrifices for the public good, Milton is influenced thereby, and contends that education should produce well-informed citizens, and good members of the state. This is one great aspect of the teacher's work. He is advancing the nation's knowledge, and he is influencing the nation's life. What the intellect and moral life of the people of the future will be, will always depend on the work in the schoolroom. There is laid either the "Seed corn of a harvest, or the powder train of a mine." But a yet higher purpose is to animate the schoolmaster—Human nature is in ruins, and we ought to seek its repair. This can be done " only by knowledge of God, love to God, and hence imitation of God, until we become like God."

We gather that Milton attaches no value to a formal routine of lessons, but requires a system of teaching that would arouse thought as well as exercise memory. This is the constant cry of the educational reformer. Forsake your mechanical drill, your setting of tasks, your burdens on memory, and give us work that will produce thinkers. In order to this the relation of language to culture should be understood. Things are to be known rather than words or rules, and the knowledge of words is best obtained through the knowledge of things. Here the Pestalozzian principle is anticipated, and also the application of it. "Certain things can be made known only by the sensible and visible. They cannot be presented at all but by concrete examples. Such are divine things. To represent the divine to us, human imagery is employed." But the same thing is true of many subjects, and thus "the same method is to be followed in all discreet teaching." Language not only embodies things, but also records for us the experience and traditions of other people and of other times. It is therefore an instrument conveying to us things useful to be known. Hence it becomes an instrument of culture, but it fails in this office, unless the things contained in it become the property of the mind. Language is the great store house of the treasures of the past, but if it is only a verbal possession, it is like a storehouse the inlets to which have been closed up. Hence though a man know all the tongues that Babel cleft the world into, yet if he have not studied the solid things in them, he is not learned.

Milton is quite Baconian in protesting against beginning where the true philosopher ends. True method is to begin with objects of sense, and to gather facts. He is strongly urgent that early instruction should begin with things that are easy, and that are obvious to the sense; and that it should be real and thorough. The result of the opposite plan is pernicious to the individual and to society. The picture is very startling. Disgust with learning, and with its babblement is of course. Nothing being ever clearly understood, there is no real knowledge, and the whole thing is consciously to the scholars a deception and a sham. Thus by being taught at school to appear to know, and to speak as if his knowledge was real, when he is conscious that it is not, he is trained in the habit of untruth. The result is that truth is absent from life, from society, and that there is no profession in which is to be found, truth, virtue, or a high aim. So that it is found that in all affairs of life persons are actuated by mercenary considerations, or they give themselves up to a loose and voluptuous career.

His scheme embraces the education of the boy and youth up to the age of twenty-one, and includes manly exercises and accomplishments. The earlier course should include good interesting books, that will allure to study, win to thought, and incite to virtue. Arithmetic and geometry should come in every day. The evening should be given to the grounds of religion and the study of Scripture. But nothing should be exacted beyond the power of the pupil, such as "the preposterous exaction of forcing the empty wits of children to compose themes and essays" on subjects which only those of enriched minds and ripe judgments can attempt. He also lays down the rule that as learners advance, they ought often to retrace their steps, and work over again their earlier studies. The whole scheme of study embraced Latin and Greek authors, first pleasant as Plutarch, then useful as those on agriculture and philosophy; astronomy and geography; architecture, fortification and engineering; religion and ethics; natural philosophy, natural history, botany, and anatomy; jurisprudence, logic, and poetry.

The motives that he would employ may be gathered from hints here and there in the tract. Learning should be made pleasant, by administering to faculties belonging to the period, and by furnishing delightful books. Careful instruction and explanation should be given on every opportunity, so that they may be drawn to willing obedience, and be inflamed with the love of learning. By mild and effectual persuasion with the mixture of some fear, if need be, they should be led to admire virtue, and they should be stirred up with high hopes of living so as to be dear to God, and famous to all ages. They should be taught to despise and scorn childish and ill-taught qualities, and they should be trained in such precepts and practice as will make them hate the cowardice of doing wrong. Finally example should gain them diligence and courage, and infuse into their young breasts such an ingenuous and noble ardour as would make many of them renowned and matchless men.

Section IV.—*John Locke.*

John Locke, "the father of English philosophy," was born at Wrington in 1632. His early education was by his father, and was conducted with great care and success. But the troubles of the time, and his father serving in the Parliamentary army, broke up this arrangement, and he was placed at Westminster school. In the remembrance of his own early career we have probably the origin of his preference for private tuition over the public school. At the age of nineteen he proceeded to Christchurch, Oxford, where, in addition to the prescribed Aristotelian course, he solaced his philosophical spirit, by the private perusal of the works of Bacon and Descartes. The latter appears to have had no special influence over him, but from the former he obtained the method, which he subsequently applied to the investigation of mental phenomena. On leaving the university he adopted the profession of medicine, but his constitution was too weak to allow him to practise. In 1665, having successfully treated Lord Ashley, subsequently Earl of Shaftesbury, in case of an abscess, "he accepted the invitation of that nobleman to reside in his house; and from this time he attached himself to his fortunes during his life, and after death vindicated his memory and honour." The studies of Lord Shaftesbury's son, and of his grandson, the author of the celebrated Characteristics, were under the direction of Locke.

The "Thoughts on Education" appeared in 1693, and reappeared invested with all the genius of Rousseau, in "Emile." Produced when the author was verging on sixty, for they were written several years before they were printed, they were the product of mature judgment, and of one whose professional studies, acquaintance with mind, actual experience in the work of tuition, active but chequered career, and habits of mind well fitted him for the work he had undertaken. The peculiar style of the book, its discursive character, and want of system are due to the "Thoughts," having been originally written in a series of letters to a friend. The book was well received, not only in his own country, but especially on the continent, being translated into German, Dutch and French; Leibnitz speaks highly in its praise, and at a later time, Rousseau embodied its teaching in his "Emile." Still, as it attacked vested interests, and advocated private tuition in preference to that of the school, and very considerably widened the sphere and altered the mode of culture, it was not universally accepted, and in fact, is now in some places, for the first time bearing fruit. A century later, Vicescimus Knox, the veriest tory in school matters, says, "For the names and abilities of Milton, Locke, Rousseau, and of others who have written on education, I entertain all the respect which is due to them. Their systems are plausible, and truly ingenious. The world has long placed them high in the ranks of fame, and with respect to their general merit as writers, they indisputably deserve their honours. But, when they wrote on education, they fell into the common error of those who attend to speculation more than to practice. In the warmth of the innovating and reforming spirit, they censure modes of treatment which are right, they recommend methods which really cannot be reduced to practice, and which, if they could, would be useless or pernicious. It is indeed easy to censure things already established, and project new institutions. The world is commonly tired of that to which it has been long accustomed, and fondly attached to novelty. It is, then, no wonder, that *visionary writers* on education are greatly admired, though their directions can seldom be closely pursued."

Locke places the formation of character and manners above mere learning, hence he is urgent that the choice of a tutor is of the first moment. Consider his work. "It is to fashion the carriage and form the mind; to settle in his pupils good habits, and the principles of virtue and wisdom; to give him by little and little a view of mankind, and work him into a love and imitation of what is excellent and praiseworthy; and in the prosecution of it to give him vigour, activity, and industry." "Under whose care soever a child is put to be taught during the tender and flexible years of his life, this is certain, it should be one who thinks Latin and languages the least part of education; one who, knowing how much virtue and a well tempered soul is to be preferred to any sort of learning or language, makes it his chief business to form the mind of his scholars and give that a right disposition; which, if once got, though all the rest should be neglected, would in due time produce all the rest; and which, if it be not got, and settled so as to keep out ill and vicious habits—languages and sciences, and all the other accomplishments of education, will be to no purpose, but to make the worse and more dangerous man."

Writing for home education, Locke gives directions for the care of the *case*, as well as that which it contains, the mind. *Mens sana in corpore sano* was a maxim he could well appreciate. Physical education has in charge diet, clothing, sleep, exercise, fresh air and cleanliness. Some of these things are removed from the immediate influence of the elementary school. Yet the teacher may do much to diffuse right views and to secure right practice in regard to them. Combe, by his work on "Physiology applied to Health and Education," happily aroused public attention to this subject, and did much to promote it in schools. Instruction in physiology and the laws of health; daily inspection and insisting on the pupil being clean in his person and clothes; inquiries once or twice weekly as to washing the feet, sponging the body, followed by friction with a flesh brush or coarse towel; attention to ventilation and keeping the school room floor and walls scrupulously clean, and school drill and healthy games are now found in many of our schools. In one district, described at the time by one of Her Majesty's inspectors as "remote from civilisation, and marked by general indifference to education," the persistent efforts of a schoolmaster led to a general improvement, not only in the habits of his pupils, but in many of their homes.

It is not necessary to enter into detail, but the

following things are noteworthy. The strength of the body lies in being able to endure hardship, hence their training should make children hardy. To this end they should not be pampered, nor should they be shielded from every risk, or a present security is obtained at the expense of danger from future exposure. Although his dictum about "leaking shoes" might seem to countenance it, yet of course he does not mean that children should be trained to fool-hardiness. The knowledge of the teacher should correct the inexperience of the child, and should lead to interference whenever the necessity existed. As exercise, and especially exercise in the open air, is essential to the strength and soundness of the body, all indications of a lazy or indolent disposition must be promptly treated. The child must be stimulated to use all its energies in play as well as work, and occasions must be provided for exercise whenever it is seen that there is a disinclination to it. But the rule now to be given is unexceptionally sound. The course of treatment in all physical education should tend to form habits. Habits of body and habits of practice are the ends to be secured. If this be so, the withholding that which is usual, or its neglect, will be a source of discomfort or uneasiness. For instance, early hours of retiring and rising may by habit save from future excess. So habit may render physic unnecessary. In forming habit the treatment should not be fitful but periodic; it should not be hap-hazard, but guided by rule and wise discretion; and in the case of exercise it should be prolonged to the point of fatigue to secure the end in view.

Locke places moral education in its right place. It

should take precedence in mental culture. Moral good is not to be bargained away for any learning whatever. A great truth this which the educator is too apt to forget or neglect. It is so much easier to cultivate intelligence than to form a virtuous character, that this is too little attempted or not persistently.

Of the *nature* of moral education Locke says, that its great aim is to secure to the child the complete subjection of his appetites and passions, his desires and inclinations to reason. In other words it is the conquest of self. These are his words:—" As the strength of the body lies chiefly in being able to endure hardships, so also does that of the mind. And the great principle and foundation of all virtue and worth lies in this, that a man is able to deny himself his own desires, cross his own inclinations, and purely follow what reason directs as best, though the appetite lean the other way."

Let us understand his meaning here and we have the key to his system, the very pith and marrow of his teaching. When he says, strength of mind lies in the ability to endure hardships, he means that there is a temper of mind that scorns to be governed by pleasure or pain, and that will not allow the desires, inclinations, or passions to control the actions only so far as reason allows. He would have a Spartan's contempt of danger with his indifference to ease and comfort; a stoic's superiority to the solicitations of pleasure or the infliction of pain; and a Christian's obliteration of self from all his pursuits and a complete subjection of his body and mind to the highest reason.

Such a course to be successful must be begun early.

It must begin on the mother's lap, be continued in the nursery, followed when sitting at table, and must not be forgotten in the presence of visitors. But, alas! early training raises barriers. Seeds are sown which, taking root, are never afterwards extirpated. In this early time there is too often the "positive teaching of vice." Children are taught to take childish revenge on anything that gives them pain, and are permitted and sometimes taught to strike those that have the charge of them. They are tricked out in finery, and are fondled for their pretty looks, and are accustomed to a mode of treatment that fixes their regards upon themselves. They are taught by example to lie. Admiration is given for what at a later time would receive reproof. Instances of clever deceit, pert forwardness, and pretty wilfulness are recited with smiling approval in their presence. Love of eating and drinking is fostered by the obvious importance attached to it by their elders, and by "dainties" being proposed as rewards. On food the right maxim is, that food is given not because it is pleasant, but because it is necessary. Schoolmasters may think that on these points they are never likely to err. What then is to be said of the practice not uncommon of keeping a child from dinner because of ill conduct at school? Such a practice elevates eating to a position it ought not to occupy. To punish a moral offence by depriving of food is to place the two things, moral duty and eating, on the same level. Nor is it quite clear that schoolmasters are guiltless in other matters. How often do they allow in younger children what they would not in older ones! Is this wise? People allow license for little improprieties, considering them harmless. Listen to Locke. The proportion of the fault to the age is the same, so that a little impropriety is as culpable in a child as a great fault in an older person. Also indulgence now will lead to expect similar indulgence at a later period of desires and passions no longer innocent. All this is culpable negligence of the mind and disposition in the most impressible time, and may be contrasted with the judicious management and elaborate attention bestowed on dogs and horses.

To educate rightly it is necessary to study the child. Two distinct classes of mental faculties offer themselves to view, those common to all, those peculiar to the individual. Of the qualities indigenous to human nature it is necessary to glance at a few which have a legitimate sphere, but which uncultivated develop into weeds that become ineradicable from the character. Amongst others of this class are love of liberty, love of dominion, sense of property, and desire of possession. From these roots, unless tended with determined vigour, spring the weeds of license, selfishness, contention, rapacity, violence, tyranny, cruelty, and injustice. Applying his great principle to these matters we have the rule that nothing is ever to be granted to a child's fancies, but only to his wants. That any fanciful or wilful preference of one thing to another must be treated as caprice, therefore not to be allowed, but rigorously withstood. He also contends that the earliest manifestations of violence, domineering, tyranny over lower animals, improper bearing towards inferiors, should be rigidly put down. He also gives us some practical rules of great value. Complaints of one against another should be discouraged, for sufferance without redress is better than an indulged sensitiveness. If notice is taken of the case, and the aggressor is to be reprimanded, it had better not be in the presence of him who complains. Still principles of justice should be strenuously insisted on, hence all instances of real injustice should be noticed and rectified. However trifling the thing or worthless in itself the act of injustice is not trifling. Nay, nothing is trifling that helps to form the character. Nor is the morality of an action to be estimated by the inconvenience it may occasion, the loss inflicted, or the injury done. Eternal justice is equally violated whether a pin or a pound be stolen. It is necessary ever to discriminate between acts of ignorance and of a perverse will. More acts that are wrong in themselves proceed in children from the former than from the latter. The practice, for instance, of children pulling flies to pieces more frequently proceeds from ignorance than from wilful cruelty. The remedy would be to exhibit a fly and a maimed specimen through a microscope. When such acts do occur, when a wrong thing is first consciously done, it should be met with a show of wonder, as inconceivable. Proceeding on the same principle, children should not be informed of evil things. They should never be named in their presence. Evil should not be brought before their minds; for talking of such things sets them thinking, and thus their minds become familiarized with things which otherwise might never enter. Never speak of evil till the necessity for it unfortunately exists. For a similar reason do not warn children against possible faults; and this for the further reason that such warning implies distrust, and distrust is a temptation to pride or bravado. Stimulate children to that which is good and you will more effectually prevent the entrance of that which is evil.

> "The odour of the wine that first shall stain
> The virgin vessel, it will long retain."

That we may educate children aright we must study their peculiarities. Differences exist. There are differences of natural endowment, difference of temperament, differences in inherited tendencies, differences in moral and emotional susceptibilities. "There will always be some predominant qualities, good or evil, and these will more or less for ever belong to him." By which is to be understood that he will ever have certain mental peculiarities that will distinguish him from others and influence all he is and does. This being the case it becomes the duty of the educator to observe and study the child, that he may know these peculiarities; and that he may strengthen that which is weak, correct that which is wrong and rightly guide and improve all that is desirable and good. The peculiarities of children are best seen when they are least under restraint. Hence, in the matter of games, they should be allowed to indulge their fancy; all should be free and unrestricted; for it is only by leaving him free in his recreations, that the child's particular bent is shown. "Such knowledge is necessary, for it is found that rules for education do not always serve because of these differences, as the same method of treatment is not always followed by the same result. It is also necessary that the right means may be adopted to mortify evil qualities, strengthen good ones, and so improve the general stock."

The *means of moral education* have therefore to be wisely ordered. It is not by rules and precepts that moral intelligence is cultivated, or moral habits formed. "It is a great fault in education to burden children's minds with rules and precepts about their conduct, which are seldom understood, and therefore, soon forgotten; and it is still more unreasonable to visit with punishment the infraction of such rules." That children may *know* what is right you must teach by example. It is thus that the precept will have meaning and force. But they must also *do* what is right. To this end you must seize on every occasion that presents itself, and if necessary make occasion. The grand business is to form habits of right practice, and not to depend on the memory of a right precept. But habits cannot be formed only by patient and continued practice, and there is absolutely no other road to morality and virtue. Laws then should be few and well observed.

The first principle that should be implanted in the child's mind is submission to authority. This is what he means by awe of the parent. The parent is to the child in God's place, and his will is the sanction of its actions. He also holds that treatment in early life should be rigid. By this is not meant that it should be severe, but that it should not be lax. There is no hardship in this. A child finds hardship not in law but in laxity. The laws of nature are not relaxed for childhood, and the child soon learns to accommodate itself to them. Principles should be rigidly carried out, else the educator is not a support to the child, when from its ignorance and weakness it needs it. But when childhood gives place to youth, and the reason and habit permit, then a rigid system is out of place. Then the time has come when the co-operation of the youth should be sought by treating him as a rational being. That which is required from him should be explained, so that he may be convinced that it is just and reasonable. (The establishment of authority early is the surest way to obtain obedience, respect, and then love. This order cannot be reversed. It is impossible to lay a basis of love, and on it to build authority.) It is an instinct to despise him who gives up his right to rule, and love cannot exist where there is not respect

How to establish authority and to secure right practice introduces the question of motive, and consequently of punishment and reward. Pain, for the purpose of reform or to deter, is punishment. Pain is bodily or mental. The former includes corporal chastisement and all other modes of reaching the mind through the body. The latter includes reproof, rebuke, censure or anything else whose direct tendency is to produce shame. (The object to be secured by punishment is an ingenuous shame for having done wrong.) In the first instance this painful emotion arises from having forfeited the good opinion of another; then it springs up with the consciousness of having done something which we know would forfeit such opinion; but it finally comes for having done wrong. Now such feeling is one of the strongest safeguards against evil courses. Hence it is the thing which we aim to secure.

Rebuke, having this end, is often an effective punishment. That it may be so it must seem to proceed from a just displeasure. It must not be conveyed in harsh language, as this can scarcely ever do good, and must often do harm. It forfeits the child's respect, it forfeits his affection, and by frequency loses its power It should never proceed from passion. In that case the teacher places himself in a position of inferiority to the child and thus loses his influence and authority.

In relation to corporal punishment, the thing to be remembered is, that it is the mind that has to be influenced. Is it desirable to do this by bodily pain? At the first blush it is seen that the motive is bad. It is an important aim in education to lead children to despise pain. It will be their inevitable lot to meet it in a variety of forms, and if they easily succumb, their future life will be worthless to themselves and others. The motive too is often inoperative. It may be but a choice of pains, the drudgery of a task or the cut of the cane, and the lad may care less for the latter than the former. It may be inoperative because some other motive overpowers it, as bravado, or the consciousness of the sympathy of others. Bodily pain is made to appear the punishment, whereas shame at being whipped, or rather shame for needing punishment, is the feeling to be excited. It often tends too to prevent shame, or to destroy it, than which nothing worse could happen, for shame in children holds the same place as modesty in women, once gone all other evils follow. Bodily pain never alters the natural inclinations, but tends to strengthen them. It is a slavish discipline and produces a slavish temper, or, it breaks the mind and makes it cowardly and timid. There is one case in which Locke thinks it necessary—obstinacy. "But be sure it is obstinacy." A recommendation on which the Brighton case, where a lad was flogged to death, throws light. In such a case as the appearance of obstinacy, there is probably a mistake, and even if there be a fit, if whipping "does no good it does great harm." Study the child's disposition, and weigh well the consequences, before resorting to this treatment. If one whipping does not improve the child, abstain from further infliction. There is one thing Locke recommends as the last resort, which might well be placed first, "pray for the child."

Locke objects to rewards on similar grounds. They appeal to motives which it is desirable to repress and eradicate. How then is moral discipline to be promoted? By children suffering the natural consequences of their actions. The desire of esteem is strong in them. They are very sensible of praise and commendation. They get their first notions of right and wrong from the manifestation of approval or disapproval by those about them. Hence right doing is attended by an unbroken intercourse. Everything runs smoothly and pleasantly. But when wrong is done the carriage of those about him makes him sensible that a different state exists, there is a "change necessarily belonging to and constantly attending one who has brought himself into a state of disgrace," and the child feels that he has fallen "into neglect and contempt." This mode of discipline commends itself as like that which we experience in the providential government of the world; it commends itself also to the sense of justice inherent in the child; and as it is of wide application, and the occasions for acting on it occur continually, it is likely to form the child to the habit of acting constantly in reference to the consequence of its actions. Since Locke's time the principle has often been urged and illustrated, but perhaps never more prominently than by Herbert Spencer.

Coming to learning, we find that Locke would have right methods and skilful teaching. Skill in teaching consists in getting and keeping the attention of the scholar; whilst he has that he is sure to advance as far as the learner's abilities will carry him. His aim must be to create a love of learning. It will help to this if the bearing of the teacher is marked by sweetness and tenderness, showing that it proceeds from love to the child; and as love begets love, the child will come to attend to that which gratifies his teacher. The usefulness of what he is taught should be made clear. He can do some things which he could not before, and thus he has real power and advantage over others who are ignorant. Advantage should be taken of the natural curiosity of children, which is an appetite for knowledge that should be carefully encouraged and kept active. Their inquiries should be listened to with patience and attention, and should be answered. Give them just what they wish to know, but no more than they can pleasantly receive. Their mistakes must not be laughed at. They should never be put off with evasive answers. In the case where the teacher cannot answer, the best way is to confess ignorance, or his present inability to reply. Children soon come to learn that no man can know everything, and they readily give their respect and confidence to him who has the courage to avow ignorance. As children like novelty, and are unable from physical causes to give attention long to one thing, there should be a variety of studies provided for them. This principle is sound, but was forgotten by Locke, when he recommended that writing should not be attempted till the child had learnt to read, and when he would withhold arithmetic until this was fairly acquired.

Locke urges that learning should be made pleasant to children, that it should at first be a play and recreation. He shows his meaning by referring to learning the alphabet and words, by means of dice. Wolsey expressed a similar wish. Is it legitimate? Speaking of Locke's plan of learning to read, Vicesimus Knox says "Reading, if it was a game, was still such a game as the child liked less than his other diversions. It was, indeed, a game at what he would never play if he could help it. I am not quite sure that it is right to give him a notion that he has nothing to do but to play. Let him know that he has business of a serious kind,—we all come into the world to perform many duties, and to undergo many difficulties; and the earlier the mind learns to bear its portion of them, the less likely will it be to sink under those burdens which will one day be imposed upon it." Upon the general question, a writer in the *Saturday Review*, has these remarks:—" Ought learning to be made as pleasant as possible? If we could turn all study into play, would children be the better for it? The answer is, that there are obvious limits to the process in the nature of things. There are some things in early training, which may be made a pleasant puzzle to the child, and may be invested with all the attractions of a game. But it is a process that does not really awaken the intellectual faculties, and if it is a common thing—common to make the learning depend on the process being pleasing or exciting—then those things which can offer no immediate interest or pleasure, will be less attractive than before. Now in every conceivable branch of study, and after every possible inducement has been exhausted, there must remain a great mass of pure wearisome drudgery. In all literary pursuits after school life is over, there have to be often months of patient accumulation of dry material, before there can be any repaying work, and much of this is simply wasted labour, having no appreciable effect on the result. In active life the case is, if anything, stronger. Every lawyer or doctor has to plod through incalculable masses of dreary details, without the stimulant of intellectual interest. With the bulk of mankind dull drudgery is to be their lot during the greater part of their lives—hence since it has to come, the preparation for it should come too. And if so, ought it not to come early? The answer is easy. If hard dull labour must come upon us, it must come; but that is no reason for introducing it too soon.

Let us look at the real nature of the process. A child must be induced to learn either by fear or by curiosity; we may awaken its intellect, or we may make it feel the dangers of idleness. The great obstacle to education is the simple dislike to all intellectual activity. An average lad resents any attempt to make him exert his intellect. If he is forced to learn some new lesson, and has his choice to learn it by rote, or made intelligible, ten to one but he will choose the mechanical method. Lads will learn if made to, but will not think if they can avoid it. You can force them to the brink; you cannot make them drink. Now the old method was powerless to deal with this state of things. The first requirement is to get some sort of intellectual interest, and the only plan is to get the child to discover by your method that there is real pleasure to be got out of intellectual exercises. Every child finds pleasure in exercising his faculties on right objects. By right method this spark may be fanned into a flame, and it is of the highest importance that this should be done early. There is no risk that the notion of play will be thus associated with school work, for from the outset work will have to be encountered that cannot be deemed too easy. Allure then by right method every child into paths of study, and do what you can to help him on, over the ruggednesses that he must encounter, but never fear that he will not meet ere long the drudgery that is to fit him for the battle of life. The more he learns, the more drudgery he will have to undergo. Climbing mountains must always be hard work, if you climb far enough and fast enough, and the same is true of the hill of knowledge. You have no need to put burdens on the back, nor to drive up the steepest ascents; there will be labour enough though the paths are zigzag, and the resting-places many."

The subjects of instruction need not detain us long. He has left little on the method of teaching to read. He is of the same mind as Milton, and would provide pleasant books, as "Æsop's Fables," and would have them illustrated, because the child finds it difficult to realize the things mentioned, and pictures and objects convey ideas, and give the means of understanding the book. To add to its educative power, the child should be encouraged and required to tell what it has read.

His method of penmanship is usually described as a method of tracing, and this doubtless is its characteristic feature. But he had a better appreciation of what is necessary to form a good penman than merely to teach the right formation of letters. "When the child comes to be entered on writing he should not be taught to hold his pen and shape his letters all at once, but the former part of the action should be perfected first. This done, the way to teach him to write without much trouble is to get a plate graven with the characters of such a hand as you like best. But you must remember to have them a pretty deal bigger than he should ordinarily write; for every one naturally comes by degrees to write a less hand than he at first was taught, but never a bigger. Such a plate being graved let several sheets of paper be printed off with red ink, which he has nothing to do but go over with a good pen filled with black ink, which will quickly bring his hand to the formation of those characters, being at first shown where to begin and how to form every letter. And when he can do that well, he must exercise on fair paper; and so he may easily be brought to write the hand you desire." Here we find that Locke would have one thing mastered at a time, and each in its right place. The management of the pen first, the right formation of letters next, then freedom and character. He would also have the pupil instructed so that his imitation might be intelligent. And he would only have mechanical aids so long as they were necessary to acquire form.

Grammar and composition should go together. He does not notice the disciplinary power of the former, but simply regards it in relation to correct speech. He rightly attaches little influence to a mere knowledge of its rules. Correct speaking is a matter of practice, association, and habit. Hence the importance of composition. This should first be oral. The pupil should read a tale, and then tell it. The next step is to write. This also after reading. The composition should be clear, succinct, and methodical. Then should come the writing of letters.

He would have French early, because it is taught conversationally, and the organs being pliant, he gets the habit of speaking it properly, which the longer it is delayed, the harder it is to be done. Latin he thinks is not needed by a tradesman. It is a waste of time to spend it first on the grammar. It is utterly impossible to understand the grammar of a language that is unknown. Hence the language should be acquired before the grammar is touched. This should be done by conversation and by interlinear translation.

Section V.—*Vicesimus Knox.*

Vicesimus Knox, master of Tunbridge school, was born in London in 1752. At the age of twenty-nine he published his book on "Liberal Education." It passed through numerous editions, and was held in much esteem by schoolmasters of his own class. It was a protest against innovations, and an exposition and defence of established practices. "Hitherto there had been many books on education, but as they were the works of speculative writers, they contained few valuable directions to the practical instructor. They were full of innovations, where innovation should ever be regarded with suspicion. He was a practical man. His whole life had been spent in school as a learner, in college as a student, and again in school as a master; hence he could speak from experience." He regrets the influence of Milton, Locke, and other speculative persons. To them was due the fact that many Adventure schools and academies had sprung up which had made a wide departure from the ancient system of education.

His chief contention is in favour of classical learning, as opposed to physical, philosophical, and mathematical studies. Classical learning produces enlargement, refinement, and embellishment of the mind. It qualifies for any particular profession or occupation. It is the best preparation for any employment above the low and mechanical. It opens sources of pleasure unknown to the vulgar. It gives an elevation of sentiment and nobility of nature. It only makes the true gentleman. He insinuates that those who oppose it are simply acting like the fox in the fable. He compares one with such training to a precious stone shining with its own lustre, while those without it have simply paint and garnish.

When you ask how these advantages are secured by classical training, you find the reply uncertain. There is confusion of thought. He speaks of them as due to the well-regulated study of philosophy, poetry, and history, found in classical authors. But this study, he says, is impracticable up to the age of nineteen, for all the attention is required by the languages, and is given to them. Yet all through his book he seems to transfer the advantages derived from the study of classical authors to the mode of learning the languages. And there is no doubt that it is this that he has in view when contending for classical instruction as the sole basis of mental discipline. He makes also important admissions. The time to be given to it must necessarily exclude from this course and its advantages all but the very few. He also admits that many have not realized the advantages, either because they lacked the parts, or were not sufficiently diligent, or were taken away too soon. But while he makes this admission he does not see its force. Few get the culture; where one succeeds, thousands fail. But the question in education is not what is the best for the gifted, even allowing this to be the best, but what is best for the many? He gives elsewhere an admirable illustration of his contention that such discipline fits for every employment, by saying that teaching to read must be irksome to a man of culture, and consequently must be ill performed!

There may be gathered from his book that certain principles should regulate school work. It is the function of the school to prepare the mind for the future. This is to be done by opening out avenues of research and culture, but chiefly by strengthening its powers. A prime aim should be to give it vigour. It is necessary to hold this position. Masters are censured for not suiting their instruction to the bias of the scholar. They use the same material for all. This complaint is in ignorance,—masters cannot do it. The school has a regular plan of study, which it is impossible to vary for individuals. It is also a misconception. School has to give a general preparation, a discipline of the whole mind, not a special culture of dominant faculties. As a tradesman does not consider of every shilling gained its purchasing power, but adds it to the general stock ; so a master has to consider the general power of the pupil, and not the special advantage of a particular course. Hence it would be a mistake. For if any faculties are really strong they may be hopefully left, and the weak ones strengthened ; or the individual will be narrow-minded, dwarfed, and contracted. It is often impossible. Natural bias seldom shows itself in the school period. Mental tastes display themselves at different periods according to the varying constitutions. Often the nobler faculties, and those that give direction to the life, put in a late appearance. It should be deemed essential that all qualify themselves with habits of constancy, vigilance, and industry. Of none should there be despair except idiots. The difference between these opinions and those of Locke is rather apparent than real. There is, in fact, no contrariety. Knox refers to faculties of intelligence, while Locke deals with the emotional nature, and here it is certainly true—

"The child is father to the man."

The scholar must be accustomed to hard labour, and any method that proposes to make the road to learning easy must be regarded with suspicion. In early lessons the agreeable may be united with the useful, but the learner must not be cheated to his task by the notion that it is a game. He must early meet the fact that nothing valuable is to be obtained without labour. The mind is naturally indolent, averse from unnecessary toil, and rejoices in means that more easily accomplish its end. This is particularly true in the season when school education begins. But in education nothing is valuable without labour. No high point of excellence is ever attained without arduous and persevering toil. That which requires great effort to gain will not be soon lost, for the impression it makes is deep. On the other hand, things easily obtained are readily lost, like money acquired at an easy rate. Ideas collected without effort make very faint impression. Hence it is no valid objection to a method that it requires effort, for labour strengthens the mind, increases its native vigour, and is favourable to the permanence of its acquisitions. But a method that proposes to lessen the labour must not be lightly adopted, for generally, as you lessen the toil you decrease its value.

These views do not sufficiently discriminate betwixt the periods of culture. In relation to the later stages of school work they may be regarded as sound, but during all the earlier stages, when the mind of the pupil is in direct contact with that of the master, and when its efforts are elicited, guided, and strengthened by such contact, all that can be done by good method to remove difficulties, or to enable the pupil to overcome them, should be done. Procedure by a good method is simply working according to mental laws, and surely it is better that the pupil shall be rightly directed and aided, than that he should be left without rudder, chart, or compass, in a sea of troubles. And let it not be supposed that any such aid will make his path too easy.

From its very nature there will remain not only enough of irksome drudgery, but of matter that will require all his intelligence and power.

There should be right culture of memory. It is strong in young children, and things may by them be acquired with ease which would be an intolerable drudgery at a later time. Latin grammar, and other things that they cannot understand, should be exacted from them. For if these are not learnt early they will never be thoroughly acquired. Knox does not see that such a practice must place obstacles in the learner's path; that it entails losses which are not covered by the gain. Such verbal use of the memory forms the habit of doing things without intelligent attention, than which nothing could be a greater hindrance to intellectual growth. In many cases it effectually bars all real progress, and where it does not it makes it greatly more difficult to acquire the power of intelligent application.

No faculty of the mind being more capable of improvement in youth, and none more in danger of decay by disease, care should be taken to store it well. If it is not filled with valuable furniture it will be crowded with lumber. It should be filled with choice pieces. Beautiful passages should be studiously committed to memory, or they will leave no more trace than the shadow of the summer cloud does on the landscape. Such passages should first be construed, then learnt by heart. Habit will render it easy. But the culture of the memory must be judicious. It is not the chief object in education. It is not to be loaded with unimportant minutiæ. It is of more importance to remember an eloquent passage than its place on the page. It is more important to get the kernel than to retain the husk. Whatever the mind receives, it should not only reproduce, but give it back altered, improved, and refined. "A good memory," says Erasmus, "is like a net that catches the great fishes, but lets the little ones escape."

The only infallible way of improving the memory is frequent, regular, well-directed exercise. "The one great secret," says Quintilian, "for the improvement of memory is exercise, practice, labour. Nothing is so much improved by care, or falls to decay by neglect." It must also be trusted. Like a generous friend it will repay habitual confidence with fidelity. It is not benefited by the practice of writing things to be remembered. Quintilian tells us that to put things in writing is the surest way to lose them, for we cease to guard them; and Plato says that the best way to keep them in memory is not to put them in writing.

The subjects taught in school should not be too numerous. Art is long, life is short. Having many subjects, children come to be talkers in all, masters in none. Early discipline will mould the future. Instruction cannot commence too early, the time must be determined by the display of capacity, but as early as possible, for earliest impressions are durable, and time is saved. Knox thinks that little need to be feared as regards the health. The instruction should be judiciously conducted, and then the spirits and activity of children will supply the antidote to any otherwise injurious strain.

Children should early learn to read. There is no

reason why it should not be attained by five or six, or at furthest seven. The longer it is delayed, the more difficult it is to acquire. Early inferiority in this is a bar to subsequent proficiency, while it is a fact that early readers make the best progress. For this acquisition the nursery is the place. and the teacher the mother. Thus the child may not have anything to unlearn. In teaching the alphabet he would have a plain card. One with cuts diverts the attention from the less interesting sign to the more amusing picture. Yet as it is a sufficiently irksome thing, he should be drawn on by interesting books, the understanding of which should be aided by pictures. But reading must not be the only source of knowledge to the infant, it is only one of several ways, and it is necessary there should be variety. It is essential, too, that the tasks should be short,—a little and with ease. The value is not in the gain from one lesson. but in the habit, the constant growth. and the accumulation of power.

Latin should be the basis of school discipline. The grammar should first be acquired. This knowledge is like the broad foundations of a building, hidden indeed, but necessary to the stability of the superstructure. But Knox abandons the early mode, and advocates a compromise betwixt it and the principle advocated by Locke. To that principle he gives his unconscious adhesion. Let the grammar be the first course for six months, then let the learner parse and construe an easy Latin author. The knowledge thus acquired gives a better hold of the grammar. With the same purpose let all the rules be learnt in English as well as in Latin. And in first going over the grammar neglect its minutiæ, as the science of language is not the object, but the attainment of a language. This compromise between a valuable principle and an absurd practice is significant both of the force of truth and the tenacity of prejudice. That no one can study the grammar of a language he does not understand seems a self-evident proposition, and would recommend itself, one would think, to all but those who consult their own ease as masters of schools rather than teachers in them. That Knox advocated as far as he did the preposterous practice of learning the grammar first, and then applying what was not understood to the parsing and construing of a book, seems to have come from that obliquity of vision which is produced by the prejudice of early custom. This compromise was the first step towards the system represented by the books of Peithman, Bryce, and Smith.

Of other languages he recommends Greek and French. They are to be pursued by similar methods, but not at so early an age. He assigns as a reason for not beginning French early, that time is required to mature the mind as well as the body. But surely this objection has stronger force against the early learning of Latin. He thinks that if the learner knows Latin, he need not begin with French grammar, but with an easy interesting book. Then the labour is alleviated; but if confined to the grammar he hates the irksome toil. He prefers learning to read French rather than to speak it, unless there is the opportunity to reside in France.

Other subjects should fill up gaps. English should be acquired through good authors. Its grammar may be delayed with advantage till the learner has intellectual strength. A paper from the *Spectator* should be taken, and treated by parsing and analysis, as a Latin author would be. Aid should be had from composition. At first Æsop, then history, Plutarch, and the *Spectator* should be read, and themes written on what had been thus prepared. Plagiarism should be discouraged. It may be prevented by avoiding captious criticism and fault-finding, and by not punishing egregious mistakes. If the boy sees that his own composition is found fault with, while plagiarism escapes, he will escape from the trouble of invention. Geography should not be learnt by rote. The first strokes that form the sketch of a picture cannot be pencilled too truthfully. In geography every idea should be presented clearly to the apprehension. The study should be begun early, but without books. Maps should be the only aids. These should not be too crowded, and should be very distinct. They should be explained, and they should be made familiar. They should be at hand for reference in other lessons. Map-drawing is a waste of time. History should be read at home as a recreation, not enter into the curriculum of the school. Euclid, astronomy, and physics belong to the university. Drawing should be taught only to such as are likely to excel in it. He who gives attention to arithmetic contracts a degree of rust totally destructive of genius. But Knox allows that as a science it furnishes a fine exercise for the mind.

We gather incidentally that Knox would have eight classes or forms, a half-yearly examination for the advancement of the proficient, and place-taking during the daily lessons as a spur to emulation.

CHAPTER II.

THE COMMON SCHOOL.

THE progress made in school education in this country during the present century has been very much promoted by the writings and labours of two men, very dissimilar in many respects,—Richard Lovell Edgeworth, born at Bath in 1744; and Henry Pestalozzi, born at Zurich, January 12th, 1746. Their plans of education have the same starting-point, and their views coincide in many particulars. But the former not only placed his own aims clearly before his mind, but was skilful in carrying them out in his practice; while Pestalozzi was more ingenious in stating and illustrating principles than apt in working them.

Section I.—The Edgeworths.

The work on "Practical Education" was the joint production of Edgeworth and of his celebrated daughter, Maria. It first appeared in 1798. It describes the practices of the former in the education of his own family, and states the principles by which education should be conducted. The first chapter is on toys, and anticipates the kindergarten system. Toys that may be handled, and whose powers of amusing and profitably employing will not soon be lost, should be provided—as pieces of wood of various shapes and sizes, squares, circular bits, cubes, balls, and triangles. These will call forth observation, make them acquainted with the properties of objects, and stimulate invention, for the child will build up and pull down, and put into a variety of forms and positions. The point here is to leave the child, and not by rash interference to break the charm and destroy the utility, for the advantage is in the child doing, not in being told how to do. "Every bit of wood," says Richter, " is a gilded flower-rod to the child, on which fancy can bud hundred-leaved roses. In the eyes of wonder-working fancy every Aaron's rod blossoms." Pictures may be early introduced. They engage attention and employ imagination. They bring back former ideas, and lead to comparisons between these and what they see in prints; they thus elicit judgments. That they may produce the best results in early infancy they must correspond to the experience of the child. Prints of a thing out of its sphere, or representing things as he is not accustomed to see them, seldom attract the attention or stimulate the fancy of a five-year-old child; but truthful representations, agreeing with facts he may have observed, will set his imagination working. "The wind blows that woman's gown back," was the suggestion of such a print to a four-year old child. After having been accustomed to examine prints, and to trace their resemblance to real objects, children will probably wish to try their own powers of imitation. At this moment place in their hands a pencil, and let them make random marks all over a sheet of paper. No matter how rude their first attempts at imitation may be; if the attention is occupied, the point is gained. Girls have an advantage over boys in the exclusive possession of scissors, and are pleasurably and profitably occupied in cutting out wonderful camels, elephants, and other things. When the period comes, in which the child wants more active employment to his mind and fingers, he must be furnished with that which will give him the opportunity of thought and invention. It will be profitable now to introduce modelling in clay and wax, making baskets, and weaving tapes. Then as skill grows, and a greater demand is made on his inventive powers, there may be supplied to him cards, pasteboard, scissors, wire, gum, and wax, that he may fashion, model, construct, and build. In all this course the purpose is to secure observation, to stimulate invention, to foster fancy, and to cultivate practical judgment. The one great rule is to teach the child to work out the things in its own mind, and not to crush in the bud its nascent faculties by hasty interference. Help may be given, but it must be judiciously timed, and it must be of a kind to stimulate originality, and not make them mere copyists. Thus the elements of a scientific character are laid. The child learns the properties of things; he becomes curious to know how certain effects are produced, destroying the toy in the prosecution of the philosophical inquiry; he inquires, combines, and invents. Such a child shows the effect of his training by asking, among many similar inquiries, "How is it that my hoop keeps up so long as it rolls, but falls as soon as it stops?"

The same principle that has guided the development of the mind should be followed in first learning. It is not verbal memory, but intelligence that should be cultivated. There must not be disagreeable associations with learning. It need not be treated as a game; but it should be made interesting by employing his faculties. Learning to read early is not a matter of such moment as some seem to think, for the use made of it is the important point; and if it should be so learnt as to disgust, and then be never used, where is the advantage of having learnt early?

The common method of teaching the alphabet is dreadful. The names of the letters and the variety of their sounds disturb the common sense of the child, and at every step stop his progress. He learns one thing in one lesson, and he finds it contradicted in the next. Having learnt *u* in "fume," he pronounces it the same way in "fun," and is blamed; he meets it again in "busy," and is again at fault; at "burial" he gives up in despair, in "prudence" he becomes reckless, and he stops at the stage of "dunce." In the reading lesson he is told to spell words by their names, but having done so through "Here is some apple pie," he finds that he cannot decipher for himself these simple words.

A better method is needed. Do not be in a hurry, let a few things be learnt at a time. It does not matter whether it takes six weeks or six months, so that it is done well, and without confusion to the learner. Take the vowels first, distinguish their several sounds by points. For instance, let a represent the sound in fame; a in fat; a in fall; ä in far. When the vowel sounds and their signs are acquired, take the consonants, but do not give their names till the child has acquired their powers. This must be by analysis and induction. Place b and the other consonants before a, a, a, ü, e, e, e, e, and so on; let these syllables be pronounced, and let the learner from such practice get the powers of the consonants. When they have thus learnt the letters and their powers let them read. In the books put the marks indicating the various sounds, and others indicating the silent letters.

This is a better plan of teaching the elements of reading, than the one it was intended to supersede. But it is needlessly complicated. It has the fault of all the earlier teaching, loading the memory with a large number of rules before supplying practice. Nor does it sufficiently recognise the truth underlying itself, that a child obtains the powers of the letters by an induction from its own practice—not a conscious induction, but one that forms itself into its habits. Hence a plan that would secure a greater amount of reading, and one that would gradually introduce the varying vowel powers, would sooner effect the object. This is now attempted in several first reading books. Langler, of the Westminster Training College, was the first to introduce it. First we have a set of lessons in which the vowels and consonants have a constancy of power, as in bat, fat, mat; bet, met, pet; bit, fit, pit: then we have a set introducing another sound, as in mate, mete, mite, where the opportunity occurs of pointing out the significance of the final e. In this way the child gradually acquaints himself with the powers of the letters, and he approaches the anomalies without perplexity. The "Phonic Method," as Edgeworth's plan came to be called, degenerated into an attempt to give the powers of the consonants by themselves, and to build up words by the process bŭ-ă-tĕ, bat. An instance this, not unfrequent in schools, of a good principle becoming the ground of an absurd practice, because carried out by parties who had no special training for their work, and who had not taken the trouble, if they had the power, to master the principle.

Spelling should follow reading. He seems here to abandon the practice of teaching to read by spelling, either name or phonic. He objects to spelling-books. They bring new perils to the understanding, and they disgust children with literature by the pain and difficulty of their first lessons. A better way is to use the words they know, and those which occur most frequently in reading and conversation. Of these a few should be taken at a time, on the maxim "a little and well." Let the children see that spelling is necessary in writing. Let them write a few words of their own daily, and others that they have been reading. When they see its use and feel its need, then they will learn with ease and precision. Spelling should not be taught before they can write. The mistakes they make in writing must be pointed out, and must be carefully corrected by the learner. This is necessary, as bad habits once formed cannot be cured, because the understanding has nothing to do with the business. It must be remembered that spelling is learnt by the eye, hence the more they read and write, the greater their progress will be in spelling correctly.

Arithmetic should be taught as soon as the child can read. This recommendation comes from Edgeworth's unwillingness to burden the child with too many subjects. But there is no danger to the child in taking arithmetic as a parallel exercise with reading and writing. The faculties it brings into play are so distinct that relief and benefit follow rather than injury. Besides, it is well to accustom the learner early to seek relief in change rather than in cessation of work. His next recommendation shows how truly he was at one with Locke and Pestalozzi in the principles that should regulate first instruction. Early lessons in arithmetic should be conducted on the same principles as have hitherto guided us. Infancy is the season for cultivating the senses, and here we find one of the reasons for proceeding in this subject from the concrete to the abstract. This, too, should be the case not only in the earlier operations, but in every subsequent stage. The intelligence of the child must go along with every process, its understanding must be preserved from implicit belief, its powers must be invigorated, and it must be saved from merely technical working.

The first thing is to combine numbers with real objects. The names of numbers must be connected in the mind with the groups they represent. He should learn these groups as two cubes, three cubes, and so on. He should see that three cubes are the same thing as two cubes and one cube. When he is able to distinguish each group and name it, then he may be taught to know and make the figure that represents it. In this and subsequent operations it is well to use half-inch cubes or pebbles, so that the eye may easily take in the group. The next step is addition. This should be first by things, then by figures. First he must be kept to numbers below ten, and the operation both by things and figures should tend to make him still more familiar with the groups and their names. The exercises might be graduated in some such way as this :—

```
                    1
           1        1 1
   1       1 1      1 1 1         1
   1  1 1 1 1 1 2   1 1 1  1  2  3
   1  2 1 2 3 2     1 2 3  4  2  2
   ─  ─ ─ ─ ─ ─ ─   ─ ─ ─  ─  ─  ─
   3  3 4 4 4 4 5   5 5 5  5  5  5
```

Before taking the next step means should be taken to make familiar all the possible combinations up to nine, to add and subtract with rapidity, and to write figures with accuracy and expedition. The process should employ the eye, ear, and mind, so that the technical habit may be acquired without injury to the understanding. These preliminary steps, if begun in the child's fifth year, may occupy a few minutes daily during half a year.

The next step, numeration, is the most difficult in early arithmetic. It may be prepared for by drawing the child's attention to the common way of speaking of one flock, two flocks, one grove, two groves, when he feels no difficulty in applying the term one to a group containing many. In the same way to speak of one dozen, two dozens, may prepare for one ten, two tens. Let dark pebbles be counted, and for each ten put aside one white pebble, then the white pebbles will each represent ten, and when there are ten of these, let one red pebble be put aside, and the child may thus see how one may represent a hundred. By exercises like these the child may learn that the terms one, two, three, and so on, may be indifferently applied to individuals, tens, or hundreds. When this is all clear, the child will find no difficulty in understanding the value of written figures by the place they hold ; indeed, he may be led to invent this arrangement. Having acquired this knowledge and skill, an idea of decimal arithmetic may be given to him, as he will find no difficulty now in understanding that the same figures may represent tenth parts as well as groups.

In subtraction Edgeworth recommends that the methods employed shall grow out of their previous work. For instance, in taking forty-six from ninety-four, the child first sees that the sum forty-six is to be taken from the larger sum ninety-four; then using his knowledge of numeration and notation, he is taught to analyze ninety-four into eighty and fourteen, then to take six from fourteen; then four tens or forty from eight tens or eighty. He would have the same principle followed in other rules. In the rule of three, as the learner can already divide and multiply, instead of the method of statement, he should first be told to find the value of one, and then of the required quantities.

Methods like these are usually spoken of as Pestalozzian, and their extensive use in common schools is due very much to Tate's "Principles of Arithmetic," but they may all be found in the works of Ward, a full century before Edgeworth; where also may be found modes of teaching mensuration on similar principles.

When we pass from the period in which the senses are the chief avenues of intelligence, to the cultivation of the understanding, the first object is to give the power of attention, or in other words, to interest the learners in what they are about. The means are now to be considered. First there must be no false associations. There should be a right medium betwixt offering the subjects as tasks, repelling the learner, and exciting his disgust, and the fashion of making learning a play, cheating him into knowledge, or paying for its acquisition by sugar-plums. This plan increases the desire to be amused, but lessens the relish for it. The mind becomes passive and indolent, and an increasing stimulus is necessary to awaken effort. Dissipated habits are formed, and the pupil never gets command of his own powers. The pupil must understand that knowledge cannot be obtained without labour. He must be incited to work, and he must be in earnest. There must be no deceit practised on him. There must be no illusion. There is no need for any. It is easy by proper methods to interest him in the subjects he has to learn; the prime thing is to carry his intelligence with you.

Edgeworth continually insists that lessons should cover short periods, but that the learner shall be stimulated to put forth his utmost strength during that period. A serious and strong effort for half an hour will do more in forming the habit of attention than the practice of assigning work that will last for hours, and where the effort is necessarily of a dreamy kind. Thorough acquaintance with what he is taught is essential to present and future attention. The pupil should be presented with little at a time, but it should be completely attained. It should become familiar. Few things so disgust a child with learning as imperfect acquaintance with it. Whenever that which he has acquired is perfectly familiar to his mind, the pupil is inspired with confidence and interest. He becomes conscious of power, and the tediousness of his employment vanishes. Those who wish thus to succeed in teaching must remember that a child can attend to but one thing at a time. Its attention must not be fatigued by variety. It is of more importance that a child should leave a lesson with a relish for learning, and a desire to return to it, than that it has made much progress. Let him find that he has made one thing fully his own, and his pleasure will stimulate him in other lessons. But while seeing that his acquisitions are thorough and familiar, the teacher must avoid the mistake of doing more than the child needs. When a thing is clear, let him not try to make it clearer. When a thing is understood, not a word more of exemplification should be added. To mark precisely the moment when the pupil is master of the subject, and when repetition should cease, is the most difficult thing in teaching, though the difficulty is in the teacher more than in the scholar. The former is so absorbed in his subject that he has no attention to give to the unmistakable signs of repletion given by the pupils. Thoroughness and familiarity may be promoted without this weariness, by asking in other lessons the reproduction of former teaching.

In instruction it is often found comparatively easy to fix the attention on the several points of a lesson, where there is utter failure in fixing it on the connection of the parts. None but teachers know how difficult this is. The dependence of one thing upon another, and the concurrence of the whole to some definite conclusion, altogether escape the scholar. Yet this, if allowed to pass, will prove a hindrance to that completeness of attainment and its accompanying consciousness of power which make the child a voluntary worker. This, then, is an important point. The pleasure of thinking, and much of the profit, must frequently depend on the learner preserving the connection of ideas. It is impossible to teach those who do not grasp each link and hold fast the whole chain of reasoning. This confessedly difficult business requires all the skill at the teacher's command. His steps must be short. He must remember the difference between his own capacity and that of his pupil. Things easy to him may test all the power of the child. He forgets how he learnt things that now seem to be received intuitively. The pupil's steps must not be hurried. Let there be time for each thing definitely to enter his mind. It is not speed, but complete attainment that is to be sought. Especially is it necessary that the pupil shall not be perplexed by talk, nor pressed too hastily to reply. Do not place a crowd of words between him and the end to which you are conducting him. Let him not be lost in a fog. Yet there must be judicious repetition. The reasoning must be repeated till the chain of ideas is completely formed.

A great difficulty in teaching, in fixing attention, and securing thorough attainment, arises from language. This difficulty has several aspects. Often the pupils want words. They have ideas, and they have the power of expressing them; but they are not connected in their minds with the words used by the teacher, hence there is no common ground on which they can meet. The language of the teacher awakens no corresponding thought in the scholar, and his ignorance of their knowledge and language makes these of no avail for the elucidation of the subject in hand. This shows the necessity of adding to the child's knowledge of words as well as to his knowledge of things. This may be done in several ways: by examining objects and associating words and phrases with the ideas obtained; by reading and by conversational lessons. Often when children begin to read they acquire a great variety of words. This is the source of a new danger. The learner speedily picks up a particular use of a word, and the teacher concludes that its whole meaning is laid bare to him. The duty thus becomes incumbent on the teacher to deal with new language. New words and phrases should never be passed without full explanation. This is absolutely necessary to the growth of the understanding, for if their knowledge of words is obscure, so will be their thoughts, and correct judgments and right reasoning will be impossible. The possession of words by children which have never been unfolded to them, and the employment of such words in lessons, are fruitful sources of inattention. The words are ever changing their meanings, to the great perplexity of the learner. Edgeworth illustrates the difficulty to the child by supposing it to be set to cast up a sum, the figures of which were being constantly changed by the teacher. The child will refuse his attention where the language is indefinite to him. He will make no effort when it is impossible for him to understand. All this shows how necessary it is for a teacher to be simple in his language, and to use it with precision.

Among motives to attention the personal one must not be overlooked. There are some persons who have the power of exciting others to great mental exertions, by the ardent ambition which they inspire, and by the value which is set upon their love and esteem. When once this generous desire of affection and esteem is raised in their minds, their exertions seem to be universal and spontaneous; children are then no longer machines requiring to be regularly wound up, but they are animated by a living principle which directs all that it inspires. Edgeworth himself was an example of this with his own children; and it was perhaps the one thing above all others that accounts for Pestalozzi's success.

Great care should be taken in the selection of books, whether for reading or technical study. Bad books are very mischievous. Early reading books should have no narratives in which forms of vice, wrong doing, or faults are described. Such books often put evil into the minds of children which otherwise would not have entered. They should also be free from false sentiment, and from urging right actions by questionable motives. They should also be in good English. Erroneous modes of speech, though sanctioned by custom, should be avoided. The practice of putting vulgar language into the mouths of the actors in the narrative, under pretence of being true to nature and to fact, cannot be too strongly condemned. Children do not appreciate the supposed humour, they are not competent to criticise, and they cannot but be injured by it. *History* is a very appropriate subject, but the books written for children are open to serious objections. It is not right to put opinions into children's heads. Care should be taken not to prejudice the mind. The characters that are drawn of historic personages, the moral reflections that are continually interspersed, the political doctrines that are expressed, are all out of place. Facts should be given as fully as may be, and the children left to form their own judgments.

Poetry should not be given too early. Descriptive poetry is intelligible to young children, but it demands little effort of attention, and therefore should not form a part of their daily occupation. It should be read but occasionally. More difficult poetry must always be accompanied by questioning and explanation; only thus can it be made profitable. When clearly comprehended it may be committed to memory. *Grammar* should not be begun too early. First lessons should not deal with technical terms. Familiar explanations of the structure of simple sentences should be given. These should be accompanied by exercises, from which the children may discover for themselves the offices of words. From these to more complicated sentences, until they have a knowledge of rational grammar. Then they may begin the more technical study.

The chapters in which the Edgeworths treat of moral discipline deserve the careful consideration of all teachers. Only one or two points are noticed here. The first notions of right and wrong which children get are from the expressions of pleasure or displeasure by their parents. They thus learn to associate pain with certain actions, and pleasure with others. In continuing their moral education the same principle should be recognised. The whole treatment of a child should lead him to associate certain experiences as the necessary consequences of his actions. This should be consistently acted upon until the association in his mind is indissoluble—that wrong actions bring painful results. In doing this the teacher will be aided by the way in which a child learns the qualities of external things, and by which its experiences fashion its conduct. The child who puts its finger too near the fire and burns it, and who finds that the same effect always follows the same action, has learnt the lesson God intended. Punishments must be of the same character. They should appear as the natural consequences of the actions, and they should be of uniform occurrence. Punishments of an artificial character have no permanent effect, for they are perceived to have no natural connection with the offence, to depend on the will of the individual, to be fitful in their severity, and not certain in their action. It is uniformity of natural consequences that creates the impression of cause and effect.

The child is placed in a relation in which its own will is to be formed by first submitting to the will of another. The principles that should guide in this are few. It is better to prevent than punish; hence care must be taken to form the child to a habit of obedience. Let first commands be about things the child has pleasure in performing. An action which the child would do of itself is thus associated with obedience to a command. At a somewhat later stage depend rather on prohibitions. Here you can enforce your will, or you may prohibit actions, which if performed will bring slight pain. Then disobedience will convince the child that the prohibition was for its good. When commands are necessary, consider whether you can enforce them, for nothing should be done by you that would suggest or foster obstinacy. In early life reasons are out of place; they cannot be understood; hence implicit obedience must be exacted. But when children begin to reason, they do not act merely from habit; and now, whenever we can use reason, we should never use force.

Section II.—*Pestalozzi and the Pestalozzian System.*

The term Pestalozzian is used to designate certain principles and methods that are employed, in this country, chiefly in infant culture. These principles and methods in their germ, along with much that was unsound and injurious, were found in the system of training established by Wilderspin. Their development and combination into—as far as it goes—a rational system of training is due to neither worker—but in other countries to Pestalozzi's fellow labourers, and in this country to the Mayos and to their co-workers. Reserving for another place the contributions of these to educational progress, we shall glance in this at the work of Pestalozzi himself.

Pestalozzi was born at Zurich, January 12th, 1746. He had reached his thirtieth year, when the failure of some speculations in which he had embarked at his place, Neuhof, gave him the opportunity to attempt the accomplishment of a dream of his youth. He set himself vigorously to pursue the means of raising man morally, and of promoting thereby his comfort and happiness. Afflicted with the misery that he saw around him, and deeply pained at the moral depravity and great degradation of the people, he intently revolved the problem of their recovery. His first notion was, that to elevate man morally he must be improved outwardly, his circumstances must be bettered, his social status raised. Entering enthusiastically into this view of the case, he spared neither himself nor his fortune. He opened at Neuhof an industrial school for poor children, an effort that was not altogether thrown away on them, as more than a hundred were reclaimed, but which was of more value to Pestalozzi himself. Convinced, by the excesses that accompanied and followed revolutionary action, of the fallacy of his previous opinion, he began to have a glimmering of the truth, that it is not the change in outward condition that brings happiness to a community, but the intellectual and moral improvement of the individual. Hence, it now became his aim to produce a condition in which the happiness of the man would not be affected from without, because its source would be within, and to raise the moral condition of the community by an entirely new method of training the young. His opinions he embodied in various works, by which he sought at once to stimulate parents to educate their children, and to point out how it should be done. Of these amongst others may be named, "The Evening Hour with a Hermit," "Leonard and Gertrude," and "How Gertrude teaches her Children."

In 1798, at the age of 52, Pestalozzi became a schoolmaster, and from this period until two years before his death in 1827, he gave himself up to the work he had chosen. His qualifications for this work consisted rather in a profound conviction that education was on a wrong basis, than in any special knowledge of what it should be, or how it should be prosecuted. He was of opinion that to enkindle right affections, to substitute real knowledge for verbal forms, to develop mental power rather than to load the memory, and harmoniously to cultivate "the hand, the head, and the heart," should enter into a right system of education. But he had only vague conceptions on these points, and he certainly saw no clear way to their accomplishment. However, he brought to his work, earnestness, a loving spirit, a fair intellect, and a simplicity, which did not object to be instructed even by a child. Possessed of these he could not but feel his way to that which he sought.

It could not but arise from this beginning, that he would fall into many errors, and that there would be contradictions betwixt his principles and practices. Besides, he lacked the power to place clearly before his mind his own purposes, and he also lacked the power to express that which obtained in his practice. Thus it happened, that his views were often vague, and his practices absurd, and things were advocated by him, or carried on under the sanction of his name, that were altogether anti-Pestalozzian. It does not fall within our purpose to follow him and his coadjutors in all their experiments, discussions, dissensions, failures, and successes, but rather, to give, as far as the confusion of statement admits, a succinct account of the principles and methods to which he gave his final adhesion.

Clear insight into the nature of the things to be acquired, rather than a verbal enunciation of a fact or a formula, is the leading principle of the Pestalozzian method. This he called intuition. The learner was to examine and compare things, and acquire ideas rather than signs, and this he was to do under direction rather than by instruction. His knowledge was to be real, made his own by examination with his senses. Clearness of perception was one thing sought, the doing it for himself the other. Both must go together; for so far as the process of observation is interfered with by the oral communications of the teacher, so far will there be want of clearness in the result, and loss of power to the child; but let the child exercise its senses —under direction—gradually on things, and its perceptions will be clear, its mind strengthened, and itself prepared for further acquisitions.

In this principle, Pestalozzi struck at the root of the common practice. He found children's time at school spent on books, on verbal forms, on definitions, and in committing to memory that which they did not and could not understand. He saw that with the many, school-work was fruitless of results. The people grew up unintelligent, their minds burdened with verbal rubbish, and themselves none the better, but rather the worse for their school course. Certainly, some struggled through the form, and seized the spirit of what they acquired, but these were the few, the gifted, the minds that in any circumstances would have attained knowledge and power. Pestalozzi aimed to do for the average intellect, what superior minds struggle to do of their own accord, or intuitively grasp. The common mind rested in the sign. Their stores were verbal. There was no life, no meaning, no thought. The mental current was not affected by anything they acquired. The daily flow of feeling and idea was governed entirely by the wants of the lower life. They never rose above this level.

Their minds had been weighed down at school, and never recovered their natural elasticity.

All this Pestalozzi desired to change. By banishing books, by employing the senses, by developing—Socratically, but in a new form—ideas in the mind, by giving realities, by following nature, by exercising every faculty in a gradual and natural way, he hoped to give the child intelligence and power, and to habituate it to live in a higher sphere of thought and feeling than was hitherto possible. But his distaste to the common school course was carried to absurd lengths. Instead of retaining what was valuable, and rejecting what was bad, he aimed at something which should be entirely new. In fact, novelty seems to have had the charm for him that it has for the veriest child. He discredited everything that had on it the stamp of time and experience. That which he sought was very well in its place. The knowledge acquired by the child would be real, but fragmentary, and this was as it should be. For infancy and childhood are storing times. Classifying, generalizing, and defining, are altogether unfitted to a state of mind in which the stores for such processes have not accumulated. But the very fact, that storing is the work of early life shows that it is but preparatory to something higher and better. Now the old school course was wrong, not in what it did, but in doing it out of place, and at the wrong time. Everything in its order would be a safer rule than that which would restrict a child to the mental operations connected with the senses, or that would give it verbal forms before the facts that underlie them. Pestalozzi, in dismissing books, was right for early childhood, but decidedly wrong for a later period. What in his practice—supposing it to end there—could compensate for the loss of the discipline to be derived from the study of the past? For what is a book but the record of the working of another mind at a former period? And what can be substituted—at the proper time—for the right use of books?

There is an objection often urged to the improved methods of training children practised by Pestalozzi, which has been partly anticipated, but which demands more distinct notice. The objector, instancing undoubted examples of progress and mental power under the former system, asks you to account for them if the method was so bad as is assumed. The answer is, either the superior quality of the mind saw that the sign was a sign, and hence looked for something more, and found it, or experience of life and intercourse with man gave the letter subsequently a power which it had not while being acquired.

This point gained, that the child's instruction must be by things rather than by words, and that it must be engaged on realities rather than on signs, the next step was easy that the child should not simply be acted upon, but should be an agent in his own education. He must be made to examine, to compare, to reflect, to think. His must be the examination of the objects brought before him, and his the expression of the ideas awakened in his mind; the teacher's place being to guide by questions, and to correct false impressions and wrong answers in the same way. Whatever the thing on which the child's attention is occupied, this must be the mode. The thing on which it is engaged is comparatively of little importance, but the mode in which its attention is engaged is of essential moment. "There is not an object so trivial that in the hands of a skilful teacher might not become interesting, if not from its own nature, at least from the mode of treating it. . . . . Any subject will do for the purpose. Not only the little incidents in the life of a child, but everything within reach of its attention, whether it belong to nature or to the arts of life, might be the object of a lesson, by which the child might be familiarized with the habit of thinking on what he sees, and speaking after he has thought. The mode of doing this is not by any means to talk much *to* a child, but to enter into conversation *with* a child; not to address to him many words, however familiar or well chosen, but to bring him to express himself on the subject; not to exhaust the subject, but to question the child about it, and to let him find out and correct the answers. The attention of a child is deadened by long expositions, but roused by animated questions. Let these questions be short, clear, and intelligible. Let them not merely lead the child to repeat in the same, or in varied terms, what he has just heard before. Let them excite him to observe what is before him, to recollect what he has learned, and to muster his little stock of knowledge for materials for an answer. Show him a certain quality in one thing, and let him find out the same in others. Do this, and you teach him to observe, to think."

That the ideas gathered may be clear, and the process invigorating, the course must be from the simple, or that which is easy and preparatory, to that which is more complicated and difficult. This course is to be pursued whether dealing with a single subject, or in the entire course of the child's training. For the latter the near and the familiar must be taken, and the circle gradually enlarged till it embraces the remote and strange; for the former, that which is elementary and fundamental must be dealt with, and gradually added to, until the full idea or subject is built up in the mind. For instance, in connection with common objects a lesson might proceed after this fashion :—the object being placed before the child and distinguished, its name is given and repeated; then the parts are noticed and named; then the form and size; the colour; the smoothness of the surface; the hardness or softness; the sound when touched, and so on, are brought out from observation. Then other objects which resemble this in any of these qualities are examined so as to bring out the greater or small degree thereof, and so on. Proceeding thus, there is a clear idea of the object developed in the child's mind, in a gradual and natural way, and besides, there is fostered an effort at observation, judgment, and expression, which, if pursued daily, could not but train the mind of the child in invaluable habits.

Pestalozzi attached much importance to this way of engaging the child on what was simple first, and then proceeding in a gradual and natural manner to what was more complex. "Often," he says, "the supposed incorrigibly dull and slow were found to make rapid progress in the very things in which they had been pronounced incapable, when these were introduced to them in this simple and natural way." So that he thought it ill became any teacher to pronounce on the incapacity of any of his pupils, for it might be that he was rather declaring his own want of skill and method than the obtuseness of his pupil's intellect.

Pestalozzi in pursuing a child's education would have such exercises employed as would be likely to fit the child for the use of all its faculties. He contends that early education should be general, not special; and should concern itself with the harmonious development of the whole nature as far as that is possible in early life. Such also was the opinion of Locke,— " The business of education, in respect of knowledge, is not to perfect the learner in all or any one of the sciences, but to give his mind that disposition and those habits that may enable him to attain any part of knowledge he shall stand in need of in the future course of his life" This consideration led Pestalozzi to seek for means to accomplish this purpose, and he found them, as he thought, on the side of the intellect, in number, form, and language. " These things, he says, not only elicit thought and train to think, but are the mediums through which all ideas come to us in later life." Now without accepting this in its entirety, it must be allowed that a rational course of training would embrace these things. For, apart from their entering into so many of our ideas, and apart therefore from their general educational value, they particularly recommend themselves for infant education, as their elementary parts admit of being presented to the senses, while there is also possible a gradual advance in them from the concrete to the abstract. Nor can it be said that Pestalozzi estimated too highly the advantages of his method when applied to these subjects. In the case of number, if things are presented to the child in groups, and the name attached to the group, there is an intelligence in the result which could not be if but the name was given. So with operations on numbers. Let these be performed before his eyes, or by himself with things, and there is a rational force in operation rather than a mechanical one; and thus taught, the child is led, even in the most advanced stages, to realize to himself the conditions of the problems he works, and to gain his results by applying principles rather than rules. Such practice also gives him analytic power, accustoms him to exact thinking, and leads him to seek for realities under the signs with which his mind works. In the case of form, such exercises as Pestalozzi intends, lead the child from the observation of lines and angles to discern at length forms and relations in surrounding things, which, but for these, would remain hidden from him. But a higher result is obtained, inventive skill, and a power of abstract conception, when the child is taught to produce, to combine, and to originate forms for himself.

In the case of language it is not so clear what was Pestalozzi's notion, or what the special application of his method to it. Certainly his practice here, in some points, was as absurd as it could well be. What advantage could arise from bawling at the extent of the voice unmeaning sounds like ba, ba, ba, la, la, la, or at a later stage all the technical terms belonging to some branch of science, does not appear. But perhaps the solution is in what has been adverted to before, that Pestalozzi often failed to put forth as well in practice as in language the conceptions to which his mind gave birth. From some of his statements, and from some of his exercises, we may gather that it was his wish to enrich the mind of the child with language; to place at its command a large store of words and their combinations, with a thorough intelligence of their meaning and use, and to give it great facility of expression in speaking and composition. Such a design, well carried out, could not fail to be a valuable discipline to the learner, and must fit him for a more intelligent and rapid progress in intellectual pursuits at a later time. Nor can it be a valid ground of objection that in the early course of a child's education this should be done, as Pestalozzi proposed, by the living voice in free communication with the pupil rather than by the dead letter in books. The difficulty in Pestalozzi's practice must have been in getting the children to attach any meaning or take any interest in exercises which consisted chiefly of verbal repetition after the teacher. The oral lesson on objects and other things, referred to in a former paragraph, would have furnished the opportunity required. But Pestalozzi, run away with by the notion of treating everything from its elements, thought consistency required from him the construction of the series of lessons which he framed on language.

There remains but one point necessary to notice in this brief sketch, but that is a most interesting one,—the application by Pestalozzi of his great principle in moral and religious training. Here, as in other things, he objects to *words* as the vehicle of moral and religious truth; he requires *facts*. Not facts of a remote time or place, but facts occurring amongst themselves or in their neighbourhood. And he wants these, not to convey notions merely to their minds, but to lead them to act for others, or to avoid evil. He saw that moral and religious truth, however clearly conceived, if not acted out as occasions occurred, was not merely inoperative, but positively injurious. Hence he sought to awaken sympathy, and thence to lead to action. This led him also to notice the great difference in its influence on children between the act witnessed, or—where that was not possible—conceived, and the precept stated. The latter, a nice jingle of words, is learnt, and in a few days forgotten, not having practically influenced for a moment; but the former conveys not only the truth, but exciting sympathy, gives it firm hold of the mind, and, if occasions are found of acting it out, fixes it as a living power in the life.

To develop religious feeling in a child, it must be, he thought, excited in the first place towards parents and friends, in connection with every-day duties and relations, and then transferred at command to God. Here is one of his vague conceptions of a great truth. That the best way to convey to the mind of a child any notion of its relation to God, is through its knowledge of the relations that exist between its parents and itself is undoubtedly true, and so the best way to make apparent to a child the nature of the feelings which should exist towards God, is by exciting right feelings towards parents; but that these can be transferred at command to God is utterly impossible.

CHAPTER III.

Infants' Schools.

"Oberlin, the pastor of Walbach, in Alsace, may be regarded as the founder of infants' schools. Louise Scheppler, under his auspices, used to assemble the little children of his parish between the ages of two and six. Their object was to interest them by conversation, pictures, and maps, and to teach them to read and sew." The first infants' school in Great Britain was established at Lanark. Its founder, Robert Owen, gave the following account of its origin to a Committee of the House of Commons in 1816:—

"The children are received into a preparatory or *training school* at the age of three, in which they are perpetually superintended, to prevent them acquiring bad habits, to give them good ones, and to form their dispositions to mutual kindness and a sincere desire to contribute all in their power to benefit each other. These effects are chiefly accomplished by *example* and *practice*, precept being found of little use, and not comprehended by them at this early age. The children are taught also whatever may be supposed useful that they can understand, and this instruction is combined with as much amusement as is found to be requisite for their health, and to render them active, cheerful, and happy, fond of the school and of their instructors. . . . In this training school the children remain two or three years, according to their bodily strength and mental capacity. When they have attained as much strength and instruction as to enable them to unite, without creating confusion, with the youngest classes in the superior school, they are admitted into it. In this school they are taught to read, write, account, and the girls, in addition, to sew; but the leading object in this more advanced stage of their instruction is to form their habits and dispositions."

The teacher of this first infants' school, Buchanan, was subsequently put in charge in 1819 of a similar school in Westminster by Brougham, Lansdowne, James Mill, Macaulay, and others. In 1820 another was opened in Spitalfields, of which Wilderspin took the charge, with whose name the methods and success of the earlier period of the movement are connected.

Section I.—*Wilderspin.*

Samuel Wilderspin was born in London. At the time of the experiment under Buchanan he was clerk at the New Jerusalem Church, Waterloo Road. The minister of this church, Mr. Goyder, introduced him to Buchanan, by whom he was induced to give himself to infant training. The opportunity offered in the school erected by Joseph Wilson in Quaker Street, Spitalfields, the charge of which was given to Wilderspin and his wife. They opened it on the 24th July, 1820, a memorable morning, when Wilderspin, at his wits' end, by exhibiting his wife's gaudily adorned cap at the end of a pole, succeeded in arresting the attention and reducing to quiet the screaming crowd that had hitherto baffled all his efforts. This was the real beginning of the infants' school system. Not only is the very name due to Wilderspin, but it was his arduous and self-denying labours, his ingenuity, perseverance, and skill that gave it form and made it a power.

When Wilderspin began his work he was literally without a plan, and almost without an aim. He had some vague notions of rescuing the little ones under his charge from the depraving influence of their daily associations, and of giving them a culture that should be beneficial to their future. But of plans he had none, of principles he had no knowledge, of what education really was or required he had no conception. His work was one of experiment. Many were his mistakes, many his failures. Much that was absurd or impossible to realize, or that was positively injurious, found a place at times in his school, and obtained his advocacy; but he gradually hit upon valuable principles, and introduced practices that have maintained their ground to the present day. His success was such, that those statesmen and others to whom reference has already been made, having their attention drawn to it, conceived the plan of a society for the purpose of promoting the establishment of similar schools. Of that sanguine and enthusiastic temperament, so necessary to the pioneer in difficult enterprises, Wilderspin was eminently fitted for the work that now lay before him. During the next twenty years we find him travelling to every part of the British islands, lecturing, establishing schools, training their teachers, and conducting examinations, wherever his services were required, or where he thought an opening might be made. Besides this, he kept open a central school in Cheltenham, conducted when he himself was away by members of his family, or by his own trained agents.

This course of life not only added to his experience, but also brought him into contact with many earnest educationists, such as Stow, Simpson, Combe, and Close, and with many good practical teachers; the result being an enlargement of his own views, and an occasional adoption of a principle or a method, without, it might be, the consciousnesss of his indebtedness. This explains, perhaps, his pertinacious and somewhat angry contention of later life, that things that were doubtless taken from others had their origin in his own experiments. In the brief sketch now to be given of his system, we neither propose to trace its growth, nor to separate what is properly his own from what he picked up from others, but simply to set forth the leading principles and practices which he ultimately advocated.

At an early period Wilderspin became aware that if he was to succeed he must adapt his measures to the nature of the child. This became his leading idea, and the clue in all his experiments to what he hoped—a rational system of training. Hence he arrived at the truth, which he sets forth as a leading principle of education, that the whole nature of the child must be considered, and his education be physical and moral as well as intellectual. Physical culture required him to pay special attention to habits of cleanliness, and to those ailments of young children by which others might be affected. Imitative actions and amusing exercises, adopted at first simply as a means of arresting attention, he continued not only on that account, but as important instruments in physical training. Singing, introduced as a recreation, was employed also for the same end. The playground, introduced for moral purposes, supplied the means of fresh air and outdoor exercises. In all these, and in clapping and marching, he says play is given to the lungs, the blood is sent with a quickened impulse, and every organ of the body is benefited.

Following his principle of suiting himself to the nature of the child, he perceived that the rigidity of the National or of the Dame's school was unsuitable. Their forced quiet, their constrained positions, were unnatural. Childhood is joyous, childhood is active, childhood is curious, childhood is imitative. The child delights in laughter, frolic, and fun; and if it is to be educated aright, these must be encouraged and provided for, not repressed. For there is a mutual reaction between the departments of human nature, and where there is a violent repression of lawful actions, unless in obedience to a higher law of nature, there must be injury. For instance, the joyousness of childhood, good in itself, is much more so as a moral agent, or at least as a favourable condition to moral growth; while certainly the opposite state is one from which may spring all manner of evil dispositions, tempers, and habits. With this truth before him, he sought to make school a happy place, and provided the child, as far as he had power, the means of acting out its real life.

Moral education was rightly deemed by Wilderspin as the chief aim of school training; in fact, that he might raise from their moral degradation, or recover from vice, the children of the poor or criminal class, was that which led to his life-long devotion to their cause. Moral education should take precedence of every other school practice. However strong the temptation—and to some it is a strong one—to give attention to what is showy, or that can be measured, it must not be yielded to. The child's best interests must not be sacrificed to a puerile love of display, nor to a wish for pecuniary gain.

Moral education embraces at least two things—the instilling of moral truths and principles into the mind of the child, and the formation of its disposition, temper, and habits. In other words, it aims " to give a moral constitution to the child instead of a moral custom." It has been too much the practice to depend on moral injunctions and the committal of Scripture texts to memory, as the means of giving an acquaintance with religious and moral truth and duty. The principle that he had hit on at an early period of his labours, that a child's education must be by things rather than by words, suggested the absolute futility of the common practice. It became evident to him that it was not only fruitless in moral results, but that it altogether failed to convey any notion of the truths themselves. He found that to give moral perceptions there must be present to the child the example or the act that embodies the truth. His only course was therefore to take advantage of the little incidents occurring in the schoolroom and playground, and to take familiar instances of conduct coming within their experience, as his means of communicating to them notions of virtue and religion. The same great truth which had served him in this also led him to see that injunction, precept, and learning by rote, would equally fail to affect the

G

feelings or form the habits It would be as wise to expect a child's health to be benefited by merely learning to repeat maxims on exercise and cleanliness. No; if the disposition is to be moulded, the temper formed, the foundation of right habits laid, it must be through example, the culture of the feelings, and by right actions. Proper feelings must be excited, and occasions found for acting them out, if there is to be any moral or religious result. To excite feeling and sympathy he depended on cases actually brought before the children, on instances which their imaginations could conceive, on incidents occurring in the playground, and on example. By means of the playground he made himself acquainted with faults only revealed there, and obtained the means of exercising the moral judgment of the whole, or of benefiting the individual otherwise not possessed. Here, also, he had the sphere where he could bring practice to his aid. Little ones were taught practical lessons in forbearance, kindness, truthfulness, and honesty. Here they learnt to give way, in little things, to the wishes of their associates, to protect the weak, to help the suffering, and generally to learn the lesson that life consists in promoting the well-being of those around. In such ways he sought to train the heart rather than the head, to bring out the good deed rather than a good precept, for he had discovered that learning to act takes precedence in the life of a child of learning to talk. While thus seeking to *prevent* the formation of evil dispositions and habits by the formation of such as were good, he also found that the only way to destroy what was evil was not by the rod, or by attempted forcible repression, but by carefully cultivating the opposite habit, practice, or disposition.

In cultivating the intelligence, the plan had hitherto been to do so through language. Wilderspin discovered that for the infant the process should be reversed. He found out, he says, on his first day in school, that if he would arrest the attention, it must be through the senses. Following this up, he obtained the truth that objects should be examined and compared, and ideas obtained, before the attempt to give them expression. This being done, language became to the children a living thing, words being then the signs of realities, instead of so much lumber lying as a dead weight on their faculties. This valuable principle, long before advocated by Locke, and shortly to be extensively known as Pestalozzian, is the key to Wilderspin's system and success in cultivation of the intelligence. Yet, had he adhered to his principle here, as in other things, of adapting himself to the nature of the child, he would have found that the principle is valuable only within certain limits. For as a matter of fact and of necessity, children do acquire much language, and much through language, that they cannot understand, and this requires both to be furthered and dealt with in a right way. How to do so was one of the problems Stow tried to solve.

From the principle that a child's first instruction must be through the senses, by things, not by words, there was but a step to—a child must not receive simply at the hands of his teacher, but must make efforts of his own, his teacher showing him *how* to think rather than *what* to think. For " the aim of the infant school should not be to give knowledge, but to lay the foundation of the habit of seeking for it." In practice, there were many departures from these principles. For with an object before them, the attention was not confined to points which could be observed or discovered, but much information was detailed of a kind totally unsuited to the mind of a child. This at length proceeded to such extravagant lengths, that many who did not discern the good came to condemn the whole thing.

The means employed for this cultivation were various. Motions with the fingers accompanied the utterance of words, as up, down, perpendicular, horizontal, parallel, angle, and so on. Objects, and where these were not procurable, or of a nature not to bring into the schoolroom, pictures were employed on which to give lessons. Those on pictures he found often more interesting than those on objects, but he failed to discover wherefore; which is that a higher power, the conceptive, is brought into play, than in simple observation, a power to which much of the enjoyment of early life is traceable. Lessons in number were given by means of the arithmeticon, and on form by means of an instrument which could be formed into triangles, squares, and other geometrical figures. To all these he added lessons in reading, though not conducted on a method in accordance with his first principle.

Since the first appearance of this brief account of Wilderspin's system, he himself has been called away. His death took place nine years ago. It attracted little attention at the time; still some portions of the press referred to his great services to education. He was the first to produce a system of infant training. But he also awakened public attention to its importance, and he did much to establish it in the country. He travelled to many parts of England, Scotland, and Ireland, establishing schools, undertaking their charge for a month or six weeks, and then holding a public examination to show the nature and results of his work. He could boast that he had thus commenced the training of upwards of 20,000 children, and had instructed the teachers of hundreds of schools. Besides this, he delivered a series of lectures in the places he visited, explanatory of his aims and plans, and he published two valuable works on infant training. It was this enthusiastic, long-continued, and self-sacrificing advocacy that led, after two or three abortive attempts, to the placing of infant training on a sound and satisfactory basis.

Section II.—The Mayos.

Educational progress has consisted in the adoption of higher ends and aims, and of improved principles and methods of culture ; and in extending the area of culture in the community. These have generally proceeded together. But among the workers in this field some have given more attention to the former than to the latter, satisfied that if they could improve the quality of education, its extension would follow. In continuing our observations, the work, sometimes of one, sometimes of the other, will come under notice ; but it is not within our purpose, even were it possible or desirable, to bring under review every movement of the past fifty or sixty years—years forming a period of educational excitement never before experienced. It will suffice to show the character of this progress, if we instance a few of the more prominent movements.

The work of Pestalozzi attracted attention to it from every part of Europe. Many visited the scenes of his labours, and not a few, captivated by what they saw, remained students of principles which they felt were to revolutionize the entire system of early education. Of those, who thus visited him, there were some whose tastes and aptitudes, improved by liberal culture, enabled them to separate the principles from the forms in which they were embodied, and by which their real nature was too often obscured, even from Pestalozzi himself. But for them, his must have been simply an example of lofty zeal and self-sacrificing devotion to the cause of education. Catching the spirit of his method rather than its form, these provided courses of instruction and training for the systematic and harmonious development of the whole nature of the child. Among these, Charles Mayo and his sister did for England what had been already done for Continental countries by others of Pestalozzi's disciples.

"Profoundly convinced," he observes in his preface to "Lessons on Objects," "of the truth of Pestalozzi's views, and warned against his errors by long actual observation of their consequences, the writer of these prefatory remarks determined to attempt the introduction of his method into England, religiously preserving the *Idea*, but adapting the *Form* to those circumstances in which he might be placed. He considered that the most effectual mode of accomplishing this end was to devote himself to the formation and conduct of a school, in which the arrangement and practical application of those principles might be made. To exhibit the system in operation, to elaborate, by means of experiments continually repeated, a course of instruction; and above all, to prepare materials for an appeal to actual results, seemed to him a far more useful and effectual, though less rapid or brilliant process, than that of dragging it before reluctant audiences at public meetings, or of advocating its merits in the periodical publications of the day. He was content that it should be buried in oblivion for a while, assured that if it possessed the life of truth, it would in due time spring up with renovated vigour. That time seems to have arrived. Attention to this subject is revived. Schools professing to be conducted on Pestalozzian principles are increasing in number, and publications issue from the press which point out, with more or less success, the manner of applying them to different branches of instruction. Under these encouraging circumstances, it is proposed to publish, from time to time, a number of little treatises of a strictly practical nature, embodying in a familiar manner the principles of Pestalozzi. They will be the results of many years' experience—the corrected and re-corrected editions of lessons actually given by different individuals." In conformity with this announcement, there issued at short intervals little books of "Lessons as given at Cheam, Surrey." But before this, as early as 1826, Mr. Mayo had directed attention to Pestalozzi and his principles, in a lecture at the Royal Institution. From this lecture we give the following summary of Pestalozzi's principles.

Pestalozzi was unencumbered by the trammels of a regular school, and unfettered by its routine. Nature became the school book; and, in the actual experience and self-acquired knowledge of his pupils, he found those elements of instruction which are usually sought in the discoveries of other minds and the abstractions of science. Pestalozzi accustomed his pupils to make observations on the objects that surrounded them, and to express with accuracy the ideas which they thus acquired. He taught his assistants that reading, writing, and arithmetic were not the real elements of instruction, but that a simpler, a more natural foundation, must be sought. The basis of all sound knowledge, argued he, is the accurate observation of things acting on the outward senses. Unless physical conceptions be formed with distinctness, our abstractions will be vague, and our judgments and reasoning unstable. The first object then in education must be to lead a child to observe with accuracy; the second, to express with correctness the result of his observation. The practice of embodying in language the conceptions we form gives permanence to the impressions; and the habit of expressing ourselves with the utmost precision of which we are capable, mainly assists the faculty of thinking with accuracy and remembering with fidelity.

This being the leading idea of his method, the following are the principles by which it should be pursued.

Education should be essentially *religious*. Its end and aim should be to lead a creature, born for immortality, to that conformity to the image of God in which the glory and happiness of immortality consists. In pursuing this end, the instructor must regard himself as standing in God's stead to the child; and as by the revelation of God's love is the spiritual transformation of man accomplished, so must the earthly teacher build all his moral agencies on the manifestation of his own love towards the pupil. Then, as "we love God because He first loved us," so will the affections of the pupil be awakened towards his instructor, when he feels himself the object of that instructor's regard. Again, as love to God generates conformity to His will, so will obedience to the instructor be the consequence of awakened affection.

Education should be essentially *moral*. The principles and standard of its morality should be derived from the precepts of the gospel, as illustrated by the example of the Redeemer. Moral instruction, to be availing, must be the purified and elevated expression of moral life actually pervading the scene of education. In carrying on the business of the schoolroom, or in watching over the diversions of the playground, the motives and restraints of the purest morality, and those only, must be employed. Moral diseases are not to be counteracted by moral poisons; nor is intellectual attainment to be furthered at the expense of moral good.

Education should be essentially *organic*. A stone increases in size by the mechanical deposition of matter on its external surface; a plant, on the other hand, grows by continual expansion of those organs which lie folded up in its germ. Elementary education, as ordinarily carried on, is a mechanical inculcation of knowledge, in the Pestalozzian system it is an organic development of the human faculties, moral, intellectual. and physical. Moral education does not consist in preventing immoral actions in the pupil, but in cultivating dispositions, forming principles, and establishing habits. Nor does intellectual education attain its end by the mere communication of intellectual truths, but rather in the development of those faculties by which truth is recognised and discovered. And, lastly, physical education, instead of confining itself to instruction in particular arts, must be directed to the improvement of the outward senses, and the increase of activity and strength.

Activity is the great means of development, for *action* is the parent of *power*. The sentiments of the heart, the faculties of the mind, the powers of the body, advance to their maturity through a succession of acting in conformity to their nature. Opportunities for the exercise of moral virtue should be carefully sought out, or, at least, diligently applied. To cultivate benevolent dispositions, the pupil should be invited to relieve the indigent; to overcome his selfishness, he should be induced to share or to part with the objects of his own desire. In intellectual culture every branch of instruction should be so presented to the pupil's mind, as to bring into the highest activity the faculties most legitimately employed upon it.

That there may be that action that leads to development, there must be liberty. It may be possible by a system of coercion, to produce a negative exterior morality, which shall endure as long as the circumstances on which it is built remain in force; but no interior moral power, that shall survive a change of outward circumstances, can be formed, unless such moral liberty be enjoyed as leaves to the judgment room for discerning between good and evil ; to the moral choice the adoption of the one, and the rejection of the other; to the conscience the approval and rewarding of right, the condemnation and punishment of wrong. Restraint is useful to check the career of passion, to arrest the progress and diffusion of moral mischief, to remove the incentives to evil, and to restore to that position in which the moral principle may again exert its influence. Still it is only a negative, not a positive means. All the real development of man, moral, intellectual, and physical, arises from moral, intellectual, and physical liberty.

This liberty must be directed by an influence essentially parental; where there is no mother there can be no child, is as true morally as it is physically. It is the order of providence that maternal affection and maternal wisdom should call forth the dawning powers of childhood ; and that the wisdom and firmness of a father should build up and consolidate the fabric which reposes on a mother's love. The Pestalozzian instructor must combine the character of each relation, but exhibit them in different proportions according to the age and disposition of his pupil.

The development of the faculties should be *harmonious*. In some cases the intellectual, or moral, or both, are sacrificed to the physical ; in some, the moral, or physical, or both, to the intellectual. A Pestalozzian educator respects the rights of each. He fortifies the body by gymnastic exercises, while he cultivates the understanding, and trains the sentiments. He endeavours to preserve the equipoise in each, as well as between each of the three departments, to mingle firmness with sweetness, judgment with taste, activity with strength. His object will be, not to develop a disproportionate strength in one faculty, but to produce that general harmony of mind and character which is the most conducive to the happiness and usefulness of the individual.

Development should be essentially *progressive*. The sentiments should be gradually led to take a higher direction and a wider range. The motives of welldoing must be by degrees elevated and purified in their character; the duty which was discharged at first in obedience to an earthly father must be set forth as the requirements of a heavenly one; the charities of life must be exercised towards those in immediate contact; by degrees an interest may be cultivated in operations embracing a wider or distant sphere of usefulness.

In every branch of study, the *point de depart* is sought in the actual experience of the child; and from that point where he intellectually is, he is progressively led to that point where the instructor wishes him to be. Thus he proceeds from the known to the unknown, by a process that connects the latter with the former, and, instead of being abruptly placed in contact with the abstract elements of a science, he is led by a course of analytical investigations of the knowledge actually possessed, to form for himself those intellectual abstractions which are in general presented as the primary truths.

With these adaptations of Pestalozzi's principles, Mr. Mayo and his sister gave themselves to the task of working them out in a private school. Subsequently they embodied them in the series of lessons to which reference has been made, and eventually secured for them a wide circulation and adoption through the agency of the Home and Colonial Training Institution. With that institution and its great work their name is intimately associated.

Section III.—Home and Colonial School Society.

It is a remarkable fact in connection with educational progress, that its gains and its advancement have been by a constant struggle against a tendency to deteriorate. So much of the success of a method, or of the application of a principle, has been due to the personal element—the zeal and enthusiasm of the teacher—that many, who thought to adopt the principle or apply the method, have failed to obtain like results. Nor is it difficult to account for this. It is much easier to get the *form* in which a method or a principle is embodied, than it is to get the thing itself. It is also a much easier thing to apply the form mechanically, than it is to work out by the principle or method involved. Hence as few ever penetrated through the form, and many lacked the spirit which alone wins success, while most were too indolent, intellectually, to incur the exertion that true education demands, there have been but few good teachers, and the majority have either sunk back into rote and rule, or have aimed at results which, while they were showy, were also unsound. This tendency to deterioration has had illustrations in every movement of the century, but in no case more noticeably than in infant education.

The primary object of an Infants' School should be moral and physical training, and laying the basis of good habits. The cultivation of intelligence—except as a matter of method—should hold a subordinate place. By Wilderspin and some of his abler coadjutors, this object was on the whole kept steadily in view. But by many, the Infants' School was made either a place of amusement—necessary to keep the little ones quiet —or a place of forcing or cram. In many schools, the number of subjects professed was appalling, and would have been sufficient to task the energies of adults. The teaching—not that it deserved the name—was showy and pretentious. The result was seeming wealth and real poverty. Words, hard, dry, scientific, took the place of things and ideas. Facts of all kinds were crammed into the children's mouths, to the injury of their truthfulness, and to the prevention of their growth in real intelligence. There was no proper method, no proper food. Ignorant of mind, and indifferent to consequences, these empirics brought the whole system into ridicule, and placed the existence of such schools in peril. In corroboration of this, we may quote the following observations of the late Joseph Fletcher, Esq., one of H.M. Inspectors of schools: "Some of the promoters of infant schools appear to have considered them merely as asylums for healthful amusement, under some degree of discipline and moral control. Others seem to have thought they presented opportunities likewise for mental improvement. . . . . The most fatal error was the leaven of intellectual display which, whatever the subjects for its exercise, appears to have crept into a good many of these establishments of earlier formation. It seems to have produced in some of them what I do not know how to designate otherwise than as the 'prodigy system,' under which the quicker children were to be wonders of envy and admiration to the rest, and the whole school in which they were exhibited one of admiration, if not of envy, to its friends and neighbours, on occasion of each 'examination,' which might more truly have been designated a little 'drama,' in which the clever children had each their little part of 'representation' by rote. Conceit, envy, and fretfulness, ill restrained by fear, were the leading moral elements of such a system; and stultifying verbal repetition, its chief intellectual exercise. Travesties of the language of science vied with desecrations of that of Scripture, and the world of truth was shut out by a veil of familiarity with its unvivified formulæ."

But there were some who knew how invaluable were well-conducted Infants' Schools They had formed a right opinion of their true purpose, they had a fairly just conception of the objects to be sought in the cultivation of intelligence during the period of infancy, and they had a glimpse of the methods appropriate to the period and purpose. Unwilling that what was good should be lost, and that institutions capable of so much real work should fail, through a mistaken or inefficient agency, they formed a society for the purpose of " *improving* and *extending* " the existing system.

This Society, founded in 1836, adopted the title, Home and Colonial Infant School Society. It included in its purpose the training of teachers, and the working out and setting forth in model schools such principles, practices and methods as a growing experience and careful experiment might establish as suitable for infant training. "At an early period of their labours, they were so fortunate as to obtain the cordial co-operation of Miss Mayo, the well-known author of 'Lessons on Objects,' who, to a clear knowledge of the principles on which Infant Education should be founded, added eminent practical skill, acquired at her brother's justly celebrated school at Cheam." They also secured the services of Robert Dunning as Training Master—a gentleman eminently qualified by natural aptitude, special study, and extensive experience, for that office, and they obtained as Honorary Secretary, J. S. Reynolds,—to whose zeal, devotion, indefatigable exertion, and educational knowledge, the Institution owes much of its success.

Ere this Society began its labours, the two most marked systems of infant training were those of Wilderspin and Stow. That of Wilderspin, as pointed out in a former section, was in its essential features the same as that of Pestalozzi. In the hands of many, however, it had sadly degenerated, until it had lost nearly all that was appropriate for infant culture. Stow, though professing to observe the same principles, really to a great extent lost sight of them in his pursuit of what he thought a higher, yet appropriate culture of the infant mind. The advent of a new society, aiming to improve and extend existing systems, might have been thought a favourable juncture for framing a system of culture that should harmoniously blend the two great methods, and do really what both professed, train the "hand, the head, and the heart." But the time had not yet come. The infant mind had not been sufficiently studied. No system was yet possible that should provide an education just suited to the nature of the being to be educated. The accession of Miss Mayo gave a decided direction in the system of training adopted to Pestalozzianism. Not that there was a slavish adherence to a name. The active agents in the work of training were too much in earnest, and too practical, not to avail themselves of whatever might more effectually promote it.

An early improvement on the existing system was the banishment of the huge gallery, and the division of the school into sections, so as to render possible a gradual system of instruction and training, adapted to the nascent power and awakening faculties of the children. The same thing had been done by Stow for juveniles above the age of seven, but he retained in the Infant School the absurd practice of addressing at once the whole school, though ranging between the ages of two and six.

The following remarks by Mr. Dunning, in 1841, set forth the purpose and advantages of this arrangement.

"I now come to the question—Why are the children of the Model School separated at gallery lessons, and not taught together as in the greater majority of Infant Schools? I like to see this spirit of inquiry into our plans and practices: we want teachers to investigate and to think for themselves, and I earnestly wish they would do so, not only when they visit the Model

H

School, but every other school. Observe first, any plans that differ from your own, and endeavour to ascertain the reasons for them : examine them with reference to the true ends and aims of education, and, having formed your judgment, adopt or reject them accordingly. . . . . Our changes are not the results of caprice or a desire of novelty; we endeavour to keep in mind the physical, intellectual, and moral improvement of the children on the standard of reason and the word of God; and as increased experience amongst the little ones has proved the inadequacy of any plans practised, they have been laid aside, and succeeded by others better calculated to promote the end in view. It is the effect produced by our machinery, and not the machinery itself, that is the object of our attention; and considering how limited is the knowledge of the phenomena of the human mind, and of the laws which regulate human thought and feeling, it is no matter of surprise that we should see grounds for changing our plans. . . . . But to return to the immediate subject before us; the principle on which children in the Model School are separated at gallery lessons is precisely the same as that which leads all teachers to separate them at reading, ciphering, or writing. We ought just as soon to think of teaching all the children to read together in one class, as to learn the elements of knowledge in one division. In teaching to read in classes, you adopt a method that economises time, that keeps all grades of children employed; the advanced are not retarded by those of slower progress, nor the slow and dull hurried beyond their power. Now this is all good as far as it goes, but it is capable of a more extended application; it is equally applicable to intellectual and moral improvement; they are precisely in the same degree progressive; they do not change their nature because they are taught in a gallery; and experience shows that there is no mode of meeting the difficulty but by dividing and classifying the children. In some Infant Schools the only object is to provide comfortable shelter to the children; then they may content themselves with a spacious apartment, an ample playground, a few pictures to amuse the mind, and a few swings to occupy the body. In such a place, the division of a gallery of children would be absurd. In other schools, the great object is the acquisition of the art of reading and one or two other mechanical exercises, whilst the songs sung, and the little lessons given on pictures, are only to relieve and amuse. Here, again, division is out of the question. In schools of a different character, however, the principles which require the classification of children whilst receiving instruction and exercise at the galleries, may be summed as follows:—1st, 'That the development of the various faculties does not take place at the same time, and that in each it is progressive.' 2nd, 'That when the internal faculties are systematically and habitually exercised, they gain strength, durability, and readiness of action.' 3rd, 'That to derive benefit from the exercise given, the strength and continuance of the stimulus must be duly proportioned to the maturity and condition of the faculty on which it operates.' In carrying these principles into practice, our children are separated into four great divisions, which may be almost called four schools. In these, the children are arranged not according to size, or age, or acquirements in reading, but according as their mental and moral faculties seem to be awakened.

"The utility of this division, and the graduated and progressive nature of the instruction given," will be apparent on consideration " of the objects kept in view in each of the four divisions. In the first division, it is proposed to exercise the bodily organs, to obtain order and obedience, preserving a tone of cheerful good humour fitting the joyous season of infancy, and to give the first religious impressions.

"In the second division, it is proposed to exercise the conceptive, as well as the perceptive faculties of the children; that is, to accustom them to reproduce and accurately express the ideas gained through the senses; to arouse and enlighten their consciences, by bringing before them different moral qualities, and particularly their own responsibility; to call out religious feeling, making use for this purpose of Scripture pictures.

"In the third division it is proposed, in addition to exercising the faculties of perception and conception, to give the children a little simple information on subjects about which they have been previously interested, and to exercise their memories in storing up the ideas gained; to make the moral instruction arise as much as possible out of the events of the day, habituating the children to try their own dispositions and conduct by the standard of the Bible; the religious lessons to be drawn immediately from the Bible, and to form a regular course by which the children may be trained to preserve in their minds a chain of events; the instruction in general to become more systematic and connected.

"In the fourth division, or juvenile section, the children become more independent of the master's instruction; they learn to acquire for themselves; the object with them is to cultivate the higher faculties, as judgment and reflection,—to give a more decided direction to those powers that have been developed, and to endeavour to fit them for a life of usefulness. Writing, ciphering, and linear drawing are more practised, and a larger share of Scripture and other important information committed to memory. They also perform the office of monitors, and thus learn to make use of what they have acquired."

It is easy to trace in this description the lingering of those forcing practices which had been heretofore the bane of many infants' schools. But the fact of graduating the lessons to the growing capacity, and of forming divisions in which to carry them out, with the evident desire that existed to arrive at a rational system, gave a warrant that as experience grew, that which was preposterous would disappear.

Having adopted Pestalozzianism as its basis, this Society's great service to the cause of infant education was the reduction of its principles and methods to a practicable shape. This it did by the preparation of graduated courses of instruction. Surveying, from the stand-point chosen, the field of infant culture, they selected such subjects as were fitted for their purpose, and dealt with them so as to illustrate their fitness to secure the end in view, and to point out the method by which it was to be attained. Their aim was by a graduated and progressive course to secure the harmonious development of the whole child, so as to preserve it from being of stunted and dwarfed proportions, a result which would certainly follow from a one-sided treatment, and a result which the system adopted would not enable them to escape. The courses of instruction provided indicated the *matter* which was deemed suitable for the specific purpose in view, the *order* in which it should be presented, and the *method* by which it was to effect its design. The latter was also deemed to equal or to surpass in importance the other, so that it became almost an axiom that *how* to teach was of more importance than *what* to teach.

Development and intuition are the two great watchwords of Pestalozzianism. The former points out that education is an organic process, proceeding from within, activity on the part of the child being essential to the end,—the growth and vigour of its faculties. It also points out the necessity of suitable stimuli being presented to the embryo faculties to excite them to action, and that these must be presented in a gradual and progressive way, so as at once to feed, to strengthen, and to stimulate for higher action. And it also points out that each phase of mind—feeling, will, intelligence—must be regarded, as it is impossible to exclude any during the presence of one, and that no child is developed where any department has been overlooked. The latter points out the condition of success; the starting-point of successful culture being the child's observation or experience. These principles and others allied therewith are set forth in the graduated courses and numerous publications of the Society in a way which leaves nothing to be desired. Other principles, more advanced and of equal importance, are often enunciated, but their application is obscured by the prominence of the other method. Nor is it, perhaps, a loss that it is so. For we have, in consequence, as complete an exposition of what Pestalozzianism can accomplish as may be hoped for or desired.

In endeavouring to form a right estimate of this work, of the fitness of any part of it, or of the end proposed, it must be constantly borne in mind what that end was. It was nothing less than the complete education of a child during the period of infancy. The claim advanced was that of having nicely adapted a variety of expedients into one harmonious system, that takes in every faculty of child-nature coming into play during the period of culture. Such a claim implies that the child has been an object of study, and that a complete knowledge of it, and of the laws of its being, has been obtained. Without this the right education of the whole child cannot be, and any scheme of education will vary in completeness according to the knowledge possessed. We may well hesitate in yielding assent to this claim. But granting a partial knowledge to have been obtained, and a theory of child-life formed, complete as far as it goes, defective but not erroneous, it may be held that in judging of their scheme of education we must regard it from their standpoint, and must consider any part, not as if isolated, but as one of many things working together for an intended result.

The object was a noble one. In fact, it was the only

way to success at all. No one can succeed as an educator who does not conceive of education as a whole; as a fitting of parts synchronously and in succession. There is nothing really isolated in a teacher's work. The close of a lesson is not the end of it. Nor is it the number of lessons that makes school work. Nor are the lessons, where education is the aim, however distinct in subject, isolated in purpose. School work, if it is to be educational, however diverse it may be, must be a unity. All the lessons, all the influences at work, in all the days of school life, must be considered and provided in order to harmoniously working out the child's education. Oneness is the characteristic of a good educational system, and this Society must have the credit of giving it its rightful prominence.

We shall begin our illustrations with religious training. It was a principle of Pestalozzi that education should be essentially religious. He regarded a child as possessing religious instincts, which had but to be properly exercised to become religious principles and habits. But this Society took a more Scriptural and evangelical view. The necessity of the Holy Spirit's work on the heart and conscience was insisted upon. It was seen that, however true the doctrine, however suitable in form, however well adapted to interest the child, to awaken its sympathies, to enlighten and quicken its conscience, it would be but a show of vain words, powerless to change the heart or improve the life if not accompanied by the direct influence of the Holy Spirit.

Religious education does not consist in furnishing the memory with texts, nor in the daily use of the

Scriptures, nor even in acquaintance with the doctrines of the gospel. Religion itself is not a belief, but a spiritual and transforming influence, pervading the whole life. So religious education consists not in the knowledge given, but in a holy influence felt in the schoolroom and in the playground, in the lesson and at play. It is not religious education unless the truth given in the lesson has a transforming influence on the character, or becomes an active principle in the life. Hence the test of success is in the child and not in the lesson. It is not, has the truth been communicated, but has its power been experienced? With such an aim as this the devoted teacher will not be satisfied with the extent of Scripture knowledge, however gratifying in itself, but will be ever watching for the dawning of spiritual light, and the buddings of spiritual life.

Still truth must be communicated. In fact it is the first step. Then what truth, at what period, and in what form? These questions receive a definite reply. The truth to be taught relates to God, His character, His abhorrence of sin, His mercy through Christ, the relations of the child to God and its duties to Him, and generally a knowledge of His will and word. Such truth, as the child is able to receive it, cannot be communicated too soon. There is no sympathy with the crotchet that would leave the mind uninformed till reason is ripe. For the truth is not given for the benefit of the intellect but for the impression of the heart. And the youngest mind capable of affection to a parent is in a position to have a similar feeling awakened towards God. The form in which this truth is communicated is the vital point. It must not be by abstract statement. It must enter the intelligence or it will not reach the heart, and mere abstractions fail to do that.

Three steps or stages are recognised as marking this course.

"*First Step.—First ideas of God.* The object at this step, is to give the infants their first ideas of God —to teach them that they have a Heavenly Father; leading them to feel somewhat of His power, from its manifestations in those works of His with which they are familiar, and somewhat of His benevolence, by comparing it with the love shown them by their parents and friends. Thus to begin with what they have seen and done, and then endeavour to raise their hearts to Him whom faith only can comprehend. . . . . Teachers should avail themselves of what is passing immediately under the children's observation. On a bright sunny day, let the blessing we derive from the sun, and the goodness of God manifested in the beautiful and useful part of His creation, form the lesson. On a wet day they might learn to understand and appreciate something of God's goodness in sending the rain, which refreshes our earth and causes it to bring forth and bud. A lesson on their food, on water—its uses and abundant supply, on fire, all might help to raise the infant heart in reverential love to the Giver of all good." The following may be taken as an outline of the lessons at this step:—" 1. The children to be led to talk about something in which they are interested—their parents, and what they do for them, or some of the works of creation—endeavouring to call out their feelings. 2. What they see and know to be made a stepping-stone to what they cannot see and do not know. To lead them from the love of their earthly parents to form some idea of God, who is love ; to lead them also to conceive from observation of His works that He must be good and great, and wise. 3. The ideas gained in each lesson to be carefully impressed on the memory by simultaneous repetition."

This step has been advocated on these grounds. "'There are conceptions to be formed of a Being that is neither present, nor can be seen, and cannot be compared (except faintly and in some remote points) to anything around the child ; who can only be known by the manifestations he gives us of himself, in nature, providence, and grace. This is to be taught to a child in the first dawnings of intellect, and to one who has no ideas at first, except what it receives from sensible objects ; whose feelings come into activity as it comes into contact with the beings around it. But whilst the child is thus circumstanced intellectually, it is constituted so as easily to go from what it sees to what it does not see, and to transfer its ideas of what is seen to that which may not be seen. Morally, it is disposed to depend on, to love, to reverence, to submit to, to conciliate the persons around it, to believe the word of those it loves, and so on, and it can be made to transfer these feelings to parties remote. The point at which we are to start at is, this little being itself, with all its ideas taken from sensible things, and all its feelings brought into activity by the actions of those around it, and the point to which we are to bring it, is God, whom rightly to know is life eternal. In the first step we endeavour to awaken the feelings of love, gratitude, dependence, reverence, faith, towards those around the child; and thus prepare him to exercise the same feelings towards God."

The first of these positions may be granted. It is not so clear that the other may. It is easy to see that a child may form conceptions of the unknown from what it knows, that is, "to transfer its ideas of what is seen to that which may not be seen;" but it is difficult to conceive how a child "can be made to transfer" its feelings at the will of those in charge of it. The fact is, feelings are excited by the presence of their objects, and where any feeling has been habitually excited and properly yielded to, there the feeling has a tendency to pass into the phase of disposition, so that the mind is in the state to take the initiative in reference to anything that contains the exciting cause. Now the difficulty in relation to the feelings, love, reverence, submission, and such like, is in placing the object really and distinctly before the mind; but let these feelings be brought into activity in connection with those that the child knows, until the child becomes disposed to exercise them towards all possessing the qualities, then if their exciting causes as existing in God can be made distinct to the child, the feelings will spring up of course. The closing sentence is a better statement of the result sought than the former one, and may be accepted as embodying the great principle on which all must act who would excite religious emotion in a child.

Second Step.—Further ideas of God from Scripture incidents, by the aid of Scripture prints. "At this step, it is proposed to carry the children through a course of religious instruction, with the help of Scripture prints. The story is to be gathered from the picture by the children's attention being directed to it by questions. A portion of Scripture should be given, that the children may connect the narratives with the Bible, and receive them as divine instruction."

"The Scripture print is to be used in various ways. First, it serves as a groundwork for questions. At the commencement of the lessons the children must be questioned in such a manner that they may obtain and give answers by looking at the print. Thus, their observation being directed to the representation, their minds will be brought to bear upon the subject, and they will long for the narrative. Secondly, while the narrative is given in the words of the teacher, or in words read from the Bible, questions are mingled at intervals with the relation, and the print is glanced at again and again, for the requisite reply. Thirdly, the print is to be used as a help to the children in the repetition of the narrative."

"The purpose of prints in scriptural instruction is to awaken curiosity, to excite observation, to engage and fix attention. That the print is needed and suited to accomplish these ends is very certain. All who know anything of the minds of children, know that their interest will be excited by the mere sight of a picture. We know, too, that when their interest has been excited, a considerable effort must be made in order to sustain their attention. If infants have not the subject of instruction set as an object before their eyes, their thoughts soon begin to wander from it. It is true they may be interested by the meaning of words addressed to them; nevertheless, without an object which meets the eye their minds cannot easily be fixed on the subject, and drawn off from all others.

. . . . . But, beside the purpose to which the teacher purposely applies the print, it benefits the children even without his effort or design. It aids the conceptions of the children, it enlivens their apprehension by embodying their ideas. While their ears receive the words addressed to them, their eyes encounter a representation of the ideas, and thus impressions are made on the mind with a two-fold impulse, and become doubly deep and permanent.

. . . . . Whatever improvement of the mind and heart can be effected by means of a Bible lesson *without* a print, may be effected by means of a lesson *with* one. In addition to such benefit, moreover, the use of the print insures greater exercise of mind, and so an increase of its strength, a more lively apprehension of the subject, and a more lasting impression on the memory." The use of prints as a mechanical aid to less gifted teachers, and as a necessary one for infants from the poverty of their language and the weakness of their attention, is no reason for the more gifted teacher with more advanced children shackling himself with such a device. A descriptive and word-picturing method has certainly the advantage of giving more scope to the teacher, at the same time that it demands a greater effort from the children.

"*Third Step.*—Scripture histories and character, religious and moral duties, and Scripture natural history. At this step, narratives are chosen, with a view to inculcate some of the chief fundamental truths of Christianity. For instance, sin—its nature—introduction into the world—its consequences—and the remedy provided for it in the sacrifice of the Son of God. Incidents and characters are also selected, with a view to inculcate some important truth or influential precept. As the children advance, lessons are given to illustrate the natural history of the Bible; and the instruction is drawn from the Bible in a regular connected course, thereby training the children to preserve in their minds the idea of a chain of events."

With respect to the general method of conducting religious instruction, it is held that a mother's intercourse with her little ones should suggest the style of communication. Colloquial and simple, while winning the confidence of the little ones, it will also be found to be the most impressive. A lesson too will be more effective if confined to developing and impressing one point. This will not make the lesson meagre, for it may be discussed in a variety of ways, and, in fact, should be, both in order to gain it admission into more minds than one mode would secure, and also to impress it more deeply. In fact, little by little, must be the motto of the teacher of infants. His charge, as pointed out long ago, are like narrow-necked phials, which subjected to a continual stream receive little or nothing, but taking in drop by drop, retain and fill.

The counterpart of religious instruction is moral training. There is a sense in which morality may exist without religion. That is, certain moral habits may exist, and certain moral practices obtain, where there is no pretence to religious feeling, and no reference to religious sanctions. But the highest morality, nay, it may be said true morality does not exist except as the fruit of religious principle. The true character of a practice, habit, or principle is the motive from which it springs, and religion recognises those acts only as moral which proceed from motives such as God approves. It is not enough that the act is one that God sanctions or commands, its performance must spring from the intention to do His will. In themselves, therefore, religious education and moral training cannot be dissociated if we would have the latter on a right basis. Religious education is a sham if it does not secure moral results, and moral training will prove a delusion if it is not founded on religious sanctions. There can be no real severance between religion and morality,— where the former is the latter must be. The latter in its true nature cannot be where the other is not. For neither is what it professes to be without the other.

This is the ground occupied by this society. "Morality is that practice which results from obedience to Christian precepts on Christian principles; the application to the ordinary events and duties of life of the doctrines and precepts of the Christian religion. Moral training is the application to children in their ordinary conduct, in the schoolroom and playground, of the precepts which they learn from the Bible." Moral training thus becomes a process which has for its aim the implanting of moral principles and the formation of moral habits, under the sanctions of the word of God. It has, consequently, much in common with religious instruction, its point of departure being the steps taken to form the practice and the habit.

To form the practice and habits, attention must be given to the springs of action. To attend to acts regardless of the feelings of which they are the expression, or which they tend to excite, would be to miss the central point in moral culture. The feelings require attention. Some are to be brought under control, others have to be strengthened, and, especially, all have to be regarded in reference to their objects. Feeling is not an end. It exists as a means. It is an incentive to action. As a feeling does or does not find issue in action, so it subserves or not its purpose in the human economy. Hence the feelings demand culture, which culture must embrace the actions allied thereto. If the feelings and their associated actions receive proper attention, the result is the formation of the disposition, temper, and habits, or, in a word, of moral character. The importance of this culture is acknowledged by this society. At an early period some of its officers expressed regret that the same success had not attended their work here as in other points. They thought that the same clear results should be expected from the culture of the feelings as from the culture of the intellect; that a teacher should be able to act upon a feeling, as compassion, as systematically and effectively as upon perception or judgment. In intellectual education it is known beforehand what effect is to be produced, and the nature of the means to be employed to produce it. It ought, they thought, to be the same with the feelings. There ought to be just as clear a conception of the end sought, and just as wise an adaptation of the means. No doubt this is very desirable, and perhaps would be attainable if our knowledge of all the springs of action in their thousandfold complications was perfect, and our control of all the circumstances which excite or modify them complete.

Two or three considerations may be offered why the same success is not to be expected in the culture of the feelings in school as of other mental or of physical powers. First, the occasions are not always at hand for the cultivation of any particular feeling. In the cultivation of intelligence, the means may be extemporized if they are not ready at hand, but it is not so with the feelings. It is true that occasions as they occur may be seized, and as Locke says, when possible they should be made, but in many cases it is impossible. And if the occasions cannot be made, systematic culture cannot be had. For instance, suppose the feeling is compassion : the proper object of this is wretchedness, and the purpose of exciting it is relief. But how provide the exciting cause? It may be said, invent it; appeal to the imagination by a fiction. Well, we might develop the feeling in this way, but we should thwart our purpose. The feeling is to be cultivated, not for itself, but for the action to which it prompts. Where no action can follow, the feeling passes into the phase of sentiment, and a moral condition is induced, the very opposite of the one we seek. A state is produced, in which distress will excite no condition but a sickly sentimentality, without moving a finger in relief.

Mistake or failure has not the same significance in intellectual culture as in moral. The intellect is not necessarily injured by mistaken action, that is by being exercised on improper objects. But the case is different with the moral feelings. Here loss is all but irretrievable, while mistaken action is doubtless injurious, and may be fatal to moral growth. Sin has a tendency to perpetuate itself. Once admitted into the soul the stain remains. The mind, astray morally, feels the effect of it ever afterwards. Hence to the culture of the moral feelings there are obstacles which have been created by former states, that do not exist, or in a very limited, and certainly not in an insuperable degree, in intellectual culture.

Besides this, there is the fact of original depravity—that disturbing element in our moral system which renders repugnant to us those objects of the feelings and those duties connected therewith which are moral and religious; and to this may be added the constant recurrence of temptation to indulgences by the enemy, which are destructive of all right feeling and action.

In this condition of things the cultivation of the conscience is the chief corrective of failings in the culture of the feelings. The office of conscience being to approve or disapprove of particular states, and of the actions springing therefrom, its culture implies that the mind is informed of that which is legitimate and right, so that it may have a standard of judgment, and that it is practised continually in deciding on the moral quality of feelings and actions, both personal and of others. In the absence, then, of a perfect scheme of culture, the next best thing in our power is to give to conscience its rightful supremacy, by continually furnishing cases to be decided by the standard of the divine word. Nor are the elements wanting of such a culture. Considering the position of a child in school, the opportunity exists of placing in its mind a right standard on such important points as justice, truth, kindness, self-denial, and so on, and to get decisions of the conscience in respect thereto on the little incidents arising out of its daily life.

A great difficulty in moral culture is in the child itself, arising from the emotions of self having been injudiciously stimulated in its earlier years. To so great an extent is this sometimes carried by those in charge of it, that the child concentrates its regards on itself, and only considers its actions as they may affect itself. The corrective is, early to divert the attention of the child to the effects of its actions on others. It must get into the habit of recognising that its own claims in every case are limited and modified by the claims of others. Supposing this to be effected, it will be comparatively easy to establish a high standard of feeling and practice in such things as honesty and truthfulness, and to save from those things which proceed from utter regardlessness of the feelings, wishes, or rights of others.

Moral instruction, culture of the feelings, and working against the emotions of self, require practice of moral duty as that which gives each its force in moral training. Those are introductory to this. "See," says Miss Mayo, "that they not only acknowledge the principle, but that they carry it out in practice, for it is essential, besides awakening feelings and instilling principles, to cultivate moral habits, and habits are formed by the frequent repetition of an action." So again Mr. Dunning: "The child's character is very much in the hands of the teacher, but then more must be done than mere teaching. . . . . Education contemplates the formation of character. But how is character formed? Much of it by training, not teaching. A teacher cannot lecture a child into good manners, or change habits of any kind by the longest speech. The physical, intellectual, and moral habits are only changed by a repetition of doings, and it is in these doings that training consists. Action is the parent of power."

The course of moral instruction should be both incidental and formal. The incidents of the schoolroom, playground, and street should be made use of to illustrate moral truths and to obtain moral decisions. But these occur too irregularly to be relied on altogether. The instruction should come at fixed intervals and follow a well-defined course. This Society recommends a course of three stages, each stage having a special purpose, given subjects, and its own mode of treatment. "In the first step the object is to awaken the moral sense, to cultivate right feelings, and to form good habits: leading the children to determine what is right and what is wrong, and preparing them for the reception of religious impressions. The lessons should embrace kindness and love of parents and teachers so as to awaken affection, the little griefs and joys of their companions so as to excite sympathy, and so on. The plan in giving the lesson is to lead the children to talk about the various actions that fall under their notice, with a view to form their moral sense and cultivate right feelings, and to make a very simple application to themselves. In the second step the object is to enable them to distinguish, appreciate, and name moral qualities. The subjects embrace duties to parents, teachers, brothers and sisters, their companions, the aged, the property of others, and so on. The plan is to lead them by observation on their own conduct and disposition, or the conduct and disposition of others, to form clear conceptions of moral qualities; or the teacher is to give some examples of the exercise of a moral quality, and the children decide what it is, and learn how it is to be called. They also tell how they can exemplify the quality under consideration, and determine whether it would be right or wrong. In the third step the object is to cultivate a quick perception and nice discrimination of moral feelings, and to teach the terms by which they are expressed. The subjects of instruction to be drawn from historical facts, fables, poetry, the playground, and proverbs. The story to be narrated, the children to determine the merit or demerit of the parties spoken of, and the kind and degree of faults mentioned in the story, and to state what would be their own duty in similar circumstances.

The principle on which these lessons are conducted is to take something as a starting-point from the child's experience, or that has come under its observation. "The rule is the same," says Mr. Reynolds, "in moral as in intellectual education. We must start from what is within the child's own experience. We must not talk to it of great sacrifices of life or fortune, but of the little incidents that occur in the schoolroom or playground, in which either good or bad conduct is exhibited. If we bring an object before a child, that it may by degrees be led to acquire clear ideas on the various properties of matter, so we must bring actions that he has witnessed before him, that he may be led to form right notions of moral qualities; to determine for himself which are good and which are bad; to trace the motives and dispositions which lead him to certain actions; and thus prepare him to see and appreciate the Christian principles by which he should be regulated."

The power of the teacher's example must not be overlooked. "One of the most powerful auxiliaries in the cultivation of character," says Miss Mayo, "is the force of example; children not only imitate what those around them do and say, but involuntarily acquire their habits and manners." It should never be absent from the teacher's mind that example is stronger than precept, and he should fortify himself with those considerations that show why it is so. Amongst others, four have special claims on his remembrance. Example is stronger than precept because it conveys truth to the mind better than precept does. Often the precept is but a form of words until embodied in an example. The action conveys to the mind what the precept did not. The truth now stands forth in strong light, so that there is no mistake as to it. Here example has the same value as an experiment in physical science, or as a construction in geometry. It exhibits and conveys to the mind the meaning underlying the words. Again, example is stronger than precept because it makes the impression that the precept is obligatory. Where the precept is understood, nothing will so strongly recommend it as obligatory as seeing another submit to it, especially if the other is an adult, and placed in so apparently irresponsible a position as a master is. Children cannot but feel, if a man consistently does a right thing, that he feels its obligation upon him, and especially so if they see it under strong temptations to the contrary. But suppose the case where a man's example is not according to his precept, then the children must feel that, whatever he may say, he cannot believe in its obligation. If he says, "You will find it better to do as I say than as I do," they will think him either a fool or a knave — a fool in neglecting to do what he says interests him so nearly, a knave in pressing upon others what he does not do himself. Again, example is stronger than precept because of the force with which sympathy and imitation silently mould the character. By sympathy we place ourselves in the circumstances, and assume the feelings and actions of those around us. This is a force more or less at work on us continually. We do not resist except consciously. That is, sympathy will operate unless we voluntarily and strenuously resist it. But in the case of ordinary example, and especially by children, there is no thought of resisting; on the contrary, there is often a great deal of interest, and sympathy at once awakes. And in those cases where sympathy is impossible, there is a strong imitative propensity, and the child copies the teacher. Finally, example is stronger than precept because in cases of emergency, when called on to act at once, it is the example that occurs to the mind, and not the precept; and if it be the example of a father or a teacher, its force is irresistible.

Moral training has a branch that is too often considered as something distinct from it. School discipline is often regarded as merely obtaining order and securing attention to work. But others, taking a wider view of their duties, regard it as obligatory upon them to do what they can to form in their pupils a right character. With these, discipline is a system of means for enforcing right conduct, of correcting bad habits, of lessening the force of evil tempers and dispositions, and of eradicating anything that would be injurious to the moral and intellectual growth of the child.

Discipline with such aims, is supposed to have its sphere in the juvenile rather than in the infant school. And this is the fact; the province of the infant school is to prevent rather than cure. Or if evil exists either in habit or bias, to uproot or change by forming other and better habits, or giving another direction to the feelings and conduct. In this view the whole course of infant school training is disciplinary. Exercises adopted for other purposes are in fact great moral forces. Thus manual exercises, intended for physical relief or benefit, have a direct influence in forming the habit of obedience, and of establishing the teacher's authority. The march, the clap, the rising and sitting at command, the loud shout, the low whisper, the sudden silence, the cessation of all employment for a few minutes, these all help to establish conditions highly favourable for more direct moral agencies.

This being the case, the attention of this Society was given to the more direct means of moral training as belonging especially to the sphere of infant culture, and not to those practices and expedients which are found necessary at an older age. Yet, even in infants' schools, evils are sometimes found, which the common course does not eradicate nor prevent. In such cases other means must be resorted to, and we are now to inquire what are those practised or recommended by the officers of this Society.

Authority, the right to command, and if necessary to enforce obedience, and also the acknowledgment of the right in the practices of those subject to it, is essential to discipline. One of the first things, if not the first, that a teacher has to work for, is the establishment of his authority. Until this is effected, the influences on his children must be wayward and capricious, and their progress, morally and intellectually, fitful and hap hazard. It is not of speedy growth. To be lasting, authority must be based on influence, and on the ascendency of the teacher's moral and intellectual character. But this cannot be attained at once. At first the teacher and child are strangers, and authority cannot exist. It is true that the child, introduced into the sphere of its influence, is affected by the tone of his companions, and is predisposed to submit; but the personal ascendency of the teacher must be a growth, and comparatively a slow one. The means to be taken is to acquire influence, and this cannot be but by studying the characteristics of children, and adapting the treatment thereto. "Those who wish to govern by influence, not by force, who desire to govern children by means of their will and not against it," must make them their study. "Authority," says Mr. Dunning, " unquestioned and unlimited authority, is the aim, and the means to be made use of is *influence.* . . . . . In studying the characteristics of childhood, in order to secure an abiding influence over them, there are two aspects in which they present themselves, which must both be taken into account in order to be successful: the one is, in the general and prominent features of a child's character; and the other is, the special peculiarities of its disposition. Now, in order to gain ascendency over children in general, we have only to attend to a few points. First, children delight in the exercise of their opening faculties both of mind and body; next, they have a strong desire for information; thirdly, they love those who sympathize with them and aid them in attaining their objects; and fourthly, they have a strong tendency to catch the spirit and imitate the action of those they love. It follows that all we have to do is to exercise the various faculties judiciously and at proper times; to present new facts and new objects in great variety, though not too rapidly; to sympathize with and assist them in all their little movements and lawful desires; and, lastly, to show in our own walk a steady, upright conduct, and the work is done, they are our bondsmen. But in addition to this we must study the child *sui generis*. What are his peculiarities? what feelings are strong, what weak? what habits has he acquired? what are his likings and dislikings? Such points being ascertained, the teacher will be well prepared to begin his work. Begin gradually, and try your authority over the child on little points."

But it is not merely the establishment of his own authority, but regard for authority in general that must be the teacher's aim. This obtained, that will be secured. This may be by giving great prominence to the claims of law and rule; the teacher showing by his own conduct that he acknowledges the authority of law. It may be furthered by his conduct to the managers of his school. It does not do for one who wishes to reign by moral force to act Dr. Busby to his managers and employers. The relation between the teacher and manager is not unknown, and the children cannot but be favourably impressed by proper deference on the part of the former to the wishes of the latter. It may also be promoted by the mode of his intercourse with their parents. Treatment of them with proper respect, because they are his children's parents, will strengthen the regard for their authority, and consequently for the authority of the master.

Punishment is a point of great moment in school discipline. It may be laid down as an axiom that there can be no government where there is no punishment. It cannot be but that offences will come, and these must be dealt with to prevent their repetition, and to produce a moral impression against evil on the witnesses. Still it is to be said that "a school is good or bad according to the frequency of the cases demanding punishment. In a good school they are seldom required. Where they frequently occur the school is a bad one, and the master unfit for his position Especially is this true when the mode of punishment is the infliction of bodily pain." In extenuation it may be admitted that a master thus acting has a strong temptation to do so amidst the many claims on his attention, and in view of the fact that force may accomplish the immediate end sooner than other means; but still no one who looks merely at present effects, careless of future results, can be considered as fit to be entrusted with the education of the young.

It will ever be the aim of the good schoolmaster so

to order his measures as to prevent the necessity of punishments. Attention to moral training, finding employment for the activity of children, giving free scope to their natural characteristics, and banishing absurd restraints, will lessen the occasions for punishment. " You will wish to know," says Mr. Ogle, "by what means severe punishments may be prevented. I arrange the means under two heads—mental and moral. . . . . There is in the child a love of employment for its own sake, and if you do not spoil the child you will have him doing much that you wish, simply because he loves to be employed; and if you manage well he will take such pleasure in working as to have but little disposition to be idle. In every case in which the child is punished for not doing something that he ought to have done in the way of mental exercise, the teacher is more or less to blame. There is also implanted in us a love of knowledge, a pleasure in knowing what was not known before. You will find that a child evidently has pleasure in receiving knowledge; he not only feels a pleasure in the employment given him while gaining knowledge, but he loves the knowledge he gains. Here, then, is a love of employment and a love of knowledge to aid the teacher. Surely, then, we have here two great means of preventing punishment. . . . . Among the moral means of preventing punishment are, first, a certain personal weight with the children. Some persons never have this, but they have themselves to blame for the want of it, and if they cannot acquire it they may as well give up all attempts to be a teacher. Apart from every other motive in a child's mind, this almost insures success. The teacher prevails by a sort of weight, with which his influence presses, so to speak, on the minds of the children. Every human being has a certain weight with, and exerts a force upon others. We may wish to do a thing; but a certain person is opposed to it—he is like a solid block in our way, and we cannot make up our minds to act against his wishes. He has expressed his disapprobation, and though, perhaps, he cannot affect us in any degree, we do not like to act against it. We hardly reason on the matter; a mere sensation is produced, and this rules us. It is very easy to have this personal weight with children. It is not always out of love to you that they say, 'I cannot do so because teacher does not like it.' It is not always out of fear of punishment, but because the teacher is a great person in the child's estimation. There is a certain sense of power and authority in the human mind, and if we act on it, we shall prevent much insubordination, and so prevent much punishment. Another means of preventing punishment is in the many little bonds which may be formed during the personal intercourse between the teacher and children, in which the children receive proofs of kindness and sympathy, and to which they yield affection and liking. Another means of preventing those misdeeds which call for pains and penalties is to be ourselves what we would have our children to be. This is a single rule containing a great quantity of momentous truth. Do you wish the children to be free from irritability, petulance, and peevishness? You must be so yourselves. Do you wish them to be interested in the lessons so as to profit by them? Then you must show that you are interested in giving them, that you know what the application is yourselves. Do you wish them to be respectful to their superiors, and deferential to their equals, their schoolfellows and playmates? Then you must be respectful to your superiors, and exhibit a kind and courteous demeanour to all. Without your example they will disregard your precept."

Still, occasions will arise in which punishments must be inflicted. Then it becomes necessary to regard the spirit in which they are administered. Punishment should not be vengeance looking back on the past, but hope and love looking forward to the future. The measure of punishment, too, must be determined by the character of the offender, and not of the offence, for it is the child's recovery that is sought, and not the expiation of his fault. The punishment, too, must vary, according to the temperament and disposition of the child. Hence a teacher requires the same kind of skill as a physician, who reads in his patient's face the specific measures his disease requires. The teacher is dealing with moral diseases, and it is as absurd to apply one method to every child, as it would be to prescribe one measure for every patient. " A frown will act on one, separation from companions another, neglect and coldness a third, public rebuke a fourth, approbation of a companion a fifth, a whipping a sixth." The same analogy will show us the folly of expecting instantaneous cures. Sudden reform is suspicious. Deep-seated and long continued disease cannot be got rid of in a moment. The teacher has no more right to expect instant cure than a physician would in a case of complicated disease. In both cases the treatment is little by little; the progress of the cure gradual. Continuous effort, then, is demanded from the teacher; and punishment, when inflicted, must not be to save the teacher from annoyance, but to restore the child to soundness and health.

Punishment should be a consequence following misconduct, and not the prospect of it an inducement to do well. Hence threatening should be abstained from. "If you tell a boy, 'If you do so and so I will punish you,' you take it for granted at the outset that the child is disposed to disobey. You should take it for granted that he is disposed to obey. The fact is children are, in many respects, predisposed to obey. There are the bit and the reins, and you have only to take care how you use them. If you menace before any offence is committed, you tempt the child to try whether you will really keep your word, and you introduce into his mind the thought of doing a thing he perhaps had no idea of doing. You will find menaces produce ill-will, and tempt the child to do the very thing you wish him not to do."

Punishments should be light. If they are severe, offences will be frequently overlooked, and evil will increase. Where they are light there will be freedom for promptness in their infliction. It is the certainty of punishment, not its severity, that is the most powerful check in wrong-doing.

On the treatment of obstinate children we have the following remarks by Mr. Ogle:—"Avoid bringing the obstinacy into action. Every sentiment, faculty and habit is strengthened by exercise; consequently, whenever obstinacy is brought into exercise it is strengthened.

The apostle Paul says, 'Fathers, provoke not your children to wrath,' showing us that children may be irritated till they do wrong, that the mischief may be begun, for instance, by the teacher. It may be asked, How can we avoid the provocation to obstinacy in a child? I answer, by habitually endeavouring to keep up in its mind that state of feeling which leaves it without inclination to come into collision with you. Endeavour by your own gentleness, kindness, good humour, and placidity to produce and promote the same feelings in the child. There is a kind of moral contagion among human beings; we catch the spirit and temper of others around us; we are subject to that involuntary entertainment of the feelings of others which is properly called sympathy. Teachers know this by experience. If you enter your schoolroom with a countenance betraying anxiety and sadness, though you say not a word, you will find that the buzz is hushed, inquiring looks meet you on every side, and soon a vague sense of distress is seen in almost every countenance. This peculiarity of our moral constitution God has ordained for wise and good ends. When the minds which act on each other are influenced by the Spirit of God, their mutual influence produces the most beneficial results. Exhibit, then, on all occasions towards your children the same dispositions which you would have them evince; and with respect to the obstinate child, in particular, strive to foster gentle and kindly feelings *in* him by exhibiting them *towards* him.

Besides this, however, we must carefully cultivate all other sentiments which, being good in themselves, are opposed to an evil disposition. And here, too, let the beneficial influence of your example aid the force of your precepts. Establish a regard for authority, for authority in general, as such, not for your own merely; if you bring your pupil to respect and submit to authority in general, he will regard yours in particular as a necessary consequence. Especially let that intuitive sense of right and wrong with which man is endowed be constantly appealed to ; let it be *strengthened by exercise*. We are too apt to forget that the moral feelings as well as the intellectual faculties and bodily powers may be, and need to be, systematically exercised ; that, whenever used, they become the more ready for use again ; and that by performing *acts* we form *habits*. Thus conscience enlightened by the word of God, may be so disciplined, in early life, as to become by the Divine blessing habitually tender and ready to act. If so cultivated, along with other moral feelings, the temptation to obstinacy will often be resisted, or the offence, when committed, will be repented of and shunned thereafter.

But it will not be enough to cherish right feelings which may counteract the obstinate disposition; we must aim to remove all occasion for its outbreak. To this end, let the rules of your school be evidently just and reasonable ; as few as practicable, and easy to be understood ; let your conduct be consistent and decided ; let it be known habitually that your will must be done or that the punishment you threaten will be inflicted; bear yourself as if you scarcely supposed that disobedience would occur, for if we seem to expect it we often call it forth. Acting thus you will leave as little opportunity and ground as possible for the occurrence of those scenes which most commonly lead to a display of obstinacy.

By all these means, then, avoid collision with an obstinate child. But if, in spite of all your precaution and provision for better things, collision is forced upon you, for the sake of the offender, and of the discipline of the school in general, you must enter on the struggle. In carrying it on, again take Scripture for your guide. The apostle who forbids fathers to provoke children to wrath, adds, "Be not bitter against them;" and in another place says to Christians, "Let all bitterness, and wrath, and anger, and clamour, be put away from you." "Bitterness." Let the meaning of the word be weighed, and we shall surely not be slow to shun the thing it means. To abstain from it is certainly the duty of a Christian teacher, and never is he more to be on his guard against it than when endeavouring to overcome the obstinacy of a child. If a little offender withstand you, he must, on no account, become triumphant; you must be master. But let neither look nor tone nor word express bitterness; because it is both wrong in itself, and will hinder the accomplishment of your purpose. Remember once again your feelings will influence him; beware that his do not influence you. Let no bitterness on your part embitter his resentment. If you would control and conquer, you must show the dignity of a ruler, not the fury of a tyrant; and the calmness you manifest will actually tend to restore the quiet of the culprit.

This struggle ought not to take place in the presence of other children. Many, from a good moral bias, will sympathize with you; many, on the other hand, will feel with their class-fellow. You will see little lips compressed, and little bosoms swelling with emotions which none dare utter; thus the order of the school is endangered. Whenever it is possible, therefore, withdraw on such an occasion to a separate room or to the playground."

Other modes of influencing children are by rewards and praise. Rewards are considered unnecessary and injurious. A reward may be considered as having a certain intrinsic value, and as being a badge of distinction and pre-eminence. Now a reward certainly ought not to be proposed for the sake of its intrinsic value. There is that in the heart of every child which if fully developed becomes covetousness. This sense of property and love of possession in general, need no increase; on the contrary, there is constant need to repress the greedy desire of gain, a desire which often becomes a ruling passion and the source of ruin to its subject. Nor should a reward be offered as a mark of superiority. Thus proposed, the feeling which is appealed to is made the motive of exertion. Love of approbation is in itself a pleasurable feeling, but no one should seek it for that pleasure no more than he should eat simply for the gratification experienced in the act. Love of approbation is a natural feeling, and exists in sufficient force as an ordinary motive without being unduly strengthened by constant appeals to it. Injudiciously stimulated, it is apt to become a ruling motive, and when it is so the chances are that it will be a power for evil rather than good. For its power either way will depend on the character of the persons whose approval is sought. If that is frivolous or evil, it is likely that the acts done for the sake of their approbation will be of like kind. Besides there can be no steadiness of character or pursuit where this is the motive of conduct. For this will take its force and direction, not from any established conviction, but from the persons with whom the individual may happen to be associated.

It is further held that rewards are wrong in principle. They are of the nature of bribes. That which should be required and enforced as a duty is solicited for the sake of the reward. This consideration shows also that the only ground on which they can be bestowed is the doing of something over and above what was the child's duty. It is also held that rewards make punishments necessary. As the prospect of rewards only influences those that are likely to be successful, the others, who would have worked from ordinary motives, these being cast aside, becoming careless and idle, need punishment to get them to work at all.

The cultivation of the intelligence, though "considered of minor importance" as compared with physical and moral training, yet received more elaborate attention than either of the others. This, perhaps, was due to the nature of the case, as the defects in infant training and in school education generally were more apparent in the department of intellect than in the others. It might also be owing partly to the forcing process which yet lingered in infant schools —a process to which this Society may be said to have given a more legitimate direction rather than to have banished from infant culture.

Adopting the principles of Pestalozzi, this Society's work was rather to frame a method for their application than to expound them, examine their soundness, or ascertain their limits. Hence its largest gifts to infant training are its elaborate plans for the cultivation of the senses. It is true that they speak of the cultivation, not of one, but of all the intellectual faculties. But the provision by this Society is for their germ, or rudimentary condition only. Such powers as conception, memory, sense of relation and analogy, and judgment are brought into early rudimentary exercise in connection with the senses, and for their cultivation, so far, provision is made. A higher or more advanced culture—as that of the conceptive faculty and sense of analogy advocated by Isaac Taylor and practised by Stow,—whether thought legitimate or not, is certainly not attempted. This claim to have provided for the cultivation of all the intellectual faculties can be received only with this limited interpretation. In fact, it is not always clear what is understood by "intellectual faculty." Sometimes it would seem as if meant to imply—with the phrenologists—that a difference in the object or in the organ, indicates a different intellectual power. But this is not true. Lessons addressed to the touch do not necessarily differ from lessons addressed to the eye, as to the intellectual faculty exercised. There is a difference of organ, not one necessarily of intellectual power. Every mental element in the one act may be precisely that in the other. Of course, with a variation of aim, even when employing the same organ, there may be a change in the nature of the mental act.

To give employment to the several senses, and to bring into activity each intellectual faculty in its rudimentary state, and recognising that each has its own place in the order of development and activity, courses of instruction were prepared in a variety of things. Besides common objects, plants, and animals, these courses embraced colour, form, size, weight and place, physical actions and employments, the human body, drawing, and number. The following remarks indicate the method. The instruction should be carefully graduated, rising step by step from the simplest elements to as high a point of difficulty as may be presumed to be within the grasp of the infant mind. Principles and practices should be presented in immediate connection, so as to illustrate their mutual dependence. All details of practice should flow naturally from the first truths on which they are founded. The general object should be not the direct impartation of knowledge, but rather the cultivation of mental powers by bringing them into healthy exercise, and the formation thereby of valuable mental habits. It is also to be remembered that the subjects are to go on side by side. Variety will thus be given, and diverse powers of mind be simultaneously and progressively developed. The first step in mental tuition should be the education of the senses and their organs. Where this is judiciously carried out, the mind will be furnished with clear and distinct ideas, without the risk of its being overstrained.

"The office of the senses," says Miss Mayo, "is to store the mind with ideas. The medium must be by real tangible objects. The first exercises should begin with miscellaneous objects, though not altogether without arrangement, as a definite aim ought to be proposed in every lesson." Object lessons hence supply what is natural for the child to learn. An infant's first impressions are from objects, and its first knowledge about them. At first but a passive recipient of impressions, he soon comes to take an active part in learning their various qualities This goes on in a desultory way all through infancy. In the object lesson this natural tendency is utilized, and the child is judiciously and systematically directed in the employment of its senses. Thus object lessons educate the senses,—they stimulate the power of observation, and they help to form the habit of accurately doing so. Without cultivation obvious qualities often escape notice, and a superficial mode of looking at things is the consequence.

Object lessons, besides cultivating the senses, lay up material for reflection. This latter habit is always the more valuable when it is based on the habit of observation. Rightly conducted, a habit of reflection will be cultivated alongside that of observation. No facts coming under the cognizance of the senses are isolated; all are related to others. Some of these facts are obvious; others only to be discovered by comparison, experiment, or other modes of inquiry. In a good object lesson, that which lies immediately under observation will be used as a stepping-stone to that which is less apparent. This lays the foundation of reflection, and to a habit of not resting in the superficial, but of tracing out connections between related facts.

Object lessons give an intelligent use of language, and add to its stores. The idea is gained, and then the word is given. Thus the idea is fixed, and the word makes it readier for use. And it is easy to see how; for here is a twofold force by which the idea becomes ready for use. The idea has its associations with others had previously or at the same time, and when these appear that will appear too; but attaching it to a word brings in the physical element of speech, and here is another though mysterious agent for recalling the idea when wanted, and for employing it. Words thus obtained will be used significantly, and will become powers for further observation and additional acquisitions.

The method of these lessons must be that of stimulating the children to discover the qualities for themselves. The teacher must not come as it were between the object and the children, by his language or mode of dealing with it. It is not by the words he puts into their mouths, but by the tact with which he stimulates and directs their senses, that the purpose of the object lesson is attained. They must hear, see, and touch, and not depend for the facts either on him or their companions. This is a point requiring constant care, from neglect of which the object lesson too often degenerates into mere word-stringing.

It is recommended that the lessons be given in a graduated and progressive course. The age of the children should be considered, and their previous opportunities and training. As a first step with young children, it will be sufficient to take the most familiar objects, to distinguish and name them, to elicit their uses, and where usually seen. A second step would be to lead to the perception of quality, but not to give it expression, except in the case of the term being familiar. As a further advance when the children are prepared for it, two objects should be introduced as subjects of the lesson; one of them chosen to lead to the observation of parts, the other to develop some striking or characteristic quality. With these views an object is presented, having distinct and well-defined parts—as a knife,— that the children may discover the parts, and learn to apply the correct names; also another object is chosen, exhibiting in a remarkable degree some particular quality—as transparency in glass,—that the idea of the quality may be developed. As a test that the idea has been gained, the children are to find examples of the same quality in other objects. At this stage the children may be aided to remember what they learn, and to arrange it somewhat methodically, if the first letter of the word naming a part or a quality is written on the black-board. As the children advance in power, they must be led not only to discover the qualities of objects, but also the purpose for which they fit the object. They must also be practised in deciding by which of the senses they have become acquainted with a quality, and what organ they exercised. They are also to be led to see that there are some qualities not recognised by the senses, but only known from experience or by the exercise of judgment. And as a final step, they are to be led to compare objects, to discover points of resemblance or dissimilarity.

During this course the children as early as possible should be set to write on slates what they can remember of their lessons,—a practice which accomplishes several good purposes: it is a motive to attention; it serves to fix the ideas in the mind; it accustoms the children to orderly arrangement and expression; and it is a good exercise in spelling.

It is recommended that, in connection with the later stages, the derivation of the chief terms employed should be given; but how this belongs to observation, or tends to quicken the organs of sense, or comes within the province of intuition, is not shown.

Lessons on shells, plants, and animals, extend the range and purpose of object lessons. Those on animals, especially, have all the advantages of such lessons enhanced by the interest they awaken, and by the opportunities they give of comparison, of tracing cause and effect, and of drawing inferences and conclusions from facts. The interest such lessons excite quickens attention, and causes observation to be more minute and careful. Such lessons, too, have a moral value in encouraging feelings of kindness and in preventing cruelty, much of what is so in the treatment of the lower animals by children being the offspring of ignorance. They have also a religious value, by awakening feelings of admiration and reverence under the manifestations of wisdom and goodness which are continually made apparent to them.

"The right principle," says Mr. Tegetmeier, "to be followed in lessons on animals is this,—lead the children to see the intimate connection between the habits of an animal, its propensities, and its formation; how an animal is so formed that it can with ease procure the food necessary to its existence, and also the wisdom of God in adapting its different organs to its habitation and mode of life. This principle may be carried out by two plans. Either the animal or its picture may be brought before the children, and they may be called upon to observe its formation, and from considering its form and structure may be led to the consideration of its habits and mode of life; or their attention may be first directed to its habits, mode of life, food, and then to its appearance and structure. Suppose, for example, the common domestic cat be taken as the subject of the lesson: On the first plan, the children would be required to observe all the parts of the animal, as its sharp teeth and sheathing claws, its cushioned feet and flexible limbs; and from them they would be led to a consideration of its habits and food. On the second plan, the attention of the children would be first directed to the habits of the cat, its noiseless step and bounding movements, to its destructive appetite, its food, &c.; and then they would be led to observe its powerful teeth and sharp retractile claws, its elastic motion and cushioned feet, and readily perceive that these parts were given to the animal in order that it might perform the actions described, and secure the food necessary to its existence. This second plan is decidedly the best. The interest is first excited, and the attention commanded by a description of the animal or anecdotes respecting its mode of life, and then the hearers are ready and anxious to find out the means by which it executes these various actions, and procures its requisite food. Again, this second plan is the most natural, for a child proceeds from what is best known to what is unknown; the habits of every animal are better known to children than their structure." In pursuing this plan the lesson will fail to awaken due interest, and will become formal, if attention is directed first to one series of facts, and then, when these are exhausted, to the other. A better plan is to take one fact and find the corresponding fitness in structure, then another, and so on.

Colour and *Form* hold a distinct place among the means of cultivating the habit of observation. Not without reason. They are two qualities of objects to which attention is continually directed, and which give material aid to the forming and fixing of accurate ideas. They also serve to prepare the children for lessons, in which pictures and diagrams are employed as mediums of instruction.

Colour early attracts the attention of the child, and on this account has claims to an early use in infant training. But it has other claims. " Colour," quoted in the Society's Manual, from Redgrave, " gives to the world of form beauty and ornament; it also assists us to distinguish form; it aids us to determine distance and space, and enables the eye more readily to separate objects and parts of objects from each other." " Colour," says Miss Mayo, "is a subject intimately connected with the consideration of objects, and a series of very interesting lessons might be formed upon it. First, a colour should be exhibited to the children, and when the idea of the particular colour is thus formed in their minds, they should be taught, secondly, to connect the right name with it. The next step should be the calling upon them to mention what they see before them of that colour, so that their sight may be well exercised in discriminating the one learnt from others. Next they should be required to name objects, from recollection, of the colour in question,—this will tend to form the abstract idea, and will also furnish the teacher with an opportunity of cultivating accuracy of observation and propriety of expression. . . . . For the commencing lessons on Colour, a few wafers on a card will be sufficient, one being added when a new colour is brought before their view. When they are learning the various shades, they should have them painted on slips of card, which should be kept as standards to be referred to; also the proper names for each should be learnt, as apple-green, grass-green, &c. Whenever they receive a lesson on flowers, or stones, or any other coloured object, they should be called upon to determine its precise hue. A cake of each of the primitive colours, red, blue, and yellow, might be kept in the school, and it could be made evident to them how all other colours may be produced by their combination in different proportions. It is not sufficient that they are simply shown two colours, and then told what they will produce if mixed together. This kind of instruction is of little or no value, for the knowledge of the fact is but of small importance to the children; it is the having called out *their* observation upon it; it is the habit formed, and the exercise given, that constitute the real value of the lesson, and this is a point but too little understood by teachers."

The graduated course adopted by the Society, is in harmony with these views.

1st Step.—Exercise observation on several colours in succession, names being withheld. (a) A pattern colour to be shown, a child to select one like it, others to determine if it is right, and both placed side by side.

(*b*) A coloured card to be taken, and a child to find one like it on the board. (*c*) Colours to be placed in a row, then a child to arrange others in the same order. The colours selected at this step should be opposed in character.

2nd Step.—*To associate names with the colours learnt.* Terms fix ideas, and render them available in intercourse with others. (*a*) A colour to be selected, and another like it to be found, the name is then to be given, and repeated by the class. (*b*) The teacher is to name a colour, the child is to find it, and all others like it. (*c*) The teacher is to point to a colour and ask its name. (*d*) Coloured beads are to be threaded— (1) according to a pattern shown, (2) under direction by naming the colours. The principles to be borne in mind by the teacher at this step are, that the children are to be guided to the attainment of clear and distinct ideas; that they are made to feel the need of a term to give them clear and definite expression; and that proof is to be given that the name suggests the idea, and that the object recalls the name.

3rd Step.—To strengthen the power of observation; to cultivate increased accuracy and facility in expression, *and to draw out the faculty of conception by reference to objects not actually present.* (*a*) A colour is to be shown and its name required. (*b*) Others like it are to be selected by the children. (*c*) Things in the room of the same colour are to be sought and named. (*d*) Things of the same colour, not present, are to be asked for.

4th Step.—*To develop idea of shades and tints, and to cultivate nicety of discrimination on these points.*

(*a*) A colour is to be shown, then a dark and light shade of the same colour are to be placed near it. (*b*) The terms dark and light are to be used to distinguish these shades, as dark blue, light blue. (*c*) Practice is to be given in arranging colours according to their intensity. A normal colour is to be selected, then all darker than it; these are next to be arranged according to the degree of intensity, and the class informed that these are shades. (*d*) All colours lighter than the standard are to be selected and arranged, and the children told that these are tints. As a final step, the children are to observe that no colour is obtained without light, that darkness destroys colour.

As a property of objects, *Form* has claims on the trainer of infants. Doubtless it may be made to yield a higher culture to riper years, but this is its legitimate office in infant training. As a means of culture, it is of higher value than colour, partly because of the greater complexity in the act of perception, and partly because of the greater distinctness with which it can be recalled in idea. In consequence, too, of the greater adhesiveness of form, comparison may be instituted of forms now present, with others held in the mind, and thus a severer mental effort may be secured than when all the objects examined are present. It becomes also, under proper guidance, a powerful aid to discrimination. Among the endless diversities of forms found in surrounding things, likeness presents itself amidst dissimilarity, and may be seized upon, and separated by an eye in search of likeness amidst adversity. With such a purpose as this, judiciously pursued, a power is at length created, than which few things could be so beneficial to the intellectual life and activity of the child. Scarcely an object can then come under its notice but it will at once discern, and mentally separate triangles, rectangles, circles, cylinders, cubes, and other forms, to perceive which its eye has been educated and the habit given. From such considerations it becomes evident that Form should hold no secondary place in infant training. This Society attaches much importance to it, and has published an elaborate course of lessons in relation thereto.

Lessons on Size and Weight form the complement to the other means of training the senses. Besides bringing into play the muscular sense, and causing attention to be fixed on personal states as indications of external conditions, they present the opportunity of making children acquainted with the actual standard weights and measures of the country. Thus a foundation is laid for their intelligent use at a later school stage

Few things connected with early instruction exhibit the value of Pestalozzian principles, in their right sphere, more than their application to number and numerical operations. So long had arithmetic in its first operations been by rote, and in its later stages by rule, that it would seem as if an intelligent mode of approaching it and studying it would never be. In no other subject of instruction, except perhaps grammar, did it seem to be so completely a truism that any disciplinary value of the study must not, if obtained at all, be so until either the pupil was engaged in the affairs of business, or had made such progress that he could work a few problems which implied at least some

L

insight into the *rationale* of his subject. It is true that Ward had exhibited a method, the same as was afterwards applied by Pestalozzi and his followers, of intelligently teaching it. But it had not borne fruit. Nor can it be said that its subsequent revival by the spread of Pestalozzian principles has secured for it anything like universal adoption. It is to be feared that many yet have no faith in its soundness, while more either cannot give the time, or will not undertake the labour that it requires. Yet in many a well-conducted school the method has been applied with success, and even with infants a way has been shown of making it a means of developing and cultivating faculties, which but for it would be dormant till a later period.

The following exposition by Mr. Dunning sets forth the ground occupied and the practices commended by this society:—"Arithmetic is a subject which, if properly treated, can hardly be overrated in its utility as an instrument of mental culture, and in its importance to the business of life. It is also the subject I would choose to illustrate some of the finest principles of Pestalozzi. Indeed, we are told that the ability which his pupils displayed on this subject, especially on mental arithmetic, was one of the chief means by which the notice of the public was attracted to his experiments.

"Arithmetic is a powerful means of developing and strengthening several powers of the mind: for instance, it promotes concentrated and sustained attention: the processes of mental arithmetic improve the memory, or rather, what we may call tenacity of mind, by requiring the question to be remembered whilst the answer is being discovered; by requiring the several numbers to be retained in the mind whilst they are being worked; and the mind to hold the distant links of a chain whilst engaged with those nearer. It also affords early and appropriate exercise for the judgment; it cultivates the powers of abstraction and generalization, and furnishes ground on which the reasoning powers may first be called into exercise.

"Arithmetic is also valuable from the habits of mind which it induces, as accuracy, activity and readiness, clearness and precision; and the habit of forming correct and precise judgments on one subject prepares the mind to form similar judgments on others, and thus the mind is educated. In a moral point of view also it acts beneficially, for the habit of making correct and accurate statements promotes the love of truth. Weak characters are often false because their intellectual vision is indistinct, but those who are accustomed to the precision that arithmetical calculations require, and have been trained to habits of comparison, fixedness of attention, and searching for truth, are likely to carry such habits and principles into their moral dealings; at least, they will be better prepared to receive the moral lessons of the Christian educator.

"Arithmetic, too, has advantages above every other study; it affords the teacher the opportunity of judging whether the pupils have really and effectively been at work, from the certainty of its results. They must be either right or wrong without dispute; he is able also to estimate the amount of work done, and he can superintend more individual efforts at this than at almost any other lesson. Again, no study affords the teacher a better opportunity of carrying out right principles of teaching, such as making the child work, and not the teacher, leading the pupil from what he knows to the proximate truth, and thus carry out the principle of proceeding from the known to the unknown, from the simple to the complex, from the particular to the general, from the example to the rule."

Arithmetic should be taught early. Dr. Mayo observes, "the obvious connection with the circumstances surrounding the child, the simplicity of its data, the clearness and certainty of its processes, the neatness and indisputable correctness of its results, show how well it is adapted both for the young and for minds of limited structure." There is, however, no subject in which, in the first step particularly, it is more important that the teacher should exercise patience, and endeavour to throw himself into the mind of the child, and actually realize to himself what is going on within the little being whom he is instructing; for whilst arithmetic is the simplest of all sciences, it is possessed of its peculiar difficulties, and these present themselves especially at first starting; and although it is true that conquering difficulties is the very means by which tone and vigour are given to the mind of a child, yet these difficulties should not be too great,—his way should be smoothed, and he should be encouraged and stimulated gradually to ascend the hill.

On this point De Morgan well observes, "It is a very common notion that this subject is easy; that is, a child is called stupid who does not receive his first notions of number with facility; this, we are convinced, is a mistake. Were it otherwise, savage nations would acquire a numeration and a power of using it, at least proportional to their actual wants, which is not the case. Is the mind by nature nearer the use of its powers than the body? If not, let parents consider how many efforts are unsuccessfully made before a single articulate sound is produced, and how imperfectly it is done after all, and let them extend the same indulgence, and if they will, the same admiration to the rude essays of the thinking faculty, which they are so ready to bestow upon those of the speaking power. Unfortunately the two cases are not equally interesting; the first attempts of the infant in arms to pronounce 'Papa' and 'Mamma,' though as much like one language as another, are received with exultation as the promise of a future Demosthenes; but the subsequent discoveries of the little arithmetician, such as that six and four make thirteen, eight, seven—anything but ten,—far from giving visions of the Lucasian or Savilian chairs, are considered tiresome, and are frequently rewarded with charges of stupidity or inattention. In the first case the child is teaching himself by imitation and always succeeds; in the second, it is the parent or teacher who instructs, and who does not always succeed, or deserve to succeed. Irritated or wearied by this failure, little manifestations of temper often take the place of the gentle tone with which the lesson commenced, by which the child, whose perception of such a change is very acute, is thoroughly cowed and discouraged, and left to believe that the fault was his own, when it really was that of his instructor."

"Having endeavoured to set forth the importance of arithmetic, the next point is the plan to be pursued in teaching it. The best tool may fail to do its work in an unskilful hand; and so, excellent as arithmetic undoubtedly is, if not properly treated, it will not accomplish the task we have assigned it.

"Some commence their instruction in arithmetic by teaching numeration, *i. e.*, calling out in succession the first hundred numbers, and, in order to enliven the exercise by a little variety, it is often accompanied by a sort of chant, or motions of the legs and arms.

" Others commence with abstract numbers, and almost all begin with the *operations* of arithmetic, without making the child first acquainted with the idea of the numbers themselves. Further, they make the child first learn the mechanical rule, and then perform exercises, without attempting to show the reason of the rule : the time of the child is mainly devoted to ciphering, where he is trammelled by the signs, and can neither see the connection of the different parts of the process he is working, nor trace the relation between the end in view and the means adopted. Perhaps the following remarks may assist us in discovering the unphilosophical character of such methods.

" 1. It is by means of the senses that a child acquires his first ideas, and amongst these the idea of numbers ; and, therefore, objects should be used in the first lessons in arithmetic.

" 2. The *abstract* idea of numbers is acquired by applying the same number to a great variety of objects ; therefore the child should see it applied, not to one object only, but to many.

" 3. Operations in arithmetic, performed intelligently, require a knowledge of the numbers employed in the operation; therefore, before the child begins any of the operations, he should be well acquainted with the values of the numbers with which he has to work.

"4. From observation and experience we find that when a child is left to the dictates of nature, his first operations in arithmetic, like his first ideas of number, are applied to objects; and that when the Arabic numerals are introduced early, they are found to puzzle the pupil, and make him much longer in acquiring correct ideas of the properties of numbers and their relations than he otherwise would be; therefore he should be helped by objects, such as the ball frame, in his first attempts to work numbers, and should have mental practice before he begins ciphering.

"5. Whilst it very seldom happens that a pupil understands a practical example the better *for* learning a rule in abstract terms, he always understands a rule or principle more easily from first performing practical examples; therefore he should be led to discover the rule or principle after he has worked many examples in it."

The following is the graduated course of instruction in arithmetic adopted by this Society for very young children :—

In the first step the child obtains his idea of number from visible objects. There is no attempt to teach the combinations till the simple idea is clearly comprehended. In giving the simple idea objects are used, because the child never sees number apart from objects, and his mind is not sufficiently opened to understand numbers presented to him abstractedly. The practice of making a young child repeat the words *one*, *two*, *three,* &c., in succession, before the idea of number is first formed in his mind, which is called teaching it to count, will not enable it to form correct ideas of numbers; he cannot do this until he sees the number itself applied to things, as two hands, two feet, two balls, &c. That the child may get the *abstract* idea, and be prevented from imagining that what he is doing has some connection with one set of objects which it has not with another, its attention is directed to a variety of objects; and the objects selected are familiar to the child, that his attention may not be distracted by what is strange to him. At first, also, low numbers, not higher than ten, are taken. To such terms as million, thousand, or even hundred, a young child can attach no correct idea, and, consequently, is put in possession of words only. Ample time and abundant variety of exercises are given to the child on this first step. Too much pains can scarcely be taken to render this, the first step, secure. Every means that can be devised should be taken to fix the children's attention, to accustom them to reflect, and to give them an accurate idea of the value of numbers. Care should, at the same time, be taken to keep up the interest of the children by varying the form or subject of the questions.

Second Step.—When the children have clear ideas of the first ten numbers, they commence operations with them in addition, and afterwards in all the simple rules in succession. The balls are continued in teaching the various processes, on the same principle that objects were at first used. The attention of the children, however, is confined to one sort of objects, as the abstract idea of number is now familiar. Addition and subtraction are not at first brought together, as one process at a time is sufficient for the mind of a child. When a child has a clear idea how to add, and can do so with tolerable facility, and when he also understands how to subtract, and can do so pretty well, the two operations may be carried on in the same lesson; and after adding by one number he may subtract by the same; and this will lead him to a clearer perception of the two opposite processes. It is found better at first not to puzzle the child by a variety of operations, but to commence with those easiest, and to exercise him by increasing his difficulties in the same operation by higher numbers, never exceeding ten. When the child has arrived at the limit of his power in one process, then another is introduced and proceeded with in like manner, then the processes that have been learnt are alternately applied.

The children learn the operation with the ball-frame that they may have a clear idea of it; but they should gradually learn to calculate mentally, that the mind may acquire power. To effect this the ball-frame is removed, and the children called upon to repeat a process which they have just carried on with it. Questions also on absent objects are proposed, and promiscuous questions given, the ball-frame being referred to, to correct any mistake made. On this plan observation is first exercised, then conception, and lastly abstraction.

Third Step.—The same exercises that constituted the second step, with a little variety, and extending the numbers to twenty, are gone over in this step, but without any reference to the ball-frame, except for the correction of mistakes. For the children should not now receive assistance from objects, that the operations *may become purely intellectual, and therefore more conducive to improvement.*

Fourth Step.—In addition to extended exercises in mental calculation, in the four fundamental rules they are introduced to a decimal system of numeration, and to signs and definitions.

The decimal system of numeration is taught as high as one hundred, that the children may be prepared for calculations involving higher numbers. The classification of numbers into tens, and the use made of the first ten names in designating the succeeding numbers shown. In this exercise the ball-frame is used. The multiplication table is also thoroughly learned. For ordinary purposes it is necessary to be able to calculate quickly and readily, and a perfect knowledge of the tables facilitates this.

The pupils being thus familiar with numbers, and next taught how to represent them by figures, and also the signs of addition and the other rules, they are also taught to form regular definitions, both of the rules and the various terms used in these calculations, that their ideas on the subject may be made more precise; and of the language of arithmetic.

Section IV.—Kindergarten System.

Amongst those who have tried to reduce to system, and to put into practical shape Pestalozzi's great principle, Frederick Fröbel holds no mean place. To him is due a *system* of infant training which has taken root extensively in Germany, and which has been winning its way in this country during a quarter of a century. Fröbel, the son of a village pastor in Thuringia, after his education under his parents' roof, found his way to Switzerland and became a pupil under Pestalozzi. Subsequently he did service in a school at Frankfort. Called away from this by the troubles of the times, he, like many others, was found fighting for the fatherland. When peace came he was appointed Inspector to the Mineralogical Museum, Berlin. But this employment could not satisfy a nature like his, in which had taken deep root the desire to live for the good of others. He gave up his office and became a schoolmaster. He was content with a very humble position —a small village school in Thuringia. Here he laboured, earnestly striving to realize the principle of harmoniously developing all the faculties of body and mind of those under his care.

It was not till he was thus cast on his own resources that he got a glimmering of what this great principle embodies. Nor was he aware till now of the almost insuperable difficulties which the errors in previous training throw in the way of carrying it out in school. Children came to him twisted and gnarled, making it impossible to train them as he wished. Thus he came to see the importance of early training, and to form the design of devoting his life to its improvement.

He began in the right way. In the cottages around him were children in all stages of infancy and childhood. He set himself to observe them, and to make himself acquainted with their characteristics. He found these marks. There is great physical activity, a force from within, partly mental, partly vital, leading to incessant action. Associated with this and springing from it is a strong craving for employment. There is, too, an æsthetic tendency which makes the child susceptible of pleasurable emotions from light, colour, sound, and form. There is also great inquisitiveness, shown by constant experiment on objects with hands and lips— a curiosity often leading to the breaking of toys, to discover something which the child wishes to know. Growing, the child shows greater mental activity, which manifests itself in occupations of an inventive kind. In the absence of anything better, he places himself in the gutter and forms mud pies, or erects a dyke and makes a lake. In the operations now carried on there is manifested by snatches of speech, or fragments of conversation, the presence of some predominating fancy, which while the hands are trying to give form to some intellectual conception, soars above it all, and invests the works of its hands with imaginary attributes, or makes them partners in a little drama, in which the child is chief performer. They have also sympathy and a strong social instinct, which leads them to prefer acting with companions of their own age. And there is great playfulness, "turning to mirth all things of earth," "pleased with a fancy, tickled with a straw."

The child having revealed itself in these aspects, Fröbel set himself the task of elaborating a system which would give free scope for their activity and make them the means of developing its powers. To the result he gave the name *kindergarten*. In this name are embodied the two prime principles which should guide and control early training. The atmosphere of the child's life should be one of happiness, pleasure, joy, beauty, and occupation; and the child should be treated as a gardener treats a plant; it should be surrounded with all the conditions necessary to the growth of its susceptibilities and powers, with no other interference than such as will remove hindrances, prevent warping, and secure judicious guidance.

Having formed his system and framed his plans, leaving his schools in the hands of a relative, he did in Germany what Wilderspin was doing in England, he travelled from place to place lecturing, and inducing others to establish kindergarten schools. The first opened in England was in 1851, by Johann and Bertha Rouge. It now forms a part of the system of training in nearly all the colleges for the training of schoolmistresses.

The apparatus for a kindergarten is very simple. It consists of a series of "gifts," which range in an ascending order. The first consists of coloured worsted balls, and the second of a cube, a ball, and a cylinder. These form the babies' portion. They amuse and they instruct. They gratify the desire to be doing. They are play, but it is play with a purpose. Using them under guidance the child becomes an accurate observer. It not only acquaints itself with their forms and qualities, but it is led to observe actions. For instance, whirling a ball, it is directed to notice the curve; then shortening the string, it sees that the circle becomes smaller. A notable feature is the accompaniment of these actions. It is taught to describe them in infantile speech—now a word, then a phrase or a sentence, assisted by the sympathy and voice of the teacher, just as a mother would when amusing her babe. How great an improvement is this on the jargon and learned stilts of the earlier infant schools!

Gifts three and four consist of small cubes and squares. They furnish a series of exercises well adapted to the first period of infant school life. These are of four kinds—forms of utility, artistic forms, geometrical forms, and first lessons in number. Left to use his cubes as he pleases, the child in handling them and building with them will at length come to notice that each has the same form, number of faces, edges, and corners. He will also learn the right meaning of many words, chiefly relating to position. Every day he will find something new. He will vary his forms. So long as he is happy it is best not to interfere. When the teacher does, it may be in one of two ways: by one or two examples, not for them to copy, but to suggest; and by naming subjects according to the advancing power of the pupils, from grandma's chair, a gate, a house, a church, a monument, to the planning of a garden or of a village. A more important work falls on the teacher. Taking advantage of the tendency to invest objects with imaginary attributes, the teacher should improvise little stories, which will assist the little ones to express their ideas, give stimulus to their fancy, awaken kindly feeling, and convey information. This series of exercises, besides calling forth invention and fancy, will give the child a motive to observe, and many an object will receive attention, and afterwards be reproduced in school. The *artistic* and *geometrical* series should proceed carefully from the simplest forms. When the child has made some progress, then let it invent as many as possible. When a very beautiful form has been invented, let the attention of all be directed to it. *Lessons in number* should begin by forming the cubes into groups of twos, threes, and so on. Then with these groups addition and subtraction should be performed. Then as the groups are series of equal numbers, multiplication and division may be acquired. One series of groups should be well mastered before proceeding with another. It is recommended that these operations shall be conducted by the class marching round the table on which the cubes are displayed, and singing. To these exercises with gifts three and four might be joined, as some skill was attained, the lath practice and drawing. Provide pieces of smooth tough wood, seven inches long, half an inch wide, and one-eighth of an inch thick. With these you can vary the lessons on form, and prepare for first lessons in reading. One piece given to each child would be used to show the varieties of position which might be given to a line. Two pieces would enable it to form several devices, and when the forms X T Y appear a sheet of letters may be shown, and the child invited to discover those most nearly resembling them. Three pieces would extend the area of design, and admit of more letters. This exercise may be followed with advantage by drawing. A chalk crayon and a slate should be given to each child, and it should try to produce with these the forms it has made with the laths.

Gifts five and six are simply means of extending the exercises hitherto given. They will be found suitable for the second period of infant school life. They contain a greater number and larger variety of pieces. By means of sections of the cube triangular pieces occur, and other forms, and prisms are added. With these more complicated structures are possible, and a larger demand is made on the inventive faculty. The first course leaves the children to themselves; but when they have exhausted their own resources, it is suggested that the teacher shall take her boys and build up before them, confining each lesson to one building. During this process she is to make such observations as she may think called for; and when the building is complete, she is to tell some pleasing story in connection with it. Of course these gifts offer the means of larger culture in form; and to extend this culture, and to carry still further the preparatory lessons for reading and in drawing, more laths might be employed. If the teacher is so minded, the variety of forms in these gifts furnish the opportunity for lessons on angles, surfaces, and solids; and they also furnish the means for an extended course of numbers, fractional parts being shown and operations on them performed, but taking care that nothing is demanded from the child but what is grouped before his eye.

The most advanced course is the best recommendation of the preceding stages. It presents sufficient variety of employment, each step preparing for the next and higher one. Exercises with *cards* of different colours and shapes impart and develop taste in the arrangement and design both of form and colour. *Stick-laying* enlarges the area for culture of form. *Pea-work* introduces outline forms of building and of other things, sticks being united by means of peas. Coloured *strips of paper* are employed in plaiting, by means of which great scope is given for taste in the blending of colours, and in the design and arrangement of patterns. The process of culture goes on in paper-cutting and in perforating cardboards, and it is consummated by modelling in clay.

Reading is to be taught on the same principle as other things. The child must do and invent. A box containing strips of cardboard of various forms and sizes is provided. It has to form letters, and it has to put together words. A common element having been placed down, as "it;" the children are to place *b* before it, and all are to say "bit;" then removing the *b* and placing *f*, "fit," and so on. This spelling exercise is to be associated with writing, each child to form on the slates the letters and words it has made with the cards. Reading is to be conducted on the plan detailed in Mrs. Tuckfield's "Education for the People." The teacher takes an object, obtains from the class its name, qualities, and uses, and writes on the black-board as she proceeds. At the close of the lesson the children read what has thus been written.

CHAPTER IV.

The Elementary School.

Section I.—Dr. Andrew Bell.

The first attempt to reduce elementary instruction and school-keeping to system was that of Dr. Bell, the founder of the monitorial system. Much that was valuable in principle, and many important practical suggestions, had appeared in the writings of Ascham, Milton, Locke, and others; but Dr. Bell was the first to make everything connected with the school do its work as a part of a machinery for the intellectual and moral benefit of the pupils. The germ of the monitorial system, or of that part of it which concerns teaching, is found in Quintilian, who maintains that one who has just acquired a subject is best fitted to teach it; but Dr. Bell hit on the expedient by accident. It was the refusal of one of the teachers of the Military Orphan Asylum, Madras, to do some part of his duty, which led him to employ a boy, who succeeded so well that eventually the adult teachers were dismissed, and the institution conducted by boys. The system was introduced into England in' 1797, and was first practised in the oldest parochial charity school in the city of London, St. Botolph's, Aldgate.

In endeavouring to determine the value of any educational system, we must not merely examine the adaptation of its parts to the objects or aims of the system; for in this respect it might be perfect as a system, and yet as a system of education be of little value. We must rather examine the aims of the system, and inquire whether these are what education —true education—requires, and then examine all parts of the system in reference to their adaptation to secure these objects.

No person concerned for the well-being of society, and for the advancement of his race in intelligence, civilization, and material and moral well-being, can be indifferent to the question, What is the province of the elementary school for the poor? The schoolmaster has a special interest in the reply, as so much depends, both in his qualifications and in his daily avocations, upon the answer. Dr. Bell's answer is short and explicit. "It is," he says, "to teach the rudiments of letters, of morality and of religion, and to prepare children for the stations they have to fill." Or, as he says elsewhere, it is "to turn out good scholars, good men, good subjects, and good Christians." Interpreted rightly, no higher aims than these could be put forth by any educationist; but when we come to inquire, we find that the views of Bell, hid under these terms, were of the most moderate and limited character. His "Rudiments of Learning" embraced only mechanical reading and writing, with some knowledge of the fundamental four. Nay, in the case of the very poor he did not go even thus far. It was sufficient for them to learn to read the Bible! It seems ludicrous in this connection to speak of "good scholars," when the ability to read the Bible well does not give the ability to read even a newspaper. Perhaps, which is very likely, the doctor, by "good" scholars did not refer to the extent of their attainments, but to their soundness, as few educationists have been so strenuous as he on having everything that is learnt done thoroughly. By the rudiments of morality and religion Bell seems to have meant a *memoriter* acquaintance with passages of Holy Scripture and with the Catechism. Many besides Bell have attached great importance to this practice, as the one calculated to make "good Christians." Locke was one of the first to suggest a doubt of its efficiency, and to point out that no moral or religious habit is formed by merely preceptive instruction. In fact, it is hard to understand what influence a merely verbal acquaintance with divine truth could have on any man unless it was his habit to submit his conscience hourly to its guidance. And we know that there are many with such knowledge who are totally unsanctified by it either in life or heart. For ourselves, we should prefer, wherever practicable, that before Scripture, Catechism, or hymns are committed to memory, means should be taken to open out their meaning, and to bring it to bear on the conscience and practice,—satisfied, too, that this would fail in making "good Christians," unless accompanied by the powerful working of the Holy Spirit. It is singular that the analogy of reading did not suggest to Dr. Bell that moral habits are not formed by learning by heart. For as no one can be said to have received the rudiments of learning until he has the power to read, so no one has the rudiments of morality until he practises it.

The province of the school in relation to the future calling of the children is an important question. There is no doubt, as Bell states, that the school should prepare them for the stations they have to fill. But should this preparation be general or special? Should it consist in the formation of such habits as are required in any employment? or should it consist in furnishing industrial occupation or teaching a trade? Now it must be remembered that every well-conducted elementary school does supply that training, does secure that discipline, and does form those habits which constitute a general fitness for success in any calling. Considered in this light, all good schools are industrial. Attention, effort, patience, persevering application, are being cultivated every hour; and if they once become habitual there will be no more difficulty in transferring them to a trade or handicraft, or any other occupation, than there is in turning them from one school subject to another.

So thought Bell; hence he claims for the monitorial school superiority in this respect, because it secured the constant employment of every child, and also invested many with offices of trust. But Bell went further than this, and maintained that the children of the labourer and of the artisan, after an hour or two in school, should be employed on some industrial occupation, or in learning a trade.

Bell here showed himself not to be in advance of the public opinion of his day, which would debar the poor from extended instruction, as utterly unbefitting their condition, and as dangerous to society. But many still claim this as the function of the school,—some as a means of keeping children longer under instruction, the parents being able to appreciate the industrial occupation; others, because many employments require a manual dexterity which can be acquired only by those who go to them young.

The essential conditions of real education, according to Dr. Bell, are attention and exertion on the part of the children. The success of a system in securing these is the *test* by which it ought to be tried, and on the ground of its fitness to secure them he claims attention to his own. Dr. Bell is doubtless right in taking this ground, as a more important principle cannot be named in connection either with elementary learning or the acquisition of right habits. Attention originates in a desire to learn, and its degree is in proportion to the strength of the desire. It seems, as employed by Bell, to imply instruction and an instructor. But here is one of the weakest points in Dr. Bell's system. As he attached little weight to what is done *for* a child, and highly valued the teaching of children by children, the result was that the instruction was mere rote, and consisted chiefly of what was mechanical and verbal. The agency employed was well fitted to accomplish this task, and nothing in later improvements even can be said to be superior, perhaps not equal to it, in securing the mastery of lessons which always involve an amount of irksome drudgery to an adult. But this system was fruitless in a higher culture—a culture that is only possible when the mind of the well-instructed master is brought to bear directly and not vicariously on the minds of his charge. The habit of attention and exertion during a succession of lessons, for several hours daily, was rightly deemed by Bell of more importance than the simple act of attention required in one lesson. Hence the weight he attaches to this as an argument for the employment of monitors, these securing both a greater variety of work and more constant employment than were possible with but one teacher.

But without looking at from the monitorial point of view, we must regard it—as indeed did Bell—as the backbone of any system of school education. Nothing in any system of education can be a substitute for a child's own exertions. No one ever became a scholar by the efforts of his teacher. Personal exertion is the only road to knowledge and mental cultivation. Therefore all methods of instruction are of value, just in proportion as they stimulate the child to put forth his own efforts on the task before him, and fit him for independent exertion at another time. This is the aim—or ought to be—of all teaching, the master, feeling that it is his province to teach only so far as to make his pupils to learn. A teacher's measure of success should always be the degree to which he can bring his scholars to exert themselves without aid. In fact, it may be laid down as an axiom, that all methods succeed as instruments of education in the degree in which they gain the pupils' own efforts, and thereby tend to form him to habits of self-exertion and reliance. Especially is this true in schools for the poor; for as school life is short—too short for the purposes of education—the work of every school should be to put the power of self-education in every one's reach.

It will not escape notice that this matter is regarded both as a means and as an end: as a means, because nothing that is really valuable in the whole range of knowledge, or in the fitness of the mind to acquire it, is possible to any one but through his own arduous exertions; as an end, because the habit of active exertion and constant employment, directed to right objects, is one of the most important, whether to his own individual welfare or his usefulness to society.

The principle which we have been considering may be regarded as the characteristic feature of school education until the introduction of oral teaching and of collective lessons. Bell's schools made no provision for it but what was obtained by the preparation of lessons in school. But in other schools—those of a higher grade—there were home tasks, which it was the chief business at school to recite and to hear.

At present, with an equal sense of the importance of securing a child's exertions, our means are multiplied of doing so by our improved methods of teaching and organization. In many schools a portion of time is given by the younger children to the silent preparation of lessons, monitors being employed to see that all are faithfully engaged. A very valuable means of securing the scholar's exertions is having in every class where practicable the oral and reading lessons reproduced as abstracts. Another means is that of requiring—where the subjects admit of it, as in grammar and arithmetic—independent examples in illustration of any principle that has been explained or proved. In choosing his subjects, whether of class or collective lessons, the teacher should give preference to those which admit of this practice. And he should be ever careful to require his scholars to work out by themselves either the same lesson, or examples of a similar nature; as it often happens that children who perfectly understand a process when shown to them on the B. B. or follow a process of reasoning under the stimulus of a master's questions, find themselves unable to do so afterwards alone.

But of all the modes of securing the scholar's own exertions, that of home exercises—if well devised—is the best. Being more purely his own work, they are highly favourable to good progress. Their evident tendency is to form habits of voluntary exertion and self-reliance, for the scholar is working alone, without either the stimulus of the master's questions, or the power to appeal to his assistance. Hence they are peculiarly favourable to habits of self-dependence, as difficulties are to be met with, which must be grappled with and overcome without assistance. That "home exercises" may secure all this benefit to the pupil, they must be of a nature to interest him. Three kinds of home exercises are found in all good schools: —Preparative, including the reading lesson, spelling, history, geography, and any other which simply exercises the memory; Repetitionary, consisting of abstracts of lessons, and the working of examples in grammar and arithmetic,—a practice valuable not only as a repetition, but as giving a better understanding of the subject; Inventive, including all exercises in composition, from a list of descriptive terms in the lower classes, to the theme or essay in higher, and also including such a preparation of the reading lessons as involves the use of a dictionary. Of these three modes the last is the best adapted to call out his powers; the work is more properly his own, and any success he meets with animates him to further efforts. "Of all subjects calculated to call forth a pupil's own efforts, those which give him something to do have the preference over those which merely give him something to say."

The principles on which Dr. Bell would have the instruction of children conducted are excellent, and so are many of his devices. To the latter he justly attached less importance than to the former, preferring that the working out of a principle should be left to the teacher himself, who, he says, should be "a man of many devices." Here is practical wisdom. No teacher should allow himself to be the slave of routine. Let him have principles and keep to them, but let his application of principles be determined by his circumstances. He will often find that where one device—successful in other cases—fails in a particular one, another will succeed; his principle meanwhile working in all. That the instruction in Bell's system degenerated into a system of rote was the fault of the agent, rather than of the principles and methods. The most essential thing to secure the pupil's attention and exertion is to excite his interest in the work he has to do. This, then, is Bell's aim. The pupil must have something to do in every lesson. This Bell partly secures by requiring every lesson to be prepared by the pupil, with or without assistance, before bringing it up to the class. He also lays great stress on *writing*, both in the preparation and reproduction of lessons. "This gratifies," he says, "the love of activity inherent in the young mind." A definite portion of work must be assigned to be mastered in each lesson. The advantages of this are, that the pupil, knowing how much he is expected to master, works with greater energy, and as he is better able to mark his own progress, he works under greater encouragement. It is necessary that all the initiatory processes be learnt thoroughly, and, in fact, that every lesson—in any way necessary to the understanding of those that follow it—be fully mastered. " Without this the pupil is as one stumbling in the dark." Hence no lesson or book in the earlier stages should be passed until well learnt. By the practice of passing through lessons without mastering them, "a load," he says, " of toil and tedium is laid up; and the scholar, conscious of his imperfect and slow progress, and puzzled and embarrassed by every lesson, everywhere feels dissatisfied with the irksomeness of his daily tasks, and alike disgusted with his master, his school, and his book." In order to this thoroughness there must be a system of repetition. Unless frequently repeated the impressions made on the memory wear off. The impressions made by one or two perusals, or one or two practices of a lesson, are very weak; but even where well learnt they die out, or the power is lost, unless frequently recalled. To obtain repetition without sameness, one requisite, according to Bell, is so to graduate the lessons that every step may prepare for, and, as it were, anticipate the following step. Another is to combine the new matter of the lesson with the old, by which means, while making fresh acquisitions, he is not losing those made before. But both these will be ineffective unless joined with recapitulation, or the going over an entire series of lessons a second or third time, but more rapidly than in the first working. The danger to be guarded from—especially in reading lessons—is their becoming simply *memoriter*.

The application of these principles to the several subjects of instruction may now be detailed.

Reading.—Irrespective of the number of classes, which would depend on the size of the school, there are five marked stages in Bell's system, each more or less distinguished by differences of method—Alphabetical, Monosyllabic Reading, Monosyllabic Spelling, Easy Reading, Bible Reading. The methods or devices were of two kinds—individual and class. The individual were confined to the first three stages, and were employed chiefly in the preparation of lessons afterwards to be heard in the class. Two children, one a tutor, the other a pupil, were placed side by side, the one to teach, the other to learn the appointed lesson. The method was to teach to read by first teaching to write. As the first difficulty encountered by a pupil in learning to read is that of distinguishing the letters and words, Bell aimed to overcome it by bringing the hand to the aid of the eye. Here he shows himself to be a practical teacher, and not a mere theorist. The attempt to produce a thing by the hand gives greater keenness of observation, and impresses the thing more permanently on the memory.

The alphabet was grouped into a series of lessons, the letters being arranged according to their simplicity of form. When the alphabet was mastered, all possible combinations of two letters, a vowel and a consonant, formed another series, before the pupil was thought fit to pass from the alphabet stage. Each lesson consisted of three steps. The letter was traced, imitated, and at last produced from memory. The second stage in the learner's course was to read interesting stories in words of one syllable. The doctor attached much importance to the scholars becoming early familiar with all monosyllabic words because of their recurring so frequently; and his making the first lessons interesting stories was intended to lessen the sense of irksomeness necessarily attendant on the first stage of a new subject. Each lesson was prepared on the *individual* method. It was first written, then spelt on the book, and then with the book closed. This formed the first step. Then the children were assembled in class, and the lesson was read, first word by word in turn, then by sentences or lines—a pause being made after every word, for the twofold purpose of securing clear enunciation, and of impressing the words more distinctly on the eye. Then the books were closed and the lesson spelt through, after which it was again written on slates. The third stage consisted in the scholar learning to spell all the syllables that enter into the composition of words. He offers two reasons for what is so unnecessary, so irksome, and so unintelligent a practice: "Children so taught will not be able to learn by rote; and henceforth they will be able, with little trouble, to read any book put into their hands." This reason is similar to that urged for the phonic method; and in both cases there is but one answer—that it is familiarity with whole words, obtained by frequently seeing them, that enables any one to read them at a glance. The fourth stage introduced the learner to such easy reading as was supplied by the narratives of the New Testament. Here "previous spelling" and "individual teaching" disappear. The methods are—word about, then by phrases; "because," as the doctor says, "the power to analyze a sentence into its parts is necessary to reading with intelligence;" then by sentences, and lastly by pauses. This course was followed by spelling with book closed, and by a *memoriter* examination. The fifth stage introduced the learner to the Bible. The methods employed were the same as before, with the omission of "word about."

Writing.—The views of Bell and of Locke on teaching to write may be taken as expository of the practices of the 17th and 18th centuries—a period, according to Lord Palmerston, marked by good writing. No doubt the *good* writing—in which the schools of the old masters excelled—was owing, in great measure, to their observance of the rules of Bell and the plans of Locke. According to Dr. Bell, writing should be taught on the principle of learning to do one thing at a time. The first thing to be learnt is the management of the hand, then of the pen; and as these are sufficiently difficult in themselves, they ought to be mastered before forms of the letters are attempted.

ORGANIZATION.—Dr. Bell regarded organization as the prime instrument for obtaining attention and exertion. Nor can he be said to have attached too much importance to it. For the objects organization aims to secure are the constant employment, efficient instruction, and moral control of every child. And it is necessary to have some means of promoting these apart from the direct act of instruction, because children have a love of activity, are so affected by novelty, have so little power of continuous attention and have so many temptations to neglect their work, that unless stimulated continually to activity and exertion, through the power of the master to act on many points at once, the work of the school will not go on.

The first feature of the Madras organization is its being *monitorial*. In other words, the teaching and management of the school were entrusted to such as were yet learners, selected for their several offices according as they showed an aptitude to teach or to manage. The primary organization embraced five officers, tutors, assistants, teachers, sub-ushers, and ushers. The *tutor* had one child to assist in the preparation of his lessons, all the children of one class becoming the tutors of the next class below. The *assistants* had charge of a class. They were overlookers and examiners. They kept the children at their lessons when with their tutors, and examined them in class after their lessons were prepared. The *teachers* had the charge of two or three classes. It was their business to take each class in turn, examining and stimulating both assistants and tutors. The sub-ushers were chargeable with the order and general arrangements, and with the supply of books and slates; and they were expected to report to the usher the names of such children as they could not control. The duties of the usher were to conduct all the changes of the school, to act as a sort of general superintendent, and to take the names of all such as continued disorderly after they had been reported by the sub-ushers. These officers were to prevent the too frequent appearance of the master in matters of discipline and general management, it being thought that as "familiarity breeds contempt," his authority would be more efficient when he did appear.

At a later period the doctor somewhat modified this plan. Tutors disappear, and to each class is appointed a teacher and an assistant, the office of the latter being simply to keep order.

It thus appears that the monitorial agency was of two kinds,—some were charged with matters of order and arrangement, others with teaching. Hence it must be obvious that any charges against the one, or advantages attributed to it, do not necessarily hold in the case of the other. The advantages of the monitorial system over the individual system which it displaced are obvious. It made provision for stimulating into activity at a number of points at the same time, and thus converted the schoolroom from a scene of idleness and mischief into one of healthy excitement. The investing so many with offices in connection with the order of the school enlisted their co-operation, and became also a means of influencing their companions, at the same time that the regular discharge of periodical duties tended to form habits which would be of service to them in later life. For employing monitors as teachers, it was argued that they are better qualified to impart instruction to each other, from their greater sympathy, and from their understanding each other's style and language. This may be admitted where the object sought is merely a mechanical one, or mere *memoriter* or fact teaching—and no wise teacher will refuse to avail himself of such services as they can render. But the limits of their power should be well understood. They can instruct, but not educate. They want that knowledge of mind, that influence of character, and those diversified attainments which are necessary to enable the teacher to develop the mind and build up the character of the children. Another argument in favour of monitorial teaching—and, in fact, that on which it is chiefly grounded—is that those who have but recently learnt a thing are better able to teach it, from remembering what were their own difficulties. Now to this reason very little weight must be attached. For, first, the difficulty experienced by one child in learning a thing is not always the difficulty of another. And second, it seems absurd to say that one who has just learnt is better able to teach than he who, having been teaching for years, is acquainted with all the difficulties, and the mode of removing or avoiding them.

The second feature of the Madras organization was its classification. It consisted of large classes formed into hollow squares, and was based upon reading only. Such an arrangement exists yet in many schools. It is thought, by its advocates, superior to having separate classifications for each subject, from the more intimate relation which thus subsists between the class and its teacher, and the greater responsibility of the latter for the progress of the children. But, apart from the injustice of retarding by school arrangements the progress of a child in an essential subject because he is backward in another, as the reading classification—even when there are different bases of classification—embraces the greatest portion of school time, there is sufficient room to hold one teacher responsible for the general conduct and character. Besides, there is great advantage, where the subjects differ, in bringing children under the action of several minds, and of throwing them into competition with others than those they ordinarily associate with. Bell adopted the system of large classes, though unfavourable to each individual being called upon with that frequency which the elementary subjects require, because he would be more likely, having fewer classes, to get good teachers. He also thought that large classes call forth superior emulation, and with fewer classes the master's supervision would be more effective. To keep his classes on competing terms, without which emulation would be impossible, when a boy kept uniformly near the head or foot of his class he was removed to the next above or below.

The third feature of the Madras organization was the arrangements of the schoolroom. The objects to be secured in this part of organization are effective superintendence, combined with such isolation of the classes as will prevent one class interfering in any way with the efficiency of another. Dr. Bell doubtless took his whole organization from the parade-ground. The arrangement into hollow squares, the gradation and subordination of officers, the platform, the precision of the mechanical movements directed and controlled through subordinate agency, are all suggestions of that military organization with which his duties as chaplain at Madras made him familiar.

SCHOOL-KEEPING.—School-keeping includes under it all those important matters in which the master is chief agent, which do not belong either to method, organization, or discipline. Thus it includes the duties which fall specially to the master respecting the working of the school—his relations with the children and their parents—his arrangements to secure punctuality, regularity, and cleanliness—the keeping of registers—the means taken to keep the school in the public eye,—everything, in fact, which more nearly concerns the material prosperity of the school. We often hear of a man being a good disciplinarian, but a bad school-keeper; of another being an excellent teacher, but no school-keeper; and men are sometimes pointed out whose *full* schools show their *good* school-keeping, although they are not remarkable either for their power of moral discipline or for their ability to teach.

Good school-keeping is comparatively rare. Many teachers think that some of its requisites are such trifles as to be beneath their attention; others, that some of the practices are fit objects of contempt rather than of imitation; while not a few are satisfied if their methods are good, their organization unimpeachable, and their discipline generally effective. But good school-keeping is an art not to be despised. It has so great an influence in *filling* a school, that no man who cares for a *full* school will think it prudent to neglect it. School-keeping, as an art, was in Bell's days in its infancy, so that there is little to learn from him, but that little is highly suggestive. An essential feature of good school-keeping is the master's influence being felt in every part of the school continually. To this Bell attached the highest importance. He says, "It is the master's unceasing duty to direct, guide, and control the uniform and impartial execution of the laws in all the departments of the school, so as to render them effectual to the purpose for which they are framed. These are to maintain quiet and order, to give full scope to the love of imitation and spirit of emulation, so as to promote diligence and delight, advance the general progress, imbue the infant mind with the first principles of morality and religion, and implant in the tender heart habits of method, order, and piety." Of the manner of doing this he says: "From his place he overlooks the whole school, and gives life and motion to every member of it. He inspects the classes one by one, and is occupied wherever there is most occasion for his services, and where they will best tell. He is to encourage the diffident, the timid, and the backward; to check and repress the forward and presumptuous; to bestow just and ample commendation upon the diligent, attentive, and orderly, however dull their capacity or slow their progress; to stimulate the ambitious, rouse the indolent, and make the idle bestir themselves: in short, to deal out praise and displeasure, encouragement and threatening, according to the temper, disposition, and genius of the scholar. He is occasionally to hear and instruct the classes, or rather, overlook and direct the teachers and assistants while they do so. It is his chief business to see that others work, rather than work himself." The fault of Dr. Bell's system here is—not in attaching too much importance to effective supervision, that could scarcely be, but in making no provision for the direct action of the master's mind in the process of the child's instruction. Yet it is of equal importance that the master should come in contact daily with each child in his progress through the school, as that he should keep the entire machinery oiled and in motion.

Another element in good school-keeping is to have arrangements by which the master may know all particulars of the progress of every child and of every class, so that he may give special attention to the dull and backward, and stimulate to activity the idle whether amongst teachers or children. Dr. Bell's plans of doing this were simple and effective. Each boy able to write made an entry every night on a sheet at the end of his book of his work for that day. The result was tabulated at the end of the month in a book called a Paidometer. "The Paidometer," says Dr. Bell, "shows each child's monthly progress, from his admission into the school, to leaving it, in twelve triple columns, in which, on the last day of every month are entered the book page, and stage of the course at which the scholar is arrived in his reading, ciphering, and religious rehearsals. A single line on a folio sheet comprehends the progress of each child for a year." Besides this there was a Weekly Register which contained a summary of the daily attendance and work kept by the teacher of each class. It must be evident that the value of such records depends on the faithfulness with which they are kept. The means to secure this was in the periodical examinations. Coming to a class for this purpose, the master asked for this Paidometer and Weekly Register, and proceeded to examine the class in the work professed to have been done.

Another element of good school-keeping is to bring before visitors the good points of a school, as well as any special things in which individual children excel. Dr. Bell attached importance to this, because of its influence alike on teachers and children in promoting emulation. He points out that it is the mark of a weak master to be satisfied with showing the first class, and he attributes the deterioration of some schools to the neglect by some masters of "trotting out" the younger ones as well as the older ones.

DISCIPLINE.—"Were it required to say," says Dr. Bell, "in one word, by what means the primary and essential requisites, attention and exertion, are to be called forth, that word were discipline. Its original meaning is learning, education, and instruction, but it has come, as often happens, to signify the *means* by which this end is attained, whether it be the method, order, and rule observed in teaching, or the punishment and correction employed." The importance attached by Bell to discipline as a system of means to secure the great objects of the school may be seen in his saying, "It is in a school as in an army, discipline is the first, second, and third essential." The means which he includes in this term "are arrangement, method, and order; vigilance, emulation, praise, and dispraise; favour and disgrace, hope and fear; rewards and punishments; and especially guarding against whatever is tedious, difficult, operose, and irksome, and rendering every task prescribed to the scholar short, simple, easy, adapted, and intelligible."

The prevention of wrong-doing is one of the objects sought in these measures—an object deserving every master's serious attention. To do this, some of Bell's measures were admirably adapted. (*a*) Many of the offences against order proceed from the lessons not being adapted in length and difficulty to the age and stage of the children. In this case, the children not being interested in their employment, either become listless, go off fairy-rambling, or seek employment of a more congenial description. (*b*) Often offences are traceable to the presence in school of boys of bad habits or evil dispositions "A master," says Long, "in taking charge of a school undertakes to govern and instruct a number of individuals, who have been brought up in a variety of ways, some with bad habits, some with good, but all with some peculiarities or propensities;" hence the necessity of vigilant superintendence, that such as are of bad habits may be restrained by the certainty of discovery, joined to a wholesome fear of correction. (*c*) All lads prefer a strict discipline to a lax one. All like method, order, regularity, and to act as one of a body. The military arrangements, the variety, promptness, and precision of the movements, therefore, introduced by Bell, were admirably calculated to prevent wrong-doing, by accustoming them to act in obedience to system, and so tended to form habits of order and attention.

A higher aim in discipline than the prevention of disorder, idleness, or noise, or even than the obtaining of military order, is to incite children to put forth efforts for their own personal improvement. The signs of such a discipline are in the willing attention, constant diligence, respectful demeanour, and kindly intercourse of the scholars. Where these are found, the basis is being laid of a high, noble, and virtuous character. Their attainment depends more on the earnestness of the teacher's character, and on the personal influence which springs therefrom, than on the means employed. So thought Bell, yet he was not indifferent to the use of means having this tendency. Praise wherever it was due, special marks of favour to those who distinguished themselves by their diligence and good conduct, were among the subsidiary means; but his chief dependence was on the principle of emulation, and on the means to bring it into operation. "Emulation," he says, "though not a new principle, is so perpetual and powerful an agent in the Madras school as to have had the propriety of using it seriously questioned." The objections urged then and urged still seemed to have proceeded either from confounding it with something else, or because of its liability to abuse. The objections are that it is unscriptural, and productive of much evil; to which it is replied, "In its strict literal signification it denotes an earnest desire and contention to outstrip others, not to obstruct them, much less to thrust them back; that in this sense it is a natural principle implanted in the human breast by the Creator for the wisest and noblest purposes; and that its being productive of good or evil depends on the source whence it originates, and the objects to which it is applied." To set forth still more clearly his view of what emulation is, he thus quotes from Aristotle:—"Emulation is a painful solicitude, occasioned by there being presented to our notice, and placed within our reach in the possession of those, who are by nature our fellows, things at once good and honourable; not because they belong to them, but because they do not also belong to us." "Contrasted with envy—a base passion, inherent in mean souls, who seek not to exalt themselves, but to depress their fellows—is this generous principle of emulation."

This principle is brought into operation by the classification of a school, and by an arrangement which quickly removes to a higher class one who has kept ahead of his fellows, or places him in a lower one if he is found invariably below them. The means introduced by Bell to test this relative proficiency, and to excite the effort necessary to fit for removal, was placetaking. The value of place-taking in eliciting emulation must depend on the competition taking place on equal terms. Bell seems to have thought that this would be the case where the children were properly classified. Perhaps he was to some extent right, when the subjects are simply mechanical; as placetaking may then stimulate to exertion, so that by this and perseverance, weakness of natural endowment may be compensated for by acquired power,—as in the power of the eye to retain *forms;* but not so in those which demand a higher intelligence because of the diversities of character, and of mental powers found among children. Hence it has been objected to placetaking that it rewards boisterous impudence and self-confidence, and punishes the higher qualities of gentleness and modesty.

The treatment of offences so as to secure "the amendment of offenders, and the deterring others from committing faults," is an important object of discipline. To secure amendment, and to deter others from wrong, Bell thought that "much depended on making every boy in the school sensible that you have in view only his good." "That their daily experience of your conduct towards them must lead them to consider you as their friend, their benefactor, their guide, and their parent." He also thought it important that a record of each child's offences should be kept. The object was twofold. To prevent the awarding of punishment at the moment of offence, and before a calm investigation of it had taken place, and to furnish evidence of the improvement or otherwise in the pupil's conduct and character. Bell also attached much importance to the influence which the opinions of boys· have on the feelings and practices of their companions. Hence he had a system of trial by jury, in which the boys themselves had to determine the innocence or guilt of their fellows. He says that he " had never had reason to think their decision partial, biassed, or unjust, or to interfere with their award, otherwise than to remit or mitigate the punishment," when the end might be accomplished by the simple expression of condemnation by his fellows.

Punishment—what is its design? Three answers have been given to the question:—

1. To expiate the offence by a just penalty.
2. To reform the offender, and to deter others from doing wrong.
3. To expiate the offence, and to deter others from doing wrong.

Now, in reference to *punishments in school*, it has ever been held of *importance* by the most thoughtful educationists to make a distinction between moral offences and those which are simply breaches of order, or of school laws in themselves indifferent. To treat both alike tends to confound in the minds of children moral distinctions with merely conventional rules. With respect to moral offences, there has never been a doubt of the duty to impress children with the fact that any punishment they receive from their parents or masters does not expiate their sin, that it does not entitle them to forgiveness, and that without real and cordial concern for their fault they cannot be treated on the same terms as before they did wrong. Such being the case, the term punishment does not rightly describe the object in view; hence the term correction would be better. The design of it is to reform the offender by correcting what is wrong, and to deter others from doing wrong by associating indelibly the ideas of sin and pain—that where the first is, the other sooner or later must follow. With respect to the second class of offences, Bell seems to have held that the punishment should be so adapted to the offence that it would not only tend to reform and deter, but in some measure satisfy the claims of right and justice. Thus, if a task was not performed when appointed, he thought that keeping the pupil from play to learn it was the only penalty the case required.

All punishment aims at a moral result. Anything short of this is not punishment. To produce a moral result the mind must be reached. Bell, aware of this, employed reproof, deprived of some anticipated pleasure, or forbade the offender the company of his schoolfellows, and, where other means failed, corporal punishment. Reproof is often a severe and effective punishment. Its being so depends partly on the degree of esteem in which the master is held, partly on the delicacy with which it is administered, and partly on its not being too frequent. Reproof should be given privately; rude exposure only tends to blunt the feelings of the culprit, and to awaken the sympathies of the bystanders in his favour. Abbott says, "In many cases where a fault has been publicly committed, it seems at first view to be necessary that it should be publicly punished; but the end will, in most cases, be answered if it is *noticed* publicly, so that the pupils may know that it received attention, and then the ultimate disposal of the case may be made a private affair between the teacher and the individual concerned." In many cases the communication may be made most delicately and most successfully in writing. The more delicately you touch the feelings of your pupils, the more tender these feelings become. Many a teacher hardens and stupefies the moral sense of his pupils by the harsh and rough exposures to which he drags out the private feelings of the heart. A man may easily produce such a state of feeling in his school, that to address even the gentlest reproof to any individual in the hearing of the rest would be a most severe punishment; and, on the other hand, he may so destroy that sensitiveness that his vociferated reproaches will, as Madame Necker observes, "pass by him as a storm, he sheltering himself the while under the cover of indifference or resentment." In cases where more than reproof is needed, Bell was of opinion that to deprive of enjoyment is more effective than to inflict pain. Bodily pain is but momentary, but to keep from play or to detain after school hours compels the attention for a longer time to the offence, and to what it deserves.

In some of the worst cases he would forbid the lad the companionship of his schoolfellows. This to a lad is often the severest punishment you can inflict. It appeals at once to his self-respect. That he is not thought deserving to associate with other boys wounds him to the quick. It also addresses itself to his conscience, which gives the sanction of its authority to the feeling that such as are doers of evil are not fit to associate with the good.

Bell objected to corporal punishment. He thought the cases *few* where it was needed. As generally employed it effects no good, as its impression is but momentary; while, on the other hand, its tendency is to degrade and harden. Bell thought that its employment could be justified only in the case of the weak-minded master, who had no other means of government. "Its use," he says, "is a sign of poverty and destitution." It betrays ignorance of mind as well as want of power over it.

Section II.—*Joseph Lancaster.*

AIMS AND PRINCIPLES.—The year following that in which Bell introduced his system into this country, Joseph Lancaster opened a school in the Borough Road, Southwark. The son of a common soldier, himself, previously to his great enterprise, a seaman in the navy, without funds, but enthusiastic and benevolent, he started the noble project of giving instruction to the destitute poor. Becoming acquainted with the Madras system, he sought to realize Bell's conception, and with so much success that ere he was twenty he had gathered a school of 1,000 children. As an example of enthusiastic devotion to the highest though least esteemed and worst paid of all professions, Lancaster is worthy of the imitation of all engaged in it.

Some degree of enthusiasm seems necessary to bring any enterprise to a successful issue, but especially is enthusiasm essential to success in the work of education. Its high and noble objects, the culture of the mind and the formation of character, can never be fully attained but by men in whom the love of education is an all-absorbing passion. Nor is it impossible to attain such enthusiasm, though it is easier in some cases than in others. Some seem to be endowed with an enthusiastic spirit, and whatever the pursuit, they engage in it with all their soul. Lancaster was one of these, but although all cannot as readily enter into the spirit of this great work, yet by accustoming themselves to think often on the greatness of the objects sought, they will succeed at length in awakening in themselves some portion of this spirit.

The province of the school, according to Lancaster, is "to train children in the practice of such moral habits as are conducive to the welfare of society," as well as to impart instruction in useful learning. Moral training was held by him—and justly—to be inseparable from religious instruction. Here, and here only, have we that sanction and that morality which the conscience recognises, and here only have we those motives by which the will can be permanently influenced. It is well to bear this in mind. While we insist on the *practice* of moral duties, and the *exercises* of the moral faculties, as the principal agents in moral discipline, we must not place religious teaching in a low or subordinate place. Nay, we must place it first—first in the class of motives—first as an instrument. Our Saviour, in His ever-memorable prayer, says, "Sanctify them through Thy truth, Thy word is truth." Now this implies that the truth is known. Let us then present religious truth to the young mind—lodge it in the memory—make it clear to the intelligence—employ it so as to call forth emotion—but, above all, address it to the conscience, and thus endeavour to secure its action on the life.

METHODS.—Method made but little advance in the hands of Lancaster. It was chiefly in the arrangements to secure progress, and in the teaching of arithmetic, that we discover any differences betwixt himself and Dr. Bell. Lancaster seems to have had a glimmering of a truth, which must have been practically recognised by every successful teacher, though often overlooked, namely, that school life has distinct periods, in each of which there is a special object, by which its subjects and methods must be determined. He divides school life into two periods. The first is one in which the child should receive all the aid which his teacher can give him, consistently with training him to self-helpfulness, in acquiring those instruments which are required to the successful pursuit of knowledge. The second in which he should be taught to apply what he has acquired to the study of other branches, being thrown, in doing so, as much as possible on his own resources. The value of thus dividing school life into periods is, that by clearly defining what you can accomplish, and laying distinctly down what you may attempt with a probability of success, your labours become more determinate, and the results obtained more perfect than when you work without a well-defined aim, or without reference to what mental development, or the acquisition of knowledge requires. The necessity of such a graduation of lessons, in which each will prepare for and be repeated in those which succeed, was practically recognised by both the founders of the monitorial system. But Lancaster had a better appreciation of what was required to accomplish it. In learning to read, the number of words to be mastered before there can be ability to read any book is so great, that only he who gets much reading—much not in a single lesson, but in a variety of lessons—can hope speedily to overtake the task. This plain fact is often forgotten, and by none so much as those who with Bell have reading taught in large classes, instead of with Lancaster, in small drafts. The small drafts enabled Lancaster to have three grades of lessons where Bell had but one, and thus provided for a larger amount of reading as well as for a better graduation of difficulties. The same arrangement also secured the second great essential to progress in this as in every other mechanical art — much practice. It is obvious that children in Lancaster's school would have three times the amount of practice which they had in Dr. Bell's, as well as three times the variety of lessons.

A great improvement introduced by Lancaster was in the teaching of Arithmetic. Hitherto the instruction, as in reading and writing, had been individual. Lancaster applied the class system to it, and with better results than were obtained in reading. This was due to all working at once, emulation being thus, more easily excited, and the attention kept up, than when only one was actively engaged as in reading. In teaching arithmetic Lancaster had the following plans :—The basis of progress was placed in a thorough knowledge of the tables. In every new rule the examples were at first short and easy, increasing in length and difficulty with the power of the learner. Each class had a definite number of examples, which were written in a book kept by the monitor, and these were worked over and over again, until they could be worked with facility and despatch. In teaching a new rule, a monitor dictated an example; he then worked it out, the scholars following him on their slates; then the slates were cleaned, the example written on the B. B., and each boy in turn took a part of the operation. This was persisted in until the mode of working was understood.

ORGANIZATION.—*Schoolroom Arrangements.*—In the plan of his schoolroom Lancaster shows the influence of early associations on the practices of maturer years. He doubtless had a ship of war in his eye when he planned his room. The length of the room was nearly twice the width, the area was filled with parallel desks, a space of about six feet was left round the room for draft teaching, and at one end was a raised platform, from which all orders were issued, and from which the whole could be inspected. Opposite each draft a black-board was suspended, that the monitor might illustrate any difficulty that occurred in the reading, spelling, or arithmetic lessons. There was fastened to the wall, at the height of about five feet, a small open box in which the books and slates of the draft

o

were kept. At the distance of eighteen inches there were slates so let into the desk as to be level with the top—an arrangement that was made to prevent noise, save time, and preserve from breakages. In all these arrangements the intention was to economize the noise and labour of working the school, and also to give the master the power to act on the whole or a part at pleasure.

Classification.—It has been already pointed out that Lancaster, recognising two great purposes in school life, one of supplying the instruments of learning, the other of teaching their application to the acquisition of knowledge, formed his school into two great divisions corresponding to these aims. In respect of the basis of classification, having seen the advantages of united practice in reading and spelling, he applied the same process to arithmetic, which had hitherto been taught, as were all the arts, on the individual method. A very little experience convinced him that class teaching was more successful in arithmetic than in reading, because of the greater difficulty in the latter case of keeping all employed. He also soon made the discovery that to keep up a healthy emulation with equable progress, it was necessary to have a distinct classification for arithmetic, as the scholar's rate of progress was very variable in the two subjects. With respect to the *size* of a class, that must depend on the number of children in a school, since the stages of the learner's progress are pretty well defined; but when these classes come to practise reading, spelling, and arithmetic, Lancaster would have only such a number grouped as would give frequent practice.

More practical than Bell, and perhaps more mechanical, and not so sanguine of a monitor's power to keep a large number actively employed, he attached value to frequency of practice. On the other hand, Bell thought that, having fewer classes and securing better teachers, he would get a higher intelligence, which would more than compensate for any mechanical loss. The truth seems to be, in relation to these opinions, that although an intelligent lad will need shorter practice than one less intelligent, yet *frequent* practice is as much required in the one case as in the other, the only difference being that the one will pass through the various stages more rapidly than the other. Certain it is that a clever fellow, applying himself at distant intervals, will not make the progress of him who—less gifted—applies himself at the lapse of short periods.

Working and Teaching Power —In working the school Lancaster had a head monitor, who was charged with the changes, the order, and the general arrangements, thus leaving the master to devote his attention to superintendence and to cases of discipline. The head monitor was assisted by monitors of order, who had charge of class lists, looked after absentees, and supplied the classes with whatever they required. To each class was appointed a superior monitor, whose business it was to test the work of the monitors of drafts, and to superintend all the work in desks. Besides these there were inspectors, whose business it was to examine periodically every class, give to each scholar a thorough sifting, and to pass on to a higher class every one who was fit for removal. This system was due to the importance attached by Lancaster to keeping every boy employed, to having checks on the work of the monitors, the progress of the scholars, and on their attendance; and to the great advantage to the discipline of the school of enlisting the co-operation of as large a number as was possible.

DISCIPLINE.—Lancaster, as might be expected, fell into some errors in the details of discipline, but he shows himself to have been well versed in the art of government, and to have had considerable insight into child-nature, and the motives by which it is influenced. Exception has been justly taken to his appealing in some instances to the lower and more sordid feelings, and also to the punishments he employed, but his general principles are those on which the success of all school government depends.

He lays its foundations in the influence of the master, the power of public opinion, the co-operation of the leading children, the distribution of honourable distinctions and rewards, the judicious use of emulation, the value of drill, of constant employment, and of conducting all movements by signals, and on punishments varying in kind, and being administered without ruffling the temper of the master.

"The personal character of the master, the influence which he establishes in his school, and the feelings with which he inspires his scholars, are now generally acknowledged as the chief sources of discipline and government. It is often said that a master has more need to watch himself than his children, as in the majority of cases, the disorder or disobedience found in a school is traceable to some omission, inconsiderateness, hastiness of temper, or want of firmness in himself." To the same effect the good discipline of a school is invariably attributed to the ascendency of the master's character, and not to the means he employs, only so far as they help to establish it. So Abbott, after detailing some admirable plans for promoting moral influence, says "that they will depend for their success, not so much on their adaptation to human nature, as on the character of the man by whom they are employed."

A thorough conviction of this would be found to be an earnest of success to the young schoolmaster who is really ambitious to be an educator. "Not that the character can be assumed at pleasure, for this, like all character, has its roots in the soil of past years. No, nothing can appear in the character of a man that has not grown there. The lesson of to-day could not be said if it had not been preceded by those of yesterday, and many days before it. And if a man attempt the deception of appearing what he is not, the moment of entering the presence of children strips him of his disguise, 'no admittance for shams' being written on the portals of every temple of youth." Still a conviction of the truth that personal character is the source of what his school will become must point out to the young master the necessity of that personal discipline without which he must miserably fail in any attempt to achieve what is great and good.

Next to the personal influence of the master, Lancaster places the power of public opinion, the latter indeed springing from the former. By the public opinion of the school, he means the opinion which pervades the mass of children respecting their school and their teacher, and whatever concerns either the one or the other. Lancaster points to the existence of such a feeling in the rivalry which sometimes exists between two schools, and urges that it shall be formed and exerted on the side of order, diligence, and progress. The importance of securing this public opinion has been held by some of the most eminent educators. Fellenberg, describing his own practice, says, "The effort is constant to excite in the pupils that public spirit which seeks to exclude everything improper from its sphere of influence, in order to preserve the order and tranquillity which are necessary to the improvement of all. . . . An influence of this kind once established, with due regulation and oversight, will often accomplish more than all the remonstrances and discipline of the teacher. The pupil can seldom resist the force of truth when he finds himself condemned by the common voice of his companions, and is often more humbled by this censure from his equals than by any of the admonitions of his superiors." When public opinion has been thus formed in favour of whatever is lovely and of good report, the new scholar will find that he cannot do as he pleases, or as he has been accustomed to, but he must conform to that which he finds established. But this is equally true whether the teacher form the public opinion of the school or not. It is not in the power of the teacher to prevent its formation. Met together in numbers, rules are tacitly adopted, and a standard of conduct is fixed by which every one is tried, and to which every one must submit. Every one entering this society, in a few days partakes of the general tone, at the same time that he imparts to it something of his own. Few can really estimate the power which thus exists in a school, and few have ever felt more strongly than Lancaster the necessity of securing it to the side of good government.

Lancaster sought to form the public opinion of the school through the means of those children whose lively, active, energetic spirits gave them influence and command with their fellows. His first aim was to attach these to himself, by furnishing them employment, involving honour, trust, and command. Having secured them by thus skilfully availing himself of what was the prominent feature in their character, his next step was to secure their co-operation in influencing others. For this purpose he would often meet them apart, and placing before them one of his plans, he would dwell on its importance to the well-being of the school, and would by every means in his power endeavour to excite their interest in the working of it out. This accomplished, he knew they would influence others, and so the thing would spread until the mass was leavened.

MEANS OF DISCIPLINE.—Two objects, according to Lancaster, are to be kept in view in school discipline. One is to procure order, quietness, diligence, and obedience, these being necessary to the children's progress in learning. The other is the *right training of the will*. The last is the most difficult problem in education. To furnish motives which will not only operate in the master's presence, but which will have a permanent influence on conduct and character—to bring the will under control, and yet impart to it strength, determination, and power of resistance, is the highest object of discipline, as it is the greatest achievement of the educator. Our judgment, then, of the means employed in school government must have reference to their adaptation to secure the one or other of these ends; and we must be careful not to confound the one with the other,—for a set of means that may be well adapted to secure the first, may be equally so to defeat the second. Order, quietness, diligence, and obedience may be obtained at the expense of everything that is really valuable in the character and the will. No; it is not by their power as present motives to secure order, that we must determine the value of the means employed, but by their power to supply principles which shall have an abiding existence as motives of right conduct and action at all times. It is highly important to bear these considerations in mind during our present review. Lancaster well understood the necessity of supplying motives of action which should be permanent rather than temporary, and he showed his knowledge of human nature in their selection. Yet at almost every step we find something to deprecate,—if not in the motives themselves, yet in the means to give them birth.

Among the means employed to secure order and quietness, besides endeavouring constantly to form a public opinion in their favour, he attached—and justly—much value to simultaneous movements and action in class work, and in school changes; to having these done as often as possible by signals instead of oral commands; to having oral commands in the fewest possible words, and in such arrangements as would render idleness impossible without being immediately detected. In these things he laid hold of sympathy, imitation, and the love of action, found in children, and turning them wisely to account in matters of easy and pleasant performance, he laid the foundation of habits of obedience in matters of graver moment. For he says truly that a child *accustomed* to obey in little matters will more readily do so in the greater.

One of the greatest difficulties in school-keeping arises from the number of children who require some external stimulus to get them to plod on with earnest effort at their various lessons. Lancaster successfully encountered the difficulty, but it was by an almost exclusive appeal to the emotions of self—the love of distinction—the hope of reward—and emulation. Every boy in class wore conspicuously on his breast the number of his position. Every one who gained the top of his class, wore as long as he remained there a badge of merit. Every one who distinguished himself in reading, spelling, writing, or arithmetic, wore a badge setting forth the fact. Every one who distinguished himself by his excellence in all the subjects, or in teaching them to others, or in his efforts to reclaim bad boys, wore a silver medal of the *order of merit*. To boys who gained the badges of merit four times tickets with a money value were given, which might be exchanged at any time for toys, books, or pictures. To those who obtained the order of merit, and who continued to distinguish themselves, prizes more costly were given—to some silver watches. Now the great objection, as it strikes one, to all this, is not in acting on such principles as the love of distinction, but in making the gratification to consist, not in the thing itself, but in parading it before others, and in the material gains which accrued from it. Hence the thing to be feared would be that even if the motive of action did not become permanent, that the lads would slacken their efforts when removed from the school. But suppose such motives to become the permanent principles of action, what would be the result ? A character in which there would be no high aspirations, where there would be no regard to what was good, unless it brought with it distinction applause, and material gain. But how low, how mean how debased, how utterly unbefitting the high destiny of man would be such a character—a character in which the love of display was the chief feature !

A mode of employing emulation, in use by Lancaster, is worthy of imitation. He set class against class. To two classes he assigned the same work, and that which excelled occupied the highest place until the next trial of strength. In this contest the *individual* was sunk in the *class*. It was not for personal distinction, but for the distinction of his class that he contended. Here self gave way before the desire that those with whom he associated should win. Each lad would work, not that *he* might win, but that his class might Lancaster states that the experiment was invariably successful, every lad putting forth his utmost ability for the success of the class to which he belonged.

Section III.—*The Intellectual System.*

The instruction under the Monitorial system of its first promoters was the merest rote. It consisted chiefly in mechanical reading, writing, and arithmetic.

It is interesting to note this fact, now that there is a tendency under recent legislative action, to restrict the work of the school within the same meagre limits. What were the results attained under a system of similar restriction? That they were not satisfactory might be surmised from the efforts of such men as Wood, Stow, Grant, Shuttleworth, Tate, and many others, to alter or add to the existing system, or to substitute something else for it. But we are not left to conjecture. Brougham's commission of 1816, Pillans' letters, and the earlier reports of H.M.'s Inspectors, have placed the matter beyond dispute. The charges against a system that only drilled in reading, writing, and arithmetic, were, amongst others, that under it progress was not commensurate with the labour bestowed; that a large majority, after years of attendance, left school with such a smattering as to be practically of no use to them; that the stupidity under questioning was in a sense appalling; that intelligence not being cultivated, the habit of reading was not formed; and that in many cases the power to read and write acquired at school was subsequently lost.

The first innovation on this state of things was—keeping a monitorial organisation, by direct culture of the intelligence chiefly in connection with the reading lesson. The success attending it was such that its promoters, distinguishing it from the mechanical reiteration of the older monitorial schools, termed it the Intellectual system. Worked out by the disinterested exertions of Mr. Wood, and made known in its chief features by the enthusiastic labours of Professor Pillans, as well as at a later period in the " Account of the

Edinburgh Sessional School," it rapidly made its way both in Scotland and England, advanced here by the fostering care of the British and Foreign School Society.

The intellectual system originated in a desire to improve the matter and methods of instruction of the elementary school, to infuse spirit into all its exercises, and to create activity, energy, and intelligence throughout the classes. To accomplish these things, it was seen that a knowledge of child mind is essential; that the memory must not be the only object of culture, but that other powers must be brought out, such as perception, imagination, and judgment: and that regard must be had to the fact that a child has passions, affections, and a conscience, if his co-operation is to be secured in the process of education. Also the special characteristics of childhood must be borne in mind. There is an aversion to mental exertion when a definite object is not before their mind; but they possess curiosity in a high degree, which, if properly stimulated will overcome their aversion to mental application; they delight to display their knowledge, and they are ambitious to excel their fellows.

Assuming this knowledge, it was maintained further that a high state of intelligence and intellectual activity required that such facts and principles as these now to be enumerated should be constantly acted upon. Both teacher and pupil should understand that there is no royal road to learning, that the path is rugged and the toil laborious; the interest of the pupil should be excited in what he is about, and this cannot be done if what he is engaged on is unintelligible to him;

all real efforts should be praised, and where a dull child finds it impossible to excel others he should be encouraged to excel his former self; as far as practicable the inclinations and capacity of every child should be studied in order to his efficient instruction; in fixing the branches to be acquired, and the extent to which pursued, regard must be had to the probable length of the school life of the scholars; and all the school should be kept intelligently, actively, and constantly employed.

Increasing attention to the nature of education, and to what is essential to intellectual and moral discipline, made apparent that a great mistake had been countenanced, in the opinion that any one might be entrusted with conducting a school, a mistake similar in kind but more deplorable in results to that which gave operations in surgery to the village barber, or the healing of disease to the rustic herb dealer. Light began to dawn on those who concerned themselves with the subject, that a being of such complicated structure as a child, and such a noble work as its training, demanded peculiar qualifications in its instructor. This increasing appreciation of the dependence of educational success on the character of its most active agent was manifested by the promoters of the intellectual system.

Enthusiastic devotedness to education was claimed as the first requisite of a master of a school. Success, it was maintained, depended on the spirit of the master. Of the school he was to be the life and soul. What he was his school would become. His enthusiasm or indifference would spread through every class, his subordinates and pupils would unconsciously imbibe his spirit. And the hourly work would be highly invigorating and compassing noble ends; or would be languid and evil in its results, in proportion to the conception the master had of his duty, and his devotion to its accomplishment.

Another step in the right direction was the claim that the instructor of others should himself be well instructed. For, apart from such low ground as that a man cannot give to others what he himself possesses not, there are so many difficulties met with by the young, and the bringing their faculties into play requires so much nice skill, that it is only the man with large stores in hand that can successfully elucidate and remove the former, or who is himself a thorough student and observer that can acquire the latter. The discipline which a liberal culture gives is necessary to enable a man to discipline others. No control can be had of child mind, no right direction given to its powers, there can be no awakening of an inner life, and no high aspirations excited, but by one who has been the subject of a similar culture in an eminently high degree. Besides, if the schoolmaster is not a well-informed man with a disciplined mind, he will be excluded from educated society, and so run the risk of becoming a man of narrow opinions and prejudices; and who would willingly commit a child at its most plastic period to the culture of such a one?

"Apt to teach" is an indispensable qualification. Long practice does not always confer this talent. Many with no "natural gift" certainly become by study and practice respectable teachers, yet those of the highest class owe their position, perhaps, to original endowment. Be this as it may, the quality, whether acquired or original, is essential to success. One who has this aptitude has the power of winning the affections even of the dullest, of identifying himself with his scholars so as to feel their difficulties—without which he will scarcely use right methods of surmounting them—and of presenting knowledge at the time and in the manner in which it is most likely to arrest attention and produce durable impressions. Such a one has the power to draw out what the pupil knows, to make him thus acquainted with his actual state, and prepared to supply with interested effort his deficiencies; he has also *tact* shown in adapting himself to the capacity, inclination, and want of each individual scholar.

Two words express the method of this system— interrogation, explanation. The first elicited from pupils what they knew, and so made it the means of teaching others less informed; the other supplied material for a similar process in subsequent lessons. Thus it was sought that nothing should be communicated until the learner had made an effort of his own; the principle of mutual instruction was employed, and the process often became one of teaching the children to work out results for themselves, instead of taking information simply at the mouth of their teacher.

The reading lesson was the great instrument of cultivating the intelligence, and may certainly be taken as embodying all that was characteristic of the system. That a child, in being taught to read, should at the the same time be taught to understand what it reads, is so simple a truism, that it excites surprise that its necessity should ever have had to be insisted upon. Yet it was the starting point of Wood, who early realised that the mechanical part of reading might be so acquired as effectually to prevent the habit of being attained of reading with attention and profit. Without such a habit any other advantage can scarcely be deemed an adequate result of the labour demanded in the acquisition of the mere mechanical power. Still it was thought necessary to defend the practice. This was done by urging that children so dealt with no longer found their reading lesson an irksome drudgery, but a pleasant employment, the result of which was greater animation and energy when engaged thereon; that as the children's intelligence was quickened by this process their progress was more rapid, as they became thereby quick to perceive and strong to retain the matter of their lessons; and that even in the mastering of new words, the child, who was taught to gather the sense as he read, was endowed with two powers, where the less-favoured pupil had but one, and thus was more likely to make them his own quickly.

Exposition of reading lessons may aim to give such a general command of the language, and such a habit of attention and thought, as will enable the reader to make his own what he reads; or it may aim at producing good oral reading, or what is properly the "art of reading." From the attention demanded for it, it would seem that the latter is deemed a more desirable accomplishment than the former. Yet regarded rightly, surely the ability to make a book one's own is of much more importance to a man than the power to read aloud so that others may understand. To be able to read aloud with intelligent emphasis and expression is certainly a valuable power, but in school it ought to be secondary, not regarded as an end, but rather as *one* of the tests of the power to read with profit. Wood seems to have formed this opinion, for he claims that the learner shall not be taught simply to understand the passage before him, but shall get a general knowledge and command over his own language, and, not to be mistaken as to his meaning, he draws an illustration from parsing, which is not taught that the learner may be acquainted with the sentences parsed, but that he may have power to deal with any sentences.

To that habit of attention while reading, to which is due the power of appropriating what is read, there must be added, if a higher discipline is sought, the practice of carefully weighing what is read, and of bringing up former acquisitions for its elucidation, confirmation, or rejection. That the foundation of such a habit might be laid in school, it was thought desirable to give information on a variety of topics such as the passage might suggest, or its full examination might require. This practice was occasion of abuse. Much irrelevant matter was often introduced—especially as a word, and not the subject read, often suggested the topic or remark.

The work of the several classes presents a few points of favourable comparison with the system which this hoped to supersede. After the alphabet was acquired, words of two letters took the place of Bell's ba, be, bi, bo, bu, and were presented to the eye in two characters, roman and italics, by which it was found the eye sooner acquired the power of recognising words. Words of three letters followed, arranged on a principle which it was thought facilitated their acquisition. Words like dry, cry, spy, the, were followed by such as act, ink, orb; these by such as den, men, ten; and these by such as die, due, dew. This course passed the child entered on books. Here an important step was made in advance. The Bible, hitherto a task book, was removed from its degraded position, and other books, interesting in matter and suitable to the intelligence, put in its place.

In the method of working a reading class, apart from what was really the life of the system, the practice of spending some time daily in explanation, the most remarkable thing was the immense activity engendered by the practice of place-taking, It is interesting also to note—probably a consequence of this practice—that on no account was spelling allowed during reading. It had a distinct time assigned to it.

Section IV.—*The Training System.*

Few men have done more for the cause of Education than David Stow. Few have exerted in their own lifetime so wide-spread an influence on education. In the schools that exist—on his system—he has revolutionized the ordinary system of teaching and school-keeping, and has affected, for good or evil, more or less, every other system, though founded on principles the opposite of his own. For a long time past his principles and methods have engaged the attention of many in Europe and America interested in education, and they have been more or less adopted, wherever they have been thoroughly examined and understood.

Like many others, whose labours have been of the greatest benefit to human happiness and progress, Mr. Stow had no purpose—in the commencement of his great work,—but to arrest, in his own sphere, a little of the tide of evil that was bearing so large a portion of the community to irretrievable ruin. In 1816, he—then a young merchant—gathered on a Sabbath evening, into a dingy apartment, in a back lane, about thirty young Arabs of the Salt-market, Glasgow. His aim was to instil religious principles ; to engage their affections in behalf of what was right and good, and to lead them to the knowledge of Him, whose mission was to save that which was lost. He laid down for himself two rules, to the observance of which he traces much of his success in education ;—never to strike ; never expel. Amid all their circumstances of rags and filth, he viewed them as on an equality with himself, rational, responsible, and immortal ; having minds as delicate, as curious, and as complicated in structure as his own ; with emotions that it would be well to cherish, and intellectual faculties and moral powers that it would be possible to train.

During ten years he laboured, making valuable discoveries, and meeting with unexpected results. At length, awaking to the fact that the training of the street was more powerful than that of the school, and that what was done on the Sabbath was but too effectually neutralized during the week, and anxious to have a wider sphere for observation, and for testing the discoveries he had made, he established an infants' day-school, and placed it under the care of that prince of infant teachers,—the late David Caughie. Calling to his aid Mr. Wilderspin, who was then engaged in establishing infants' schools, he introduced the system of that gentleman, supplementing it with those other principles and methods of religious and moral training which had borne, and were still producing such good fruit in the smaller sphere of a Sabbath-evening class. For seven years this work went on. During them, by labouring in his Sabbath-class, by daily visits to his school, and working therein, by earnest inquiries in all directions, he increased his experience, added to his principles, improved his methods, and enlarged his views. Convinced of their soundness, and anxious to give wider scope to the application of his principles and plans, he now added to his establishment a juvenile school. He also made it, as he had done the other, the means of confirming or correcting his views, and of diffusing a knowledge of his aims, principles, methods, and results, by opening them as model schools, where teachers could be trained.

Already his work had drawn to it a large share of public attention, and many, besides those going forth as teachers—ministers of the Gospel, and missionaries about to depart for their fields of labour,—visited the schools, and attended courses of lessons therein, that they might acquaint themselves with methods and principles at once so simple and effective as these seemed, for the communication of religious and moral truth. At length so much had his earnest advocacy, his untiring zeal, his enthusiastic labours, and his remarkable success won upon his townsmen, that the

Glasgow Educational Society erected a Normal Seminary, established his system therein, and gave him its oversight as honorary secretary.

The establishment of the Training System in a Normal Seminary, forms an era in the educational progress of this country. Before this, others had, like Mr. Stow, opened their schools for persons to "learn the system" prior to taking charge of schools. But this was an attempt to give students, intending teaching as a profession, a knowledge of educational principles, to furnish them with the knowledge they had to impart, to set before them the best examples of teaching addressed to children in well graduated divisions, and to give them opportunities of teaching under criticism in the presence of skilled masters, after the models and to the same groups, as the lessons in their own presence. The system itself, as now established, was the first formal attempt in these islands to combine and exhibit in practice some original principles and methods, with whatever had been found valuable in other systems, with the object of training the child in its whole nature, physical and mental, religiously, morally, and intellectually. "The Training System," says its founder, with a rare modesty, "is not so much any one system, as a combination of what is valuable in other systems, with additions, not, so far as we know, hitherto engrafted on juvenile schools, and the sole aim is to arrive at the best mode of cultivating the whole man."

The designation "Training" was adopted partly as the best one for embodying the fact that no child can be educated unless its whole nature is harmoniously cultivated; and partly as setting forth what was thought to be the peculiar distinction between teaching and the process now contemplated. The former consists, it was maintained, in simply setting forth before the child's intelligence what it should know or do; the latter in taking means to have carried into practice and habit, what should be. But it admits of question if any such distinction can be maintained. "Teach me to live," in Ken's well-known hymn, certainly includes all that Stow intended by the term *train*, and the same is true of other uses of the term. Hence the designation was unfortunate, because seemingly pretentious, and produced opposition from many who were conscious that their term teaching included all his term training.

The proper function of the school in the education of a child must be understood by all who would rightly appreciate Mr. Stow's great work. With many the school is simply a place of instruction and of learning —a place where certain arts are first to be acquired, and then applied to the acquisition of other things. This is their sole end and aim; and if these are secured, then the school answers its purpose, and all further responsibility is escaped from. To such it matters nothing what are the habits or character of the children, or the influences at work upon them, except so far as they affect their progress or the convenience of their instructors. There are others who—especially when regarding the school for the poor—would make its aim to be, in some cases the formation, in all the growth of those habits that are necessary to the proper discharge of the duties and relations of life. With these, school learning is simply an instrument for the acquisition of such a fitness ; its value being not in itself, but in the self-restraint, steady application, and habit of obedience required from the learner. Stow claimed for the school a higher function, and pointed out a nobler aim. The idea of the family must be added to that of the school, and the duty of the parent to the responsibilities of the teacher. The school ought to be a place of education—of education, not in its popular sense of instruction, but in its real import as implying the formation of character. Looking upon the child as in preparation for immortality, Stow considered that both Scripture and reason point out that the formation of its character should be the great purpose of the school, as it is of the family, and as it is of life.

That the school has a special function, none will deny ; that it is a necessity of our social condition, for the discipline of the intellect and the acquisition of the means of continuing it, is readily granted ; that the family does not and cannot supply that which the school undertakes, is true. All that is clear. The error to be avoided is making this its sole office. For no one, really impressed with the importance of the subject, can doubt whether religious and moral training, the culture of the affections, and the discipline of the will, which belong especially to the sphere of the family, should also be continued in school. Whatever in these things is the duty of the parent is also the duty of the schoolmaster. For children cannot lose their right of having their highest interests cared for during so large a portion of their waking life as that spent in school, because sent there for another purpose. Certainly there is the highest obligation on all entrusted with young immortals in their most plastic period, when surrounded by so many claimants to their affections, and acted on from without by so many evil influences, to do for them all that the most tender, most conscientious, and most Christian parent would do to save them from evil and train them to good.

The function of the school is to assist and supplement, not to supersede the work of the family. It has to continue and strengthen that which has been begun and is being carried on there. But, alas! there are thousands of homes where these obligations are not felt, where these duties are not practised. A child from such a home has, if possible, a stronger claim to religious and moral culture than others. Here evil, already in possession, has to be neutralized, vicious habits and practices have to be uprooted, right principles have to be implanted, and virtuous habits formed. Religious truth and duty, and the moral obligation of right conduct to others, and of right regard for itself, have to be brought home to its conscience, and it is to be trained to feel their force and to yield itself to their sway.

In claiming these things as belonging to the sphere of the school, Stow cannot justly be charged with raising too high a standard, nor to have sought what is impracticable. To have done so would have defeated his purpose, for those practically engaged in·school work, not realizing their aims, would become discouraged on comparing the results attained with the expectations formed. Interpreted by what was actually done in the schools under his supervision, he aimed at no higher results than every Christian teacher is taught to expect, and at nothing more than was accomplished in numerous instances under his eyes.

Entertaining such views, it was a natural sequence that school education should be conducted on a distinctive religious basis, and that he should place moral training before the special work of the school. So strong indeed was his conviction that moral training should have precedence of everything else, and so urgently did he enforce it, that a distinguished writer on education has declared that the prominence given to it by him, and to the means of obtaining it, was the chief benefit his system had conferred on the cause of national education. Nor was this conviction weakened by advancing age and experience; rather was its hold of his mind the stronger, and his advocacy of it the more earnest. In fact, that those adopting his system should ever keep the importance of moral training in view, he urged in his later years that such schools should be designated Moral Training Schools.

Moral training he places in leading the child to feel right, and thence to act right—that is, to act rightly from right motives; and this is to be sought until the habit of doing so is formed, as no moral result can be permanent unless it exists as a habit of the mind. Such training implies in its course the cultivation of moral intelligence, the right culture of the feelings, and the proper discipline of the will. The developments of character, and the habits sought in such training, should include amongst other things "truthfulness, justice, punctuality, kindness, courtesy, forgiveness of injuries, fidelity to promises, and habits of obedience, docility, attention, perseverance, and self-control." That these results may be obtained there must be such a cultivation of conscience that it will act rightly within its proper sphere ; and that it may do so, the ground of his duties to God, to man, and to himself, must be clearly shown to the child to be in the relations he sustains to God and man—relations involving the obligation of love, reverence, and obedience to God, of benevolence and justice to man, and of purity, patience and humility in himself.

First among the means for this training is religious truth - religious truth in its precepts, these alone supplying the purest morality; religious truth in its doctrines, these only furnishing effectual motives to its observance. Instruction in this truth should teach the child the nature of duty, should furnish reasons for its performance, and should supply powerful motives to obedience. But there is a kind of teaching which fails of these results. Not that teaching—not worthy of the name—that is merely verbal and textual, but a teaching that really aims to make the truth clear to the intelligence, though it goes no further than building it up in the mind. Such instruction, often found fruitful in later life, and therefore not to be despised in the absence of something better, often fails altogether to influence the conduct of the child. This may arise in some cases from the fact that verbal instruction, from the very nature of the case, fails to convey a true conception of the truth to the mind. In others, because it does not come with an authority that the child has learned to yield to, the great Master's will not being as yet felt as obligatory upon its conduct. But Stow thinks that it is due often to the form in which the truth is presented. It has not approached the child's mind in conformity with the laws of its nature, and therefore fails to awaken its attention. It should so come to the child as to enlist its feelings, awaken its sympathy, excite its conscience, and stimulate its will. And this it cannot do unless it is presented in such a form as the child can vividly realize in its imagination. Now it requires little knowledge of human nature to see that there is really nothing of a moral character where feeling is not an essential element. It must therefore be conceded to Stow that what he demands in religious instruction is absolutely essential to its having a moral power. It must awaken feeling, or the moral result cannot be produced. Take, for instance, the command "Thou shalt love the Lord thy God." This may be understood, assented to as reasonable, kept in memory, and yet be a dead letter. Why? Because, though it has penetrated the intellect, it has not reached the heart. Now before it can do this, that which is lovable in God must be brought to bear upon the feelings. Again, how shall we get the observance of the golden rule? Not by simply making it clear to the intelligence, but by presenting it in instances in which it is applicable, and bringing these out in such a way that the children shall transfer themselves into the circumstances of others, and thus have brought home to them their present duty from what they would expect in such a case to receive. In this, then, we have one great service rendered by Stow to the cause of moral education. The matter must be brought out before the imagination, that the children may place themselves in the circumstances of others and so enter into their feelings, or shall have in vividly described cases of conduct, the means by which they may compare themselves with a right standard, and so obtain those conceptions of duty, and those motives to do it, which are the objects of religious and moral instruction.

Next to religious truth among the means of moral training, and in fact its essential counterpart, is to associate doing or action with knowledge or feeling. The child must know, feel, and act. Knowledge without feeling is moonshine, clear but cold; feeling without action is mere sentiment. In all possible circumstances, therefore, doing must be enforced, and in such things as the teacher cannot enforce, pains must be taken to compare the feelings produced under a lesson, with the feelings and actions which come under the teacher's notice in their every-day life. "Training can only be termed moral training when precept is turned to practice. For example, a child may know that it is right to give what he possesses to a poor man, but it is not a moral act until the corresponding feeling and external act follow. Neither is the action itself moral without the understanding and feeling of duty. Knowledge, feeling, and practice thus combined form complete moral training." "I am no more under training by being told and shown how to make a watch, or hem a frill, or paint a landscape, than I am under moral training by the truths of Scripture being presented to my mind, provided I am not placed in circumstances to practise them: I am only under training when I am caused to do the thing specified." "Train to generosity, or obedience, or cleanliness, or any other thing, by making the child practically so, no matter how trivial the action it has been told to do. If a child does a thing improperly, or neglects to do a thing it has been told to do, the simplest way to check such impropriety is to cause the child to do the thing. This method will produce the habit when a threat or a scold may be instantly forgotten. The certainty of being obliged to do is better for the memory than the longest speech or the severest threatening." "The point here insisted on," says Mr. Currie, "is one of vital importance; it constitutes the difference, indeed, between education or training and instruction. The greatest merit, as it seems to me, of Mr. Stow's excellent volume on the training system, is the prominence it gives to *action* in moral training as distinct from *rule*:—' The only way to do a thing is just to do it.' Locke long ago enforced the same truth on an age not prepared to understand him. 'And here give me leave to take notice of one thing I think a fault in the ordinary method of education; and that is, the charging the children's memories upon all occasions, with rules and precepts which they often do not understand, and which are constantly as soon forgot as given. If it be some action you would have done, or done otherwise, whenever they forget or do it awkwardly, make them do it over and over again till they are perfect, whereby you will get these two advantages:—First, to see whether it be an action they can do, or is fit to be expected of them; secondly, that by repeating the same action till it be grown habitual in them, the performance will not depend on memory or reflection, the concomitant of prudence and age, and not of childhood, but will be natural in them. Pray remember that children are not to be taught by rules which will be always slipping out of their memories. What you think necessary for them to do, settle on them by an indispensable practice, as often as the occasion returns, and, if it be possible, make occasions. This method has so many advantages, which way soever we consider it, that I cannot but wonder (if ill customs could be wondered at in anything) how it could possibly be so much neglected.' This is the germ of the training system."

Other reasons present themselves for thus insisting on the necessity of action to moral training. There is an intimate connection between action and knowledge. On the one hand, many moral truths are simply abstractions, and the language in which they are expressed bare terms, until they are seen in action. What conception can a child form of justice, honesty, or kindness, unless it has been exhibited before it? On the other hand, there are some truths which cannot be learnt, some states of feeling and of intelligence which cannot be reached, until there has been doing. This is true not only of divine truth, but of much that is good and evil in every-day life. Another reason for insisting on action is found in the fact that where feeling and action are not associated, the mind becomes callous and utterly indifferent to the claims of duty. This is experienced—alas! how widely!—in connection with the great concerns of religion. Its truths, from not being obeyed, come gradually to lose their power of stirring up the sensibilities, until at length the most appalling descriptions can be listened to, not only as if we had no personal concern in them, but as if they were mere fables. The heart is hardened and the eyes are blinded, so that hearing we hear not, and seeing we see not. The truth, falling on the outward ear, never penetrates to the mind, never touches the heart. Another reason for insisting on action is that no other method can be adopted for undoing the bad habits with which many come to school. The only possible way of removing the evil habit is by practice in its opposite.

The great means of moral training being thus established, the next step was to find the conditions which these means require for their effectual application.

First, he claims that there must be a development of the natural aptitudes, tastes, and tendencies of the child, and of its acquired dispositions and habits, before there can be any training at all. Until these are known, the clue is wanting to the procedure in any given case. "There must be a development of character and disposition ere the process of training can be commenced. We must actually see the habits and actions, hear the words, and observe the bent of the affections of the child." One of the things that he contends for in this is, that the child shall not be lost in the mass, shall not be treated by a method which, seeing no difference in children, puts them all into one crucible, passes them through the same mould, and subjects them to the same routine; but rather that each child's nature should be studied, and means employed adapted to its case as circumstances arise or opportunities are found. Doubtless, in view of the endless varieties of child-nature, if we accept practice as *the* means of moral training, it is a fair deduction that there shall be this study of the individual, and this provision for its wants and aptitudes. But how far is this possible in school, or how far within its sphere? Where, of necessity, there is much that is common in pursuit and purpose, the means must be wisely adapted to the many rather than to the individual, and the one must be reached through what is designed for all, rather than by special provision; and even when, as cases arise, the individual is cared for, he alone must not be thought of in the measures employed, but through him *all*. Still, the necessity of practice to moral training being allowed, and that such practice must be what each child needs, it is evident that the study of character, wants, and aptitudes is a responsibility of the teacher, as is also an adaptation of his measures to the individual, so far as the circumstances of the case admit.

But it is chiefly as giving the knowledge of the child's character as necessary to the use of means for its benefit, that Stow requires a previous development of its habits and tendencies. Without such knowledge the work of the teacher must be haphazard. Whether he attempt the individual, or adapt his measures to the many, he cannot be certain that they are the best he might employ. Means that in some cases might secure a coveted result are found ineffective, because at random. Features of character, bias, or habit exist, which, being unknown, have not been provided for. Nay, often the purpose is defeated because the teacher, wanting the knowledge required, works in the opposite direction and for a different result than he intends. On the other hand, acquainted with the minds on which he has to work, he can economize his forces, and wisely order all his means to his end. Nothing then is at random. If he fails—as he often must,—it is with the consciousness that it is due to no omission on his part, nor to the inaptitude of his means, but to the presence of influences—not unknown —beyond his ability to reach.

It seems to have been Stow's opinion, that to allow of the development he sought there must be great freedom from restraint, and circumstances provided in which the children would have not only opportunity but temptation to do wrong. He seems to have thought the former necessary to that perfect confidence of the children in their teacher which would allow them "to make him their confidant," with all openness and freedom, of everything that related to them. And he required the latter as giving the means of pointing out what duty is, and as necessary to the growth of virtuous principle. Practically, in the schools established by him, under the excellent masters placed at their head, these opinions were much modified in their operation. But standing apart they are open to the gravest doubts, if taken without very great limitation as to their educational soundness.

Perfect confidence was thought to be impossible where fear existed. Hence his objection to corporal punishment and to every other practice that would be likely, as he thought, to induce fear. But fear is a legitimate state of mind, and one that it is desirable to produce; not abject fear, not the emotion which makes its subject its slave, but that state of mind which avoids the wrong action because afraid of wrong itself. Nor is such fear incompatible with love; nor is punishment, administered with this view and in the right spirit, inimical to that feeling of regard which would make the teacher a confidant of all that concerns the child. But seeking to establish that state of feeling betwixt the teacher and the child, in which it would freely act out itself in his presence, is not sufficient to warrant freedom from restraint or fear. It is very probable that the evil of such freedom would exceed the good. Restraint may often preserve the child from that "first act" which is the beginning of its ruin. Who can estimate the influence on the child's future of a first act in what is a wrong course? Before that how many struggles it has had, how many victories it has won! A few more struggles and a few more victories, and its safety is secured. But that first act breaks down the bulwark that was its protection. In that first act the citadel is taken, and the child lies prostrate at the foot of its foe. Freedom from restraint is freedom to the aggressions of evil, not freedom to the child. A recent popular book on life at a public school, where Stow's principle was the leading feature in its management during the head mastership of a man of world-wide fame, has shown the peril incurred by the removal of restraint, by the absence of fear. Where a few were benefited under that regime, hundreds, it is feared, were irretrievably ruined.

Whether a child should be removed from temptation, or should have temptations put in its way, are questions of vital moment in moral training. Stow advocated the establishment of schools to remove children from the temptations of the street; but at school he would not remove temptations, he would rather place them in their way. Now it must be granted that it is impossible altogether to remove a child from what may be temptations to it. And as the attempt would be vain it would be foolish. It would also be unwise because it would be attempting to get free from what is necessary to its training. Much knowledge has to come by experience, especially that which fits for the material and social life. It is better to let a child touch a hot teapot—it would not do it a second time—than to excite a vain feeling of dread by a hasty "don't touch," but it would be criminal to allow the child to bring the scalding contents of the pot on itself. It would be folly to try to keep a child from those temptations which come necessarily with its daily life, but it would be criminal not to screen it from those temptations by which it would be certainly overcome, and which would be its ruin, until the power acquired in unalterable circumstances fits it to meet them. Then the best interests of the child require that it shall not be prevented from the encounter. So far we are guided by the analogy of experience in a lower sphere. But to place temptations in the way of a child—different from those met by it in its ordinary life—cannot be good for it, nor yet necessary to its moral discipline. For a temptation is something that we know will excite a strong desire to do or get, and until there is an acquired power of resistance, the result would be, not to prepare the child to conquer, but to make it the slave of every fleeting desire.

Claiming this development of character under circumstances comparatively free from restraint, and with temptations not put out of the children's way, Stow adopted from Wilderspin the playground as a necessary part of every moral training school. To his earnest advocacy of this—the "uncovered schoolroom" is due the fact that few schools are now erected, and none are thought complete without a playground. Without a playground the means of moral training are very imperfect, and where it is wanting, Stow would not recognise the school as on his system at all. Apart from its physical advantages, yielding the means of drill, games, and fresh air; apart from its advantages to school work in letting off "steam," and invigorating for fresh intellectual effort; it is, in his opinion, the only place where the master can get that knowledge of character, habits, and actions, which he has to turn to account for the individual, or use for the general good. The master— or "trainer," as he delights to call him—"may join in," but not "interfere with the sports;" he must allow every child "to follow its own bent;" he must observe "the varieties of tastes and dispositions" as shown in the occupations going on around him, "he must not place things out of the way, but in the way;" "amidst the busy scene" he "must be present, not to check, but to encourage youthful gaiety." All must be "free as air. If otherwise a full development of character would not take place, and while he takes no notice at the moment, he nevertheless marks what he sees amiss."

The complement of all this was the use made of what occurred in the playground. "A moral review" of the occurrences must take place immediately on the return to the "covered schoolroom," or at some more fitting time. This he claims is necessary to the moral power of the playground. Without it, its power would be in the direction of evil. The master must conscientiously take up the cases of wrong, or it would be better to have no playground. But such a review, however wisely conducted, must establish a sort of restraint on the conduct of the children, and the more constant the review the stronger the restraint. Certainly it might be as he says a moral restraint rather than a physical one, but nevertheless, so far as it was a restraint at all, it would prevent that freedom of action he was so anxious to secure. But the practice itself we regard as an unmixed power for good, if carried out as Stow, or as Abbott—who so admirably carried out the practice—would have it. All being calm, no feeling excited, no passions at play, the conduct is to be quietly but graphically described—the actor not being indicated—the points in which the good or evil consisted brought out strongly, the consciences of the children appealed to as to the moral quality of the action, the teachings of God's word referred to, that there may be no misgiving, and then the whole thing approved or condemned by a simple expression of the moral judgment of children and teacher—with a "go and do likewise," or a "sin no more," as the final solemn appeal.

Stow, though claiming such freedom for the child as would induce it to exhibit itself in act and speech, yet was aware of the hazard run, supposing the forces, at work wherever many are associated together, were in the direction of evil. He next claims that we shall possess ourselves of these forces and give them that direction which will be for the benefit of the children.

These forces are sympathy, example acting through sympathy and imitation, the public opinion, and the moral atmosphere or moral tone of the school. It is to these he seems to refer in the expression "sympathy of numbers." Nowhere has he defined this term; but as it is of frequent recurrence, it is easy to gather from its connections that he refers to one or other, and at times to all of the forces now enumerated.

Children, especially if nearly of an age, are strongly attracted to each other, and the sympathy which thus draws is a great force in stimulating into activity powers which would otherwise lie dormant. Thus it is frequently observed that a child, with no natural bias or aptitude, when placed with other children, after a time develops a certain amount of the same power as that for which these are remarkable. "You place a child that has no natural talent for music among children who possess this gift, and under their tutelage he will soon learn to sing. This fact has been fully substantiated in schools." Now it is important to notice that this force, which attracts child to child and stimulates each to be what it observes in the other, becomes much intensified by the mere aggregation of numbers. Here the power of sympathy becomes irresistible in leading the child to attempt what it sees in others. Hence sympathy is a great moral agent, and may be powerful for good or evil. In the hands of a skilful operator it may be the instrument of unlimited good. A consequence of sympathy between child and child is poignant distress, when a child finds itself excluded from the sympathy of its fellows, and this distress is much the greater if the sympathy of his associates is against some act of his own. In such a case the very nature of this feeling would lead him to try to regain his place in the regard of his companions, and to obtain their sympathy in his favour, by avoiding that which their sympathy was against.

Oneness of feeling is likely to pervade a gathering of children who are witnesses of the same act, or who are listening to the same narrative. But this feeling is much greater from the participation of many than if it were confined to a few. The hidden consciousness that it pervades the mass gives it an intensity which otherwise it could not have. It is the same under some circumstances with adults. Let such a catastrophe as that of the Surrey Music Hall occur, and the feelings experienced become intensified by the very fact of many possessing them. Here, then, is a power which judiciously used may be made greatly instrumental of good. Stow would have it brought into exercise in moral lessons and in cases of discipline. Incidents of conduct should be so described—not indicating individuals—as to produce the desired feeling either in favour of some excellence, or against the carelessness or guilt of some fault.

A common result of bringing many together with similar objects and pursuits is to establish—tacitly it may be—certain rules and customs by which everything is tried, and to which every one must submit. Any one coming into such a community is soon aware that this is expected from him. Nor can he remain long in it without wishing to stand well with it, to avoid its censure, and to have its approval. Every one desires the approval, and has a reverence for the judgment of the society to which he belongs. So it is in school. Here are rules, customs, and opinions, as stringent as in any other society; and each of its members has a desire for its approval, a reverence for its judgment, a fear of its condemnation, and a dread of its scorn. It is in this condition that we have what is termed the public opinion of the school, and in it we have a force which insensibly moulds the actions and habits, and gives tone to the thinkings and feelings of all that enter it. "From the day that a youth enters this new circle," says Long, "his thoughts and actions become unavoidably affected by the thoughts and actions of others; it is, in fact, the beginning of his career as a member of society. He has exchanged the narrow circle of his family for a wider circle, which gradually embraces all the relations of social life. On entering the new society he is like a stranger who enters a foreign country; he cannot do as he pleases, or as he is accustomed to do, but he must conform to that which he finds established. His words, his thoughts, his actions, in a few days partake of the general tone, and the individual character is lost in that of the mass." Besides, the very fact of the tendency to desire the good opinion of his associates, and the influence of sympathy, will lead him to seek in them his example and rule of conduct rather than in the instructions of his master. And for the same reason there may be a force and effectiveness in their opinions and judgment far exceeding any influence or authority of the master.

Hence it appears that the public opinion of the school is that which really moulds the character of its inmates. How important, then, that it shall be on the side of goodness and virtue! How desirable that healthy influences shall be at work to give it the right tone! How necessary that the influence of the master, his discipline, his moral control, his incessant activity, and his highest intelligence shall be brought to bear upon its formation and direction! Else nothing but evil can be the result. For a school so unhappily situated as that where the master lacks the power or the disposition to establish a right public opinion and to work through it for the good of its members, must be a place of unmixed evil. In such a case the remarks of Reid are too true. "The influence of youth on each other, anywhere but in the well-regulated family, tends to be vicious—indeed, very generally is so, where numbers are long together. There is no seriousness, no sense of responsibility for what they say or do about them; they are full of levity and frolic, light-hearted, short-sighted, and careless—

"Turning to mirth all things of earth."

Their public opinion is all in favour of a bold, reckless jollity, turning the most serious subjects to ridicule, laughing at any very properly behaved one who may come amongst them till he becomes as bad as themselves; sneering at the moral lessons of the teacher, which they often mimic in his absence. While thus subdued before the master, they are often rude, rough, tyrannical, and unfeeling to each other, and where they escape the practice of grosser vices (by no means a frequent case), they learn amongst each other to laugh to scorn those minor virtues, delicacies, and proprieties, which are the outposts of the greater. In any indolence, carelessness, neglect, or lesser vice, each is supported by the example of others, by the opinion of his fellows in its favour, or at least by the want of that opinion against it. The master is in a minority; the energetically well disposed are in a minority, and the majority, with more than the usual tyranny of a majority, carry the day in favour of recklessness, and a careless indifference to virtue. With beings so impulsive, so unreflecting, with little sense of duty, not much sense of decency or propriety, not even worldly prudence, the spirit of ridicule, the spirit of freedom and enjoyment, are supreme; the idle and careless are encouraged, the good contaminated, good principles and good habits gradually undermined, and a foundation is laid for evil on which the world soon raises a large superstructure."

Stow, with many others, fully aware of this tendency of public opinion to become a power for evil, would have the master bend all his energies on entering a new sphere, if he found it did not already exist, to create a right state of opinion. But he was also aware that the ability to do so would depend altogether on his character. He would fail unless he had the power of winning regard, of attaching the children to himself, and thus of inspiring them with respect for his opinions and wishes; he would fail unless there existed as elements of his character consistency, justice, impartiality, disinterestedness, and kindness; he would fail unless his example was what he wished their conduct to be. But supposing the master to be the right man, then his first efforts must be directed to the formation of the public opinion of his school. Everything else must give way, or be subservient to this. There could not be any right moral training until this great source and medium of influence was established. But let it exist, and then there would be not only a force ever working for good, but there would be an influence ready at any moment to be brought to bear in respect of any action on which a common judgment might be sought.

The joint action of sympathy, intensified by its participation by many, and of public opinion, is to produce that oneness of feeling and sentiment which, when in favour of right, constitutes what Stow calls the moral atmosphere of the school, and which, as the ultimate result, forms pre-eminently the "sympathy of numbers." "By oft-repeated simultaneousness of thought, action, and emotion," says Currie, "the mass becomes welded together, takes on one stamp, breathes one spirit. . . . This is that state of feeling so much spoken of as 'the sympathy of numbers,' a conventional expression, but one which indicates what is in the first instance an absolute necessity to any training at all, and what when established is a lever of irresistible power in the hands of him who can wield it. When the school collectively has come to have a soul which the teacher knows how to stir up, when he can lay his hand upon its pulse and feel how it beats, then has he the training power; not otherwise. It should be well noted that this training power is not a thing resident in the teacher alone; it lies in the society which forms the school. The teacher's duty is to form it and guide it. It is a power capable of great things; available in every direction of activity; at once the stimulus and the guide to progress. And when in the exercise of his prerogative he brings it to bear on the faults or excellences of the pupil, it is instantly felt and acknowledged. The effort to acquire it is the teacher's first trial; the establishment of it his great triumph."

Such were the aims and principles advocated by Stow for the moral training of children. He sought to enlighten the conscience and to exercise it; he insisted on action in every case in which it was possible to enforce it; he required a playground where, amidst fun and frolic, the children might exhibit themselves as they were; he claimed that the conduct of the playground should be reviewed, and moral judgments elicited in the light of divine truth; and he insisted that there should be a constant effort to form and guide that "sympathy of numbers" which he looked upon as the most powerful agent in moulding the character. Possessed of these he could do away with inferior and selfish motives, such as corporal punishment, and would train the children to act from the highest principles of virtue and goodness. Such a "moral training school" he deemed to be one of the greatest blessings that could be conferred on any commmunity.

The points in this system that have challenged most discussion are those relating to the principles and methods of intellectual culture, and to the peculiar organization which the former seem to require. Many things found in operation in Stow's schools were no doubt common to all schools, and others had been adopted from Wilderspin and others; but there were distinctive features which, though not new, were yet original. Starting with no pre-conceived theory, and having no purpose at first but the elevation of those whose degraded condition had taken such hold of his mind, his main principles and methods were the offspring of his experience. This much must be conceded. Doubtless many an earnest worker had taught on similar principles and had employed similar methods, and here and there in some forgotten book there might be found expositions of similar practices. Yet Stow was not indebted but to his one work for his knowledge of them. It is to this fact that must be traced both his excellences and his defects. His own practice was not extensive enough to show him that principles which are quite sound when applied to some subjects or to some ages, are quite inapplicable in other circumstances. His wonderful success, too, in the application of his principles in the sphere in which they were tried, prevented him seeing the limits within which each was sound and efficacious. Hence he pushes things too far. He does not see that seemingly opposite principles, which within certain limits harmonize in their working, when pushed beyond their sphere, neutralize each other. Here is the secret of the opposition which his system has in many cases encountered. Had he but claimed for each principle or method its legitimate value, had he but well-defined the nature, operation, and sphere of each, he would have secured acceptance where, as it was, he too often excited scorn.

A leading principle of Stow relating to the culture of the intellect is that the master's mind should be the constant source of the pupil's activity, instruction, and training. Others than he "might gain great expertness in forms of questioning, in dealing with the mechanical, and in points of order; but for awakening thought, stimulating and directing inquiry, and evolving energies of intellect," none but he could succeed. "To submit for hours daily the finest mechanism on earth—the human spirit with all its intellectual energies and capabilities—to be handled or tossed about" by inexperienced youth or crudely-formed minds, such as those at work in the schools of that period, was thought to involve peril to the agents themselves, and to be one from which valuable results to the pupils— not to say the highest—could never be obtained. Those employed were too young to make impressive or attractive, or anything but a drudgery, what was necessary to stimulate the intellect or to awaken moral power. The character was too immature—wanting in depth and power—to mould rightly by its own silent influence those around. The ability to create an atmosphere— genial and gladdening—the moral life of which should be of the healthiest, could not exist. And it was thought that the very poor, whose school life is of the shortest, and whose means of intellectual culture are of the scantiest, have peculiar claims to be put into constant intercourse with the highest order of mind and intelligence that it is possible to secure.

That the mind of the master and of the pupil might be in immediate contact all the livelong day would require not merely a new arrangement of existing schools, but an altogether different class of school. Hence, as a proper sequence, there grew up at Glasgow the system of "graded schools," where each school was in fact but one large class, pursuing the same studies and receiving the same lessons under an adult master. In these schools, the large group forming each school was broken up into smaller groups only for the repetition or recapitulation of lessons previously given by the master. In other places not so favourably circumstanced, or where the thing was misapprehended, the grossest absurdities were practised by attempts to carry out this principle. Thus, a huge gallery was erected, on which were gathered children of ages varying from six to thirteen, and of course of very different attainments and capabilities, to be instructed at the same time in the same subject. The idea is sufficiently ludicrous. It would be thought that no sane man or practical teacher could ever dream of instructing with equal efficiency, at the same moment, in the same lesson, a hundred children varying to the extent these did in age and attainment. Yet the thing was attempted in hundreds of instances. Naturally it broke down, and though such schools were said to be on his system, yet Stow's first principle was sacrificed or acted on but in a very modified form. In other places, especially in America—a few years ago Ohio alone possessing 120—groups of graded schools were established, and the principle fairly worked out.

But is the principle, broadly stated as it has been, itself a sound one? A principle which gives the entire intellectual culture of the pupil into the hands of the master—nay, more, that requires that every mental effort of the pupil in school shall be stimulated and directed by the action of the master's mind—is this sound? We think not. But let us be understood.

We strenuously advocate that the master shall place himself frequently every day in contact with his children's minds for intellectual and moral culture. But we think that an unsound principle, which seems to make no recognition of the learner's independent efforts in order to his intellectual growth. Fully carried out this principle would do away with text-books as useless things, would do away with the independent exertion of the pupil's own mind, and prevent him having the opportunity of employing any of his previous acquisitions, except as required by the master. The pupil is simply an instrument on whose strings it is only the master's privilege to play. In fact, Stow is too sweeping. It is the swing of the pendulum to the opposite extremity of the arc. Up to this time too little value had been attached to the living voice in elementary training. The work of the teacher was only to hear and correct what his pupils had prepared. Stow discovered that oral lessons made lads sharp and intelligent, and from the extreme of doing nothing for them, he rushed to the opposite of doing everything. Now there can be no question that in early childhood and in the commencement of entirely new studies, the master's mind should be the source of the pupil's acquisitions and of his activity. But it is of equal importance that as he gains power, he shall have opportunities to exert it without aid. It is also true that a master's help is often more valuable to a pupil after he has exerted himself, than it would be in removing difficulties from his path, or even in enabling him to master them.

The mistake of Stow on the one hand, and of those whose practices he wished to avoid on the other, is not seeing that for the intellectual growth of the child two things are necessary. Teaching, which belongs to the province of the master, is the one; learning, which is the work of the child, is the other. The former requires that the master shall provide suitable nourishment for each mental capability, that he shall stimulate each mind to action, that he shall direct the employment of its energies, that he shall solve its difficulties, and that he shall enlarge its views.

Learning, on the other hand, requires the independent exertion of the pupil's own mind, and the opportunity of employing, unaided, any of his previous acquisitions. It requires that suitable books be placed in the learner's hands, that he shall be taught to prepare his lessons, to dig out meanings for himself, and to meet and if possible master difficulties. To combin teaching and learning is one of the severest problems in an elementary school; but that teacher who sets himself resolutely to solve it will be more successful than even his more talented neighbour, whose sole dependence is his ability to teach.

Another principle advocated by Stow is that in teaching nothing should be told, that by a proper use of analogy, experiment, instance, or other mode of illustration the pupil may be led to discover. This valuable principle is really but a part of a more general expression that in everything relating to the formation of character there is required a training to action and self-help. This principle fully carried out would be found materially to limit the operation of the former one. In fact it would make imperative that the learner shall be trusted in all those cases in which he can

B

master difficulties without extraneous aid. But it has not full scope in Stow's system, as the child's mind is always supposed to be in contact with a superior one, no provision being made or intended for unaided effort by the child. Still as a principle to be acted on in oral lessons it received his earnest support, and indeed is often put forth by him as the special feature of his system. It forms on the intellectual side that distinction between teaching or telling and training, which distinguished, as he contended, his methods from those ordinarily prevalent. Though how there could be teaching of the highest kind where this principle was absent, it is impossible to see.

Another leading principle of Stow's was that the pupil shall commit nothing to his memory but what has passed through the understanding. Strong objection has been taken to this by many opponents to his system. Is it certain that they have understood his meaning? It has become an axiom through the labours of the followers of Pestalozzi and of Wilderspin that in the training of infants "ideas shall precede words." Stow would have the instruction of boys and youths carried out in the same sense. Clear insight into a process should be substituted for blindly following a rule, and a general cultivation of the intelligence for that of the verbal memory. Other meaning than this it may be safely predicated he had not. Some opinions attributed to him are opposed to many places in his writings, and certainly to the practices of his schools. Yet as there are very important principles involved, a brief notice of some of the suppositions may not be without its use in defining the limits of the points in dispute.

Some have attributed to him "that no facts shall be acquired by children unless the principles under-lying them are first made clear—no words shall be committed to their memories, *nor even employed in their hearing*, unless previously explained and thoroughly understood." To state this is to answer it. No man of ordinary intelligence, with opportunities of observing childhood, and with the habit of reflecting on what comes under his notice, could for a moment imagine such a thing. Take for instance—words. How often, from earliest infancy, must many fall as mere sounds upon the ear, and how long through this must there be familiarity with them, before there can be the least glimmering of the things they represent;—and as to their full import, that can be reached only by many steps of approximation. How many words children acquire, with whose meaning it is impossible for them to become acquainted, is matter of daily observation, nor could it be prevented even if it was desirable. Words are often to learners the instruments by which they become acquainted with things. Many a quality would escape notice, many a thing be unobserved, but for stored words quickening the senses and stimulating the faculties.

To get at Stow's meaning, we must have before us what was in his mind when he so strenuously insisted that words and things should be broken down to the intelligence of the young, as the means of finding them a permanent place in the memory. He had in view the almost universal practice then of making school lore a mere matter of rote. Verbiage, by dint of repetition, stimulated by the twigs of the birch, was laid on the memory, to the great peril of the intellect, often to its extinction. Yet it was thought that this loading of the memory with forms, signs and rules, was the surest way, permanent though not speedy, of ensuring the discipline of the intellect. Schooltime was not the period of such discipline, but the storing time of the material. The real discipline would be at the later period, amid the facts, realities, and opportunities of life. Then that laid up in school would come to have meaning and power, and he that had the largest store would win the most. There is something in this : for instance, one whose mind was well filled with the principles of English, would obtain sooner and perhaps a better discipline from sterling writers of English than others wanting that preparation. But would this be the case with all ? Would not the majority be deterred by the recollection of schoolwork, from following the pursuits that were to give such work its value? Stow doubted of the many, and found in the early life of the child a warrant for the other practice. From its birth, ideas enter the mind through the senses of the child, and rules of action are acquired from experience of realities; hence Stow sought to continue the process in school. Much that the child learns is not understood. Many words are picked up by it whose meanings are hidden till a large experience sheds its light over them. The same thing must go on in school and in life. But alongside of it Stow demands that the other process shall run—that in the work of the school the learner's attention shall be directed to the sense as well as to the form. Though it be true that much that a child learns in school must remain without significance till a later time, though it be true that much of the real discipline coming to him from his school course will be the result of applying what he learns there in the pursuits of later life, yet great advantage in present discipline and future power must accrue from cultivating the intelligence in school.

Some have understood this principle to warrant the offering to children reasons for everything taught to them, while others have understood it to advocate the training of the logical faculty from the earliest period. Such as would give reasons for everything are of course opposed to dogmatic teaching, and in their practice appeal continually to the understanding to justify everything they teach. Now, apart from the point whether children should be confined to what they can understand—and, if so, how narrow, how contracted the area of instruction,—it cannot but be full of peril to a child to be continually addressed, as if it must be convinced by argument and reason, before it receives what is taught. Conceit would be the least evil fostered by such a course. A sceptical habit must be induced, a habit of rejecting everything the reason of which is not on the surface. But the thing itself is wrong; for not only are many things, which children cannot be prevented knowing, beyond their insight as to causes or reasons, but childhood is especially the season of faith, and to this principle of faith it is incumbent on us to address much of our teaching. Let us make matters as clear as we can. Let us be careful to give where we can ideas with words, to make clear processes, to bring within the intelligence the facts we give, but let us not appeal to our pupils, as if their understanding was to be the arbiter of truth, or their ability to see the reasons of a thing the ground on which they are to give it their assent. No! The principle of authority is essential in early education, and if not rightly employed then, submission of the intellect to divine truth at a later period must not be expected.

Nor does Stow's rule imply that the logical faculty, as such, is to be trained from the earliest period. This faculty works by signs, which are representatives of generalizations from a large experience. There can be no proper culture of its higher functions until the materials on which it has to work have been laid up in the intelligence. Its office is to elaborate from multitudes of facts and ideas more general ideas, from premises already in possession to draw conclusions, and by a gradual but constant approximation to arrive at truth. Now, ere this can be attempted, the mind must have been stored with ideas, words must have been acquired, and facts of all kinds and from all sources must have been lodged in the memory. Hence it follows that the cultivation of the logical faculty, as such, is not merely out of place at an early period, but impossible. But, nevertheless, there is an "implicit exercise" of this faculty, long before the individual comes to the conscious exercise of it, in its ultimate sphere. Judgment and its associated acts of mind, are manifested from the very earliest infancy, the mind then acting on things present to the senses in a similar way to what it does at a later time on its own creations. Comparison and inference are not strange acts even to a young child. Now, so long as the matters are within the sphere of its intelligence, most valuable results may be expected from the right culture of this implicit judgment and incipient reason, care being taken not to tax the nascent faculty beyond its power.

This is what Stow would have done. Thousands of things exist around on which a child may be exercised in discovering relations, resemblances, and proximate causes. Many things may be brought before it in such a way as to elicit "how?" to be followed by "in this way," each involving an intelligent act of the mind, and an implicit exercise of the understanding. And many a process may be made to excite a higher intelligence, by evolving it from the simple reasons not beyond the child's ability to master—which underlie it.

Another principle advocated by Stow is that in teaching any subject its outlines should be given first, and in subsequent lessons the details. As thus stated, few things could be imagined more absurd when placed alongside of his *dictum*, that things must pass through the understanding before being charged on the memory. Outlines express results. They are summaries, generalizations, chief heads. To give these first would be to do what he so strongly condemned as the vice of the school system of his time, and would effectually prevent the admission of any subject into the understanding. The natural order is to gather facts first. There can be no science until the facts are known. There must be language before there can be a grammar, and the facts of a language must be known before the study of its grammar can commence. Begin the study of a language by taking an outline of its grammar, and intelligence will be slow to follow. The more meagre the outline the more difficult the process, and so with other things.

Stow meant no such thing. Yet two of his followers, earnest workers for thirty years past in the educational field, run away with by this notion, have introduced extensively into schools lesson books in science and Scripture, professedly framed on the plan of giving the outlines first, the result being what might have been expected. In the former books the young mind, which longs for flowers and fancies, is put into a valley of bones, very many and very dry. In the others, every little touch of nature that gives charm to the narrative, or that would come home to the sympathy of the child is rigidly excluded—shut out by the rule of giving the outline first. Stow intended no such thing; in fact, he means the very reverse. Employing the figure of a painter as descriptive of the work of the teacher, he urges the latter to give those facts connected with a subject that are prominent—likely to fall within the child's experience, and with which it will readily sympathize, ere he offers those facts which from their very nature demand a large acquaintance with the subject before they can be approached at all. Thus to give the outlines of grammar would in Stow's meaning include such special facts as would come under a learner's cognizance, and prepare him for an intelligent study of the subject. He would have patent facts acquired before niceties of inflexion, peculiarities of idiom, or any such details were approached. Such a course is, in fact, the only legitimate way of bringing any subject within the grasp of children, or of making the course of instruction to accord with mental aptitudes and development.

Dealing with rude and untutored minds, whose

energies he wished to awaken and direct to noble ends, it was an early problem with Stow as to the most effective means of doing so. Seeking willing co-operation at their hands, he must have a method, which would not only convey truth to the intellect, but that would exercise strong interest in the process, and that would make them fellow-helpers in working it out. Knowing the power of such works as "Cinderella," "Children in the Wood," "Jack and the Bean Stalk," with young children, and of "Robinson Crusoe" and "Pilgrim's Progress" with older ones, he found in them the method he sought. Soon he became aware that an engine of great educational power was possessed by him who could excite the conceptive faculty, operate on the fancy, or bring the imagination of children into play. "Picturing out in words" henceforth became a constant feature of his method, and a chief instrument for awakening intellectual and moral life. "Picturing out" aims to transfer a picture, idea, or conception, from the mind of the teacher to that of the pupil. The analogy is that of the painter, who does by the pencil what the teacher is expected to do by his words. This analogy suggests a sufficiently difficult process. It being much harder to paint to the imagination by words, so as to give distinct and complete conceptions, than it is by the pencil. Words, as they pass from the lips of the teacher are evanescent, while each stroke of the pencil is permanent. Besides the pupil has to form his own picture from the materials with which he is provided, and can do it but gradually; but the scene on the canvas is presented as a whole, and may be taken in at a glance, or examined in detail. This process of painting in words—" picturing out," consists in graphic description, aided by analogy, familiar illustrations, and suitable gestures. To these Stow would add interrogation, ellipses, simultaneous answers, and sympathy. But here he evidently confounds devices which a teacher may employ to carry his pupils along with him, or to discover how far successful he is in getting them to form the picture with what alone is essential to the picturing process. These things may be of advantage where picturing in words is employed, but do not constitute any part of the process itself.

Stow offers the method of picturing in words as applicable to every subject and at every age. This is akin to the offer to cure every ailment by one specific. It is as if the mind had not a variety of powers, as if these had no law of development, and as if there were not differences in the subjects on which it employs its energies. Into this absurdity Stow was led by a very preposterous notion, or perhaps it would be nearer the truth to say that paternal affection for the method led him to adopt the notion, " that every word either represents an object or a combination of objects, or may be represented by words representing objects." Now, to this, it is sufficient to reply that words not only represent things, but processes and relations, and that while some of the former admit of being "pictured out," the latter are out of its sphere. The origin of many words is involved in obscurity; other words, though derived from sensible objects, have completely lost their original meaning, and are now expressive of purely mental states ; others relate to intellectual operations which have no counterpart whatever in the world of sense. Hence the sphere of the method is much more contracted than was claimed for it, but in that sphere it is not only effective but indispensable.

First, it must be conceded that certain classes of words admit of the application of this method. It will help to determine what these are, when it is remembered that to picture out words is to take the ideas embodied in the words, and to spread them out before the mind, so as to make the things for which they stand visible to the mind's eye. Picturing out words, therefore, may be looked upon as the means by which a child is enabled to form an idea of the thing which the word represents when there are no means of presenting the thing itself to the child's senses. It is thus one of three ways by which a child's mind is furnished with ideas or mental pictures of things. These ways are, presenting the object itself for examination, presenting a drawing of it, and describing in words aiding the description with suitable gesture and familiar illustration. The last is picturing out, and is inferior to the other two, except as a preparatory process, when it excites interest and leads to an examination of the object with closer attention. Suppose, as a simple instance, that the word cube occurred in a reading lesson, and it was found that no child had any knowledge of the thing, the idea would be best given by placing a cube before the class for examination, and drawing attention to what was essential to it, in comparison with other things; or a fairly correct idea might be given by drawing a cube on the black-board. But supposing that the means are not at hand to adopt either of these modes, then by a verbal description, illustrated by reference to a slate, or a page of the book, or anything at hand for the ideas of a square and of surface, and by a motion of the hand describing a cube a child might be led to form an idea, so far accurate as to enable him to pick out a cubical figure from a number of dissimilar objects.

Such a method of verbal description of things represented by words is indispensable to every teacher who would rightly deal with the reading lesson. Occasions are demanding its exercise every day, and it deserves—as from the teacher alive to the importance of vivifying the reading lesson it will receive—the most strenuous efforts to acquire skill in it. But it is to be feared that few teachers know its value. Few students in training at Normal Colleges, except such as come from infants' schools, ever attempt more than to explain—that is, to give synonymous expressions, or a loose paraphrase of words, when engaged on what they misname exposition of a reading lesson.

But the method is of wider application than to words. Scenes, persons, and things, near or remote, of other times or other lands, or at home and now, admit of being vividly presented and conceived. When words as representatives of things are dealt with, the idea-forming faculty alone is brought into exercise. But now a higher effort of mind, though one involving this, is required. Imagination is appealed to when a scene, or a person not present, is to be realized. In common with the process on words, the conceptive power must be in play, either in forming new ideas or recalling old ones. The materials entering into the picture must be of familiar things, and these must be summoned vividly into the mind. This is essential. Mistake here will spoil the process. If the parts of the picture are not ideas which the pupils have already formed, the picture as a whole cannot enter their minds. The want of attention to this is a fruitful source of failure. Many a good lesson in promise is spoiled because care was not taken to ascertain that the children actually possess the ideas attached to the words employed. 'Twas but the other day that a teacher discovered, at the close of a lesson, that a very animated and graphic description was ineffective, because he had not thought it necessary to ascertain if his children had the idea of a *plain*, before commencing his picture.

Taking care, then, that nothing is introduced into the picture of which the children have not a distinct idea, care must be further exercised that out of the materials thus presented they do construct the picture intended. This will always be the more difficult as the object or scene differs from the children's experience. The further removed from this, the greater the difficulty they will have, and the greater the graphic power required in the teacher. One thing to be guarded from is the children losing themselves in the details: they will fail, unless the teacher is watchful, to combine the parts together. It is a mistake often made, that because children see clearly each part as the teacher goes on, they therefore see the connection between them, and grasp the whole. Another point to be secured is that the analogies and illustrations employed to aid the children to form a picture of the whole, are drawn from the surroundings of the children rather than from the reading of the teacher. In the latter case there is the danger of supposing that what is familiar to his own mind will be equally so to the minds of his pupils. When illustrations are not drawn from the sphere of common life, they themselves need illustrating; and analogies not so formed are riddles.

The importance of picturing out during the period of child-life to which it is applicable, will be readily acknowledged by all those who know the part played by the imagination in the process of mind-growth; and especially in child happiness. Picturing fills the mind with bright images, on which children will love to linger, long after drier lessons would have faded away. These pictures should be drawn from the whole field of natural phenomena, from the manners and customs of other lands, and from the records of the past. Special value belongs to word picturing in Bible Lessons. Here it is invaluable in giving point, purpose, and permanency to incident and narrative, that would otherwise fail to impress, because of their familiarity.

"Picturing out" was intended by Stow as part of a larger process, having for its object the discipline of the intellectual faculties, rather than the communication of knowledge, or the furnishing the mind with ideas. Not undervaluing the latter, and knowing well the power of his instrument to effectually accomplish it, yet he wanted something higher for the scholar than this of itself could supply. He desired that children should go forth to the encounter of life with minds disciplined by right modes of culture. Mere knowledge acquired at school is necessarily scanty and fragmentary, and is soon lost after school life is ended, but the discipline accruing from the action of right methods remains the heritage of the pupil, and the means of his future advancement. The method he proposed was embodied by him in the formula, "Not to tell anything to children, which by a proper use of analogy and illustration, they can be led to discover." To this method he applies the term "training," or "training out."

This term we deem an unfortunate one. It seems to imply that what you have to teach is already in the pupil's mind, and that you have but skilfully to educe it. Besides, it is apt to be confounded with the term development, as applied by Pestalozzi to the calling forth by appropriate exercise some latent faculty. It is a faulty term, then, because it does not exactly describe the process intended. It is faulty, also, because the same term is applied by him to a dissimilar, though in one particular, analogous process. It is in this analogous fact, that we find his reason for using the term. Self-exertion is the predominant feature in moral training, and as this is involved in "not telling," Stow applies the same term to both processes. By "training," doubtless he meant to indicate a process in which the pupil was *to discover* rather than *to receive*, and as the former implies more energetic *doing* on the part of the child than the latter, he thought he was warranted in applying to the intellectual what had been long before appropriately applied to the moral process.

It is somewhat difficult to state in words what the method is, so as to give an accurate notion of it to those that have not witnessed it. Its principal ideas may no doubt be clearly set forth, but though these may be understood, it is not clear that the method itself is. The absurdities that have passed under its name, practised even by those who had had the advantage of special training, sufficiently show this. A notice of these, with a few slight sketches of its right application, may perhaps convey a faint notion of the method.

The leading ideas involved in the method are, that children shall from facts known or communicated infer other facts, or establish for themselves the principles underlying the facts; and that in doing so, they shall receive no assistance from the teacher in the way of suggestion. It is his business to supply the data on which their minds have to be exercised, and to employ analogies to indicate the course to be pursued. The method may have been suggested by that of Socrates—whose was a method in which, by a skilful adaptation of his questions to the previous answers, it was made to appear as if the pupil was instructing himself, rather than being instructed.

Among the absurdities that have passed under the name of "training out," may be mentioned the notion that has run away with some people, that in teaching nothing is to be told. This is absurd. Many matters of fact must be communicated. To attempt otherwise is a waste of time, if not attended by even worse results. The *art* of the teacher is shown in communicating what is indispensable and no more, and in communicating it as material out of which the pupils are to frame their own ideas and thoughts under his guidance. From the notion that nothing is to be told, or from an entire misapprehension of the method, some question in such a way as to elicit nothing but guesses, or they string a lot of questions together so as to get out what they want, but at the same time to be as far as possible from getting it by legitimate inference. This fear of telling anything is carried sometimes to the ridiculous length of not telling even the subject of the lesson. That is to be got at by a succession of guesses. On one occasion a lesson was introduced by a question as to what would be found in the Great Exhibition? After expending half-an-hour in fruitless guesses, in in which every imaginable thing was named, one lucky urchin exclaimed, "a button," when the class was gravely informed "Yes, our lesson is to be on buttons."

Another mistake, which passes under the name of "training out" is, that it is the getting of words from the class. Sometimes eliciting words is a valuable process, especially in connection with reading, as it serves to bring out the distinctions between nearly synonymous words, and besides adding to the learner's stock of words, is a good analytic exercise, but the doing so is not necessarily an inferential process. Sometimes time is wasted in trying for a word, where the better plan would be to give the word required. For instance, it often occurs that after a teacher has clearly developed an idea in his pupils' minds, he questions them for the most appropriate expression, not seeing that this really implies that the idea had been theirs before. But supposing that in this case, by some happy chance the right word is obtained, still the process was not one of training, inference, or induction. Of other modes of word getting, there are two varieties. Sometimes a teacher wanting a word puts out a feeler for it. His question elicits an answer, his treatment of which gives the clue to his class, and they ransack their stores for all words similar in sound or sense, it matters not which, until they put their hands on the right one. The other mode is of so ludicrous a nature as to have attached in the minds of many teachers the utmost contempt to "training out," nothing better under that name having been under their notice. We refer to the not uncommon practice of getting out two or three words, and of combining them to get the word sought. This, instead of being a training process, is a suggestive one, and seldom fails to involve the employer of it in the ridiculous. One or two actual instances may be given to show our reference. A teacher in a lesson on the cuticle, for which he wanted from the class the name scarf-skin, proceeded to get it by asking for an article sometimes worn round the neck, and after some trouble got the word "scarf;" then pointing to the skin obtained the word skin. "Now," said he, "this skin is *therefore* the scarf-skin." Another, giving a lesson in geography, and wanting the name of a town evidently unknown to his class, proceeded—What are the people in Wales called? Obtaining his answer, and describing a hole filled with water, he led them to call it a pool—"*then* the name of this town is—*Welshpool*." Another, giving a lesson on the lever, and wanting the term fulcrum, proceeded thus—"When your mother pours your tea into the cup till it can hold no more, what do you say the cup is?" Full. "And when she has been cutting bread, what is there on the table about the loaf?" Crumbs. "Then this is the—*fulcrum*."

Nothing could be more ridiculous, as specimens of teaching, than the foregoing, yet they are not uncommon instances of what are deemed training-out processes.

The simplest instance of the right application of the method is where you lead to the discovery of facts by the way of inference from other facts. For example, in a lesson on the Rhine, two points are named, its source and Basle, and giving the rapidity of the stream the children infer the great difference in level, or giving the difference in level they infer the rapidity of the stream. A lengthier example is given by Stow of a teacher leading children to infer that in Egypt kilns were not used in making bricks.

A higher application of the method is in reading or Scripture lessons, when it is employed to discover the meaning of the writer. Thus, in the question put by Job, "How oft is the candle of the wicked put out?" After showing that according to the placing of the emphasis, and by the tone in which it is uttered, it is susceptible of opposite meanings, the question comes up, Which is the true one? In conducting to the answer, reference is made to hot countries, to dangers from serpents, to the fact that lights are used to scare them away—then Who can afford to keep lights always? The rich. Now, suppose a house always lighted at night suddenly ceases to be lighted, the candle is put out. What is the inference? The man has become poor. Then refer to the scope of Job's argument. His friends had maintained that afflictions in this life are signs of God's displeasure; he contends for the opposite, and asks—How oft is the candle of the wicked put out? The children are then expected to infer the truth for which Job was contending.

Another application of the method requires the highest teaching ability, and secures, where practised, the best mental discipline. It is sometimes called the historic method, or when applied to the right class of subjects, the inductive method. It consists in conducting the pupils through the various processes of thought, by which a certain result is reached; or in taking them along the path of observation, hypothesis, and experiments by which discoveries have been made. Thus in a lesson on the Davy lamp, the matter was so treated, that the learners suggested the doubts, hypotheses, and experiments through which it might be supposed that the inventor himself passed ere he succeeded in his object. It must be remembered that the essence of the method consists not in laying before the pupil the processes of thought, as is done in Euclid, but in so skilfully touching the intellect with questions or facts, that he may discover and pursue these processes for himself. Than this no other method yields, when employed at the proper age, such valuable results. For while books give the results of others' thinking, this leads the pupils along the path by which such results were obtained. Suppose a boy acquainted with addition and multiplication, to sit down without the aid of books or tutors, to discover for himself the methods and rules of division. Suppose him after much thinking, after repeated efforts and repeated failures, to hit upon them and to be able to verify each of his conclusions—no one would deny the mental discipline of such a process. Well, suppose the same done under the stimulus of a teacher's questioning, and under the correction of a teacher's knowledge, and you have an example of "training-out" and nearly the same amount of mental discipline as in the first supposition.

Other points connected with intellectual culture in Stow's system are those of oral or collective lessons in which a text-book is not employed, and the use of ellipses and simultaneous answers. These were adopted from the infant school, partly from the life and vigour which their right use excites in a large group of children, and partly because they allow just that degree of assistance from the teacher which stimulates but does not supersede the scholars' efforts. The independent oral lesson was advocated on other and higher grounds, as in fact the only one which gives the teacher the opportunity of taking his pupils through processes of discovery, and of thought leading to discovery, and as furnishing the only occasion in which the higher form of training-out can be employed. These were extensively adopted, even where Stow's methods were not accepted, but there has come lately a reaction, which threatens—to the great detriment of educational progress—to banish them from the elementary school.

In concluding these imperfect notes of the training system, it is but right to refer to the great services rendered by those employed in the Glasgow Institution, both in working out the system, and in putting some of its methods into a practical shape. We extract on this point the following remarks from a recent article

by Mr. William Sugden, who was himself an able and energetic worker for years in that institution, and who has conducted with singular ability and success a Normal College in London on the training system :—
" Like most men who have been eminent in carrying on great works, Mr. Stow seems to have been skilful in selecting and attaching to himself able fellow-labourers and associates. In carrying on this institution at Dundas Vale, he was aided by a band of teachers of noble spirit and of great ability; among whom it is not invidious to others to name Mr. Robert Hislop, at that time its rector, and Mr. William Fraser, now the minister of the Free Middle Church in Paisley. No one could be more ready to acknowledge the assistance derived from men like these than was Mr. Stow."

CHAPTER V.

Amateurs and Helpers.

THE interest now so general in the cause of the education of the people, is a growth of the present century. It originated, doubtless, in the zealous labours of Bell and Lancaster, Wilderspin and Stow, and was greatly promoted by the societies which were formed in connection with them. But it was the condition of the people, and the dangers which seemed to threaten the very existence of the nation, that gave it an impetus, and made it grow to its present proportions. Leading statesmen and eminent philanthropists came to regard it as the sole means of securing the safety and promoting the prosperity of the nation. Educational societies were formed in many parts of the country for the purpose of gathering statistics, and of united action. Public meetings were held for discussion, and for agitating the question of educational reform. Committees of Parliament sat to gather information, and at length action was taken by the legislature.

Foremost in this work was Brougham. In 1816 he obtained a Committee of the House of Commons to inquire into the state of education. Somewhat later he was one of those who established the first infants' school, and in 1824 he formed the first infants' school society. But his greatest work was the formation of the Society for the Diffusion of Useful Knowledge. He convened the first meeting in 1826. Its first publication was in 1827. It was incorporated in 1832. This Society did much indirectly to promote education. Amongst many invaluable publications, it issued the *Journal of Education*. The scope of this serial was to bring into an accessible form the best contributions to education of ancient and modern writers, to make known the educational systems of other countries, to bring into prominence all efforts that were made for elementary, industrial, and secondary education, and to publish articles by good writers on educational topics. In 1836, a selection of articles was published in two volumes, with the title of "The Schoolmaster."

In 1836, some of the more prominent members formed with others the Central Society of Education. The object of this society was to take measures to place education on a scientific basis, to establish training schools for teachers, to make education compulsory, to throw its support upon the rates, and to have it under the direction of a permanent board and a minister of education, who should be a member of the Cabinet. It also proposed to supply information on the existing state of education, on the several modes of teaching the poorer classes, on the systems of education extant, and generally to discover the means by which all classes may be best fitted in health, in mind, and in morals, to fill the stations they are destined to occupy in society.

The formation of the society was the occasion for an outburst of bigotry and invective. It was denounced as secular, as intending to put out the Bible from schools, and as intending to prepare the way for the establishment of Popery. It did good service. One of its first works was to make inquiry into the state of education. It did this very thoroughly, but not without opening itself to the charge of desiring to make out a case against the British and National schools, than to ascertain the real benefit conferred by them. They charge these schools with having nothing in them that deserves the name of education; their methods as having a tendency to crush the mental energies, and to extinguish all moral life; and their public examinations as a gross deception. Its other work was to publish a series of volumes, in which educational topics were discussed; one of these consisting of prize essays, being one of the most valuable contributions to professional literature of recent times. The growth of education during the last forty years owes much to this movement, and we shall mark its character by some brief notices of its more prominent agents.

Section I.—*Thomas Wyse*.

Thomas Wyse took an active part in the establishment of the Irish system. He was the author of a book on Educational Reform, in which he sketched a system of national education. He had a large acquaintance with ancient and modern education, and he was the advocate of principles and practices far in advance of the age he addressed. " Education should fit each citizen for the duties which his several relations enforce upon him, by giving to the physical, intellectual, and moral faculties the full perception of which they are susceptible. That such education may be effectual there must be on the part of the educator a knowledge of mind and body. In physical education it is conceded that a knowledge of physiology is essential; but it is equally true in that of mind. Take the very lowest point, the furnishing of the mind; a mind taught at random without a knowledge of its capacities and forces is a lumber-room, but a mind educated is a well-ordered storehouse. To think of working on the human mind without a knowledge of it seems an absurdity so glaring, that it would never have been maintained in practice if the real object of school work had been education. The science of mind, at least such portions as bear on practice, is essential. Without it the schoolmaster may blunder into right, but at best he is but an empiric, and never sure that he is not wrong."

Education must be moral, and in order to that it must be religious. First consider the relation of moral to intellectual education. These two cannot be separated. Those who would do so attempt impossibilities. Half of our being cannot be torn from the other half, they are so intertwisted. It is also difficult to say where one ends and the other begins. Sentiment and reason are the two prime movers of the moral nature. The first takes precedence in early education. Sentiment is the foundation of all morality and religion. It thus becomes possible to train very young children morally and religiously. The feelings which may be excited in a child towards the Author of all good, differ in no way but in their object from those with which a parent should be regarded. It is thus too that He is first made known to the child. But a later stage is reached when conviction is required, and judgment comes in as well as feeling. Otherwise the child grows into a mere creature of chance and impulse, vacillation, and incoherence. Thus it is evident that true morality requires the presence of intellectual as well as of moral elements."

Charged with secularism by those who opposed his system of unsectarian instruction, he is anxious that no mistake should exist as to the real nature of moral education. There can be no moral education without religion; and no religion supplies the standard, the precept, and the motive power, but the Christian. This introduces the question, first mooted in the controversies of the time, whether the Bible should be the source of this instruction? Wyse is clear on the chief point. "The Holy Scriptures alone, in their speaking and vivifying code, teaching by deed, and sealing by death, give that law of truth, of justice, and of love, which has been the thirst and hunger of the human heart in every vicissitude of its history. In all stages of life this ought to be the book of books. But everything depends on the manner in which it is taught. It is not enough to teach the Scriptures, we must remember whom we are to teach, and by what instruments we are to teach. We are to teach children. We are to teach by the means God has put into our hands. These means are human intellects and human affections; but though the same in both, they are not developed to the same extent in children as in men. Therefore there must be adaptation to the actual condition. A child materializes and localizes; a man spiritualizes and abstracts; hence the routes to the same end are different. The ideas of every one are limited by his experience, a child's being very contracted. Yet we can only build with the materials we have got. To comprehend new ideas we must employ the ideas we have. Further, a child's vocabulary is even more circumscribed than its ideas. Yet it is only through words that spiritual things can be conveyed to its mind. Now these facts must govern the teaching of Scripture to young children. Go contrary to them and there will be positive and enduring evil. Children form associations with marvellous rapidity in despite of their teachers and in despite of themselves. If they meet obscurity where there should be light, if pain where there should be pleasure, the associations cling and the Bible remains a closed book, when free to choose for themselves.

Meet the difficulty by following the law of God and nature. Scripture must be taught, but so taught as to be understood. Such parts then as can be understood are to be given to children. This implies selection, and therefore exclusion. Selections first should be placed in their hands, differing according to their age and understanding; but as education proceeds, the Sacred Volume itself may be intrusted to their study and inquiry. In the selections for such a course of Scripture reading two rules should be observed, they should be adapted to the capacity, and they should be accompanied by needful explanation."

Turning to the cultivation of the intellect, Wyse lays done two principles. The first is that the materials of intellectual education are the human faculties; evidently meaning that the discipline of these is the object to be sought, rather than the storing of the mind with learning. Early education is important, for every motion of mind or body tends to the formation of a habit, and of habits the man is formed. Hence the importance of a right culture of the senses. These are the great instruments of knowledge. If not cared for at school, when wanted they will be found rusty or blunted. Without culture all is haziness, with it vividness and freshness. The difference is that betwixt a waking state and a dream, between reality and unreality. Right culture of the senses tends to clearness of ideas, accuracy of language, and justice of reasoning. He is also of opinion that each sense has its organ benefited by its acquiring greater delicacy and sensibility. Education from the very first ought to be general. All the powers of a child are in action contemporaneously. We do not discover the action of the higher powers so readily because the child is working with ideas and not with language, but the results prove that the processes were there. Of course there is order. We must begin with the beginning. We live before we think. The senses are the first objects. But when cultivating the mind through these, we must not act as if it was only recipient or perceptive. It is impossible thus to contract its operations. As growth proceeds it becomes still more necessary to keep in exercise all the faculties, or the product is only half a man. Proportion and symmetry are the two great rules in education. No single chord should be left untouched or unstrung. Sounded singly there is monotony, sounded without order it is discord; harmony is the result of the scientific culture of all.

His second principle is that the instruments of intellectual culture are right methods. There is no method adapted to all stages and to all subjects. That which is suitable at an early period may be pernicious at a later. Method should be eclectic. He instances Pestalozzi and Fellenberg. The former was dominated by an idea, and when in a region where it was inoperative he egregiously failed. The latter, with a fuller conception of a child's nature and of a child's needs, had methods adapted to all stages of development, and to the object in view.

Much of his book is devoted by Wyse to the methods of teaching school subjects, and contains on these points many valuable hints.

Section II.—Horace Grant.

Horace Grant was another amateur whose labours have aided educational progress His friend Chadwick, in a notice prefixed to a recent edition of his books, classes him with Comenius, Pestalozzi, and others who have devoted themselves zealously to the especial study of the minds of children, and to the best means of cultivating them. Having been obliged by failing health to resign the East India Company's service, he devoted himself to education. He found grievous defects in the construction of schoolbooks and in methods of teaching. The chief fault of the former was, that they were calculated to display the knowledge of the writers than to interest the children. The chief faults of the latter, that they imparted matters by rote, and were utterly unfitted to develop and discipline the mind. He framed lessons and wrote them out on this principle, that each lesson was by its own intrinsic interest to sustain the attention of the learner. He borrowed children for the purpose of his trials and observations, and he circulated in manuscripts the lessons he had tried amongst intelligent and practised teachers, and obtained the results of their experience. He embodied the results of his observations and experiments in a series of volumes first published by the Society for the Diffusion of Useful Knowledge, and recently issued afresh by Bell and Daldy. They include exercises for the senses, two treatises on arithmetic, and others on geography, drawing, and elementary geometry.

Grant brought to his adopted work valuable qualifications, the most important of which was his knowledge of mental science, and especially of mind as it develops itself in young children. He himself held this to be an essential thing for one who would successfully educate. Mr. Chadwick gives the following extracts from a letter:—" A gentleman would scarcely presume to break in a colt or a pointer puppy, without first ascertaining the precise object to be obtained, and studying the character, habits, and organization of the animal, and the fitting mode of acting upon it. Yet surely a common child is as difficult to be understood as a pointer puppy." " You cannot act upon children unless you understand them, and you cannot understand them without studying them attentively, having first discarded all previous notions gathered from the cloister or the desk. It will not do for gentlemen to retire to their study, like German metaphysicians, and extract from their inmost consciousness all that is necessary for understanding and instructing their juvenile fellow creatures. . As teachers of children, it appears to me, that your masters have everything to learn ; that they have no suspicion of this, and that unless they will first condescend to go among children as learners and students, their zeal and industry as teachers will be of little avail."

His study of children made him in favour of short lessons. "There is a variety of temperament and a difference of capacity arising therefrom, which shows itself in the degree and duration of attention. Very young children cannot give attention longer than a few minutes ; the power increases with training and growth, but even with other children lessons requiring mental effort should rarely exceed half-an-hour." The remedy is in change of work. For though it is a law of their nature that they cannot be engaged on one thing long, it is equally true that they cannot remain idle. "They make innumerable short essays in all directions, by which mind and body are trained. Keep them always at one kind of bodily labour, and they become deformed and stunted, and attain not the proportions and powers of the perfect animal. Train one, or but a few of their faculties, and they are ever afterwards dwarfs in intellect, or at best ill-proportioned spirits. Train their moral faculties in the same injudicious manner, starve many, over excite a few, and you produce immoral or morally diseased beings."

Children must be employed. A healthy child at liberty to do what he likes goes through great bodily and mental exercise. "There are innumerable objects observed, inquired into, and experimented on; endless reasonings, imaginings, inventions; and there are worlds of fancy into which his old materials are constantly being marshalled. Yet all this hard work is pleasure to the child,—it is play; but such play makes men." "Overwork is most pernicious; but one thing is worse: forcibly to restrain him from that active employment which his constitution craves; thus imprisoning mind and body. Children rarely suffer from overwork, but often from improper work, the smallest quantity of which is pernicious." Anything which strains the attention, as rote work of every kind, without employing the faculties, does mischief.

Not many but much is a good rule in teaching. Where many things are attempted, there must be brevity, and consequently, poverty. "Half-a-dozen simple points investigated and discovered by the pupil, will be of more value than a book-full of geometry, to which he merely gives a cold assent. In the one case, the knowledge forms part of the mind; it is remembered, is ever present when wanted, and is ready to be connected with, and to aid, other knowledge; it assists in building up an intellect as well as furnishing it. In the common mode, however frequently a thing is gone over, it forms no part of the mind: it is joined with nothing useful or experimental; it is kept at an out-station apart from our trains of thought, and it can have little influence on the intellect or character."

The right starting-point is with the senses, and in all subjects the natural development of the mind suggests that the concrete shall precede the abstract, the near shall be taken before the remote, and the particular shall be given before the general. It is also necessary that the illustrations and experiments shall be interesting, for the great purpose is that the child shall find pleasure in its work. His careful study of children led him to observe that certain subjects are more suitable than others for the development and discipline he sought. Thus observing the vast amount of time and labour spent by every child in the first ten years of its life in investigating the forms and qualities of things, and noting the influence of the former in giving the child the power of analysis, of distinguishing things, and of forming clear ideas, he gives a prominent place to form in early culture. He also attaches great importance to arithmetic, when it is so taught as to be

T

a matter of investigation to the children, as well as of reasoning based on operations presented to his senses. His two works on arithmetic should be in the hands of every teacher; they are invaluable contributions to right methods of instruction.

The following remarks from the *Saturday Review* set forth distinctly the principles of Grant's books on arithmetic. "The main principles upon which instruction in arithmetic to young minds is founded are simple and sensible. The first is that children should learn to realize the meaning of arithmetic by concrete symbols. They should not only know but see, that two and two make four. The number nine should not only be thought of as produced by the addition of a unit to eight, but should spontaneously call up a vision of nine spots arranged in various diagrams which show its identity with sets of five and four spots, or with three sets of three spots. The mere blank expression is thus translated into a sensible reality, and is much more easily dealt with by the childish understanding. And, secondly, the child should be made to understand the more difficult rules by a process resembling that which must have led to their first discovery. Instead of having a magical formula stamped upon his memory, the application of which will, for some mysterious reason, bring out the desired result, his infant powers should be gradually stimulated until the rule presents itself to him as the summary and complete expression of his crude anticipation.

"The old method was the reverse of this. It gave the logical instead of the natural order. The abstract conceptions which had been slowly reached by the mature intellect were impressed upon the childish mind, and the rules founded upon them explained in the most abstract language. Instead of developing the principles latent in the childish mind, a complete and ready-made system was thrust in, and frequently remained as a mere set of rules obstinately refusing to assimilate with previous acquisitions. But it is true of the matter with which arithmetic deals, that a vivid realization through the senses of its first truths is the best mode of approaching its difficulties. This study, like all others, has really its base in outward fact, and it must, like all others, be attained through the medium of sensible experience." The result will come the sooner, if every operation is given as a problem to be solved, and not as an example to which a rule is to be applied; and if the work given exemplifies in every new question a distinct principle or rule from that in the operation just completed.

Section III.—*Shuttleworth.*

Till within the last forty years primary education in England was left in the hands of individuals and societies. The prevailing destitution was however too widespread to be met by voluntary associations, and it consequently became necessary that the State should take some share in the education of the people. So early as 1807 Whitbread made an ineffectual attempt to move the House of Commons to take up this duty. Brougham, more fortunate, obtained the appointment of committees of inquiry. Many others were engaged in efforts to awaken and inform the public mind, through the press and on the platform, until at length the duty of the State to aid in the education of the people was owned in 1833 by parliamentary grants distributed by the Treasury. The obligation having been once admitted the necessity of further aid was soon apparent. In 1838 evidence was laid before a Parliamentary Committee that was quite appalling, and especially the statement by prison authorities :—"That the leading characteristic of the vast majority of those unhappy beings who came under their charge was a heathenish ignorance of the simplest principles of morality and religion." The conscience of the best part of the nation was grieved that such a vast amount of misery should arise from its own neglect. It found expression in the increase of the Parliamentary grant, and in the appointment on the 10th April, 1839, by an Order of Council of a Committee of the Privy Council to administer it. Of this Committee Sir J. P. K. Shuttleworth was the first secretary. Under his auspices were inaugurated a number of measures that have done more to place education on a satisfactory footing than all previous measures. Though it is perfectly true here as in physical science, that the labour of the present worker would have been impossible had it not been preceded and prepared for by those who have gone before. Amongst the measures of importance set on foot soon after his accession to office were the appointment of inspectors of schools, grants towards the erection and fittings of school buildings, provision for the training of teachers, and aid towards the maintenance of schools, by payments of the stipends of pupil-teachers, by gratuities to their teachers for instructing them; and by certificates to teachers, with a money value, the amount being determined by the grade of the certificate, and made dependent on the report of the inspector. Subsequently, after Shuttleworth had retired from the secretaryship, the modes of aid and the regulations respecting school were so frequently changed, that teachers were in a state of constant alarm, not knowing what a " Minute " might bring forth.

Amongst the services rendered by Shuttleworth was the drawing up of instructions on method in the form of minutes. His first minute describes a form of school organization which he introduced into the practising school at Battersea. It was an attempt to combine the advantages of Stow's system and that of monitorial schools. Four groups of paralled desks were so arranged that two contiguous classes could be formed into a division for a collective lesson by the master, while the other classes were worked by pupil-teachers. He called this the mixed mode, but it came to be better known as the Battersea Method. Other minutes dealt with methods of teaching. A tour through Europe, to acquaint himself with principles and methods of teaching, had imbued him thoroughly with a preference for synthetic methods. He bases his preference on what he supposed was nature's mode of educating the child. " During infancy the child has to become acquainted with the external world; his senses are in incessant activity; the sense of sight has to be placed in harmony with the sense of touch and of muscular movement; the distance, form, weight, and other qualities of objects have to be determined; the child is making continual discoveries; it constantly presses upon the region of the unknown. This process is chiefly synthetical. It is by the acquisition of new facts, and their combination with those already known, that the child gradually acquires knowledge, and corrects the errors into which he has fallen. In the acquisition of language he is greatly aided by his faculty of imitation. In the use of this faculty he proceeds in two separate directions. In the imitation of sounds he first tries those which are shortest and simplest, and gradually acquires the more complex. A similar law determines his progress in all that relates to the structure of sentences. He acquires the names of objects with which he is familiar, and first of those which interest his affections. Then he learns to name the qualities of those objects. Their motions, actions, and influence on other bodies follow; and in these and every other part of his acquirements the simple precedes the complex. By this constructive process all his early acquirements are made." Now it is obvious in these cases the infant mind had gone through a process of analysis before entering on the constructive stage, and every practical teacher knows that the success of educational efforts depends on the proper combination of both analytic and synthetic methods.

The application of a synthetic method to reading he endeavoured to secure, by obtaining the services of two foreigners, one to analyse the English language into its elementary sounds, the other to arrange in a couple of books the characteristic words of the language, in a series, which would admit of the Phonic Method. This compliment to Englishmen was made with full knowledge of the fact that the Phonic Method was first applied by Edgeworth. In favour of the Phonic Method he observes, " It recognises in the child a being whose reasoning powers are immature, yet a rational creature, whose memory may be most successfully cultivated when employed in subordination to the reasoning faculty. It depends to a large extent for its success on the truth that it is more difficult to remember contradictory facts (or those which seem so) than classes of consistent facts which express a rule or law satisfactory to the reason. In the former case, each fact has to be separately remembered, and the memory is therefore vexed with numerous independent efforts. In the latter, the pupil remembers classes of facts associated by some law more readily than he remembers the individual facts when presented to his mind without any attempt at arrangement. In the former case, the facts appear to be not merely separate, but contradictory; and in proportion as they are irreconcilable with any effort of the reason will they be difficult to remember. On the contrary, to show to a rational creature the mutual relations and dependences of facts presented to its intelligence, is to afford the greatest assistance to the memory, by enabling it to associate those facts in consistent groups, under comparatively a small number of laws. For a child to commit to memory that which it cannot understand is a difficult and by no means salutary exercise of the intelligence; but to conduct the instruction of a child, not only without any attempt to cultivate its understanding, but to require it to charge its memory with facts which, because contradictory, must be repulsive to its reasoning powers, is worse than useless. By such means a child at an early period separates all ideas of pleasure from instruction. The tyranny of schools commences when any unreasonable effort is required. In this way, likewise, is repressed that earnestness which characterizes the early efforts of childhood. Its generous spirit can only be cherished by leading it from one truth to another, and not from one contradiction to another. It is hurtful to the moral sense to commence the instruction of children by requiring them to commit to memory what they do not understand, or what is contradictory, and therefore revolting to their understandings. The moral sense can only be successfully cultivated by inspiring the child in every process of education with a love of truth.

"The first step to this result is to satisfy the intelligence on every point which can be rendered clear. The means to this end are the arrangement of the facts presented to the mind of the child in such order that each new truth may naturally succeed, and be supported by those which have preceded it, so that the child may require neither any great effort of the intelligence to comprehend, or believe, or remember, that which it is the object of the master to teach."

Now all this is excellent, but it is irrelevant. It has force against the method of teaching to read by teaching to spell with the names of the letters, but it does not support the phonic method. It is rather true of a synthetic arrangement of reading and other lessons than of the method to be used in each lesson. Here he is decidedly wrong in maintaining that analytic methods should be reserved till a very late stage in the child's progress; and only synthetic ones employed in the earlier, for following the rule he himself lays down, of following nature, every teacher must employ both analytic and synthetic methods.

"In observing the process which nature pursues in developing the intelligence, we see the senses of the infant first in activity; they are employed in collecting facts; the mind then gradually puts forth its power, it compares, combines, and at length analyzes the facts presented to it. Thus the child raises his attention above material objects. But whatever may be the differences which mark these successive periods of intellectual progress, the method of education which suits them is always the same. From the most elementary knowledge to the highest speculations one method is universally applicable. This consists, first, in carefully examining the constituent parts of any object before us, *i.e.*, in *analyzing it;* secondly, in classifying and separately considering these component parts. This is the work of the teacher in elementary schools; thirdly, in reconstructing the object which has thus been decomposed by the analysis of the educator, *i.e.*, in operating by synthesis. This is the work of the pupil, by which he is prepared for the more difficult work of analysis. When his mental powers are exercised in this way the attention is actively engaged." Holding these opinions he had prepared besides reading-books, manuals, and tablets for the promotion of writing and vocal music, the former on the method of Mulhäuser, the latter by Hullah.

Other services were rendered by Shuttleworth to the cause of elementary education. He was the founder of

Battersea Training College, and this institution retained for many years the impress of his mind. That the system he tried to establish, taken from Switzerland, was ultimately abandoned, arose from its being not suited to English habits and circumstances. His able coadjutors at Battersea were Tate and Macleod, men to whom English education is so much indebted. To Shuttleworth was due the system of school inspection, for which he drew out an elaborate scheme, a scheme that has not been improved by the departures therefrom.

Section IV.—Inspectors.

The earlier reports of Her Majesty's Inspectors of schools contained many valuable contributions to common school education. It was the practice to scatter these reports broadcast over the land. Many a teacher labouring in a remote district found himself encouraged and stimulated by what he found in them. Many a teacher had his mind first awakened to the importance of his work, and himself set on the right track, by the earnest spirit which breathed through the writings of Moseley, Fletcher, and others. To these early volumes, coming into his hands just as he was beginning his work, many a young teacher was indebted for many valuable hints, and for many important principles. Here he first learned the real nature of his work, and the spirit in which it should be conducted; and from them he obtained invaluable plans for its accomplishment. It was a pity that the *low* estimate of the work of the school, and the false parsimony which attended it, ushered in by the Revised Code, led to alterations in the reports themselves, and to the stoppage of their gratuitous circulation.

The reports of Professor Moseley cover a period of eleven years, and touch, amongst many other topics, some of the most important in elementary instruction. On religious instruction he observes, "I see the desire to implant principles of sound doctrine, and to furnish the memory with Scriptural truths,—all, in short, effected that may be learned as a lesson and enforced as a task,—but little, I fear, that appeals to those sensibilities which are the springs of action in childhood, and the elements out of which the Christian character collects itself in youth and manhood. The way to the hearts of children is easy to those who seek it; and I know not why the schoolmaster, who can call to his aid that power which is given him over the affections by the sympathy of numbers, should pass it by in the matter of their religious teaching, seeking rather to store their memories with the language of Scripture hereafter to be applied—if, indeed, religion ever becomes to them a matter of personal application,—or exercise their judgment with questions of controverted doctrine, in anticipation of a period when they may be called upon to defend it." "Religious truth should be presented to children so as to awaken the sensibilities and arouse the conscience, for they act not from what they know, but from what they feel. Their characters are forming themselves not upon principles, but upon feelings, reiterated until they become habits of feeling and laws of action. Religion is best presented to the mind of a child under the form of a principle of action. Appeals of Scriptural truth find their way most readily to the heart when supported by admonitions of conscience." "We are too much accustomed to confound our notion of a religious education with that of religious instruction, and not to consider that a place should be sought for religion in the heart and affections of children, as well as in their memories and understanding." "It is often difficult to know how religious principles are to be applied under certain practical conditions, and this stands in the way of the application of them. As, then, in secular, so in religious education, the science of application is of great importance. Our elementary schools should in this respect be schools of application,—of application by precept and by example; application so simple as to include the experiences of the child, but based upon principles which involve the destinies, for time and for eternity, of the man. The example of a school life controlled by Christian principles—of the mind that was in Christ, is a result which the faithful teacher will not fail to pray for, and which by God's blessing he may hope in some measure to attain to."

On discipline and moral training the following remarks are especially valuable :—" I have often been struck, in intercourse with teachers, with what appeared to me a want of faith in education. They have seemed to me not to have that confidence in the resources of it which, on the authority of Scripture and of reason, we are justified in having. We know that if we could but 'train up children in the way they should go, when they are old they would not depart from it;' and every day's experience tells us that men and women are very much what they were trained up to be as children. Yet very little attention is given to the training of children in schools. I believe the root of this lies in a want of faith in the power of the school to do anything for the training of the child, but only for its teaching. Yet the child is for six hours a day in the presence of the teacher, looking up to him for everything, at that period of its life when it is most open to the influence of example, when habits of thought for good or for evil are most readily formed, and when the heart and affections lie near the surface. It is, too, a great resource to the teacher to minister to the understanding of the child its daily food, to have the first tottering steps of its mind stayed upon his, to have the will of the child absorbed into his; and, if he be a skilful teacher, to command the public opinion of his school; and all this at that age when thus to be fed with the first elements of knowledge, thus to be supported in the first uncertain steps of the understanding, thus to yield to authority, is natural." The schoolmaster possesses vast power for training the children of his school, and he is always for good or evil unconsciously exercising it. "As I go from school to school I perceive in each a distinctive character, which is that of the master; I look at the school and at the man, and there is no mistaking the resemblance. His idiosyncrasy has passed upon it. I seem to see him reflected in the children as in so many fragments of a broken mirror. What importance this gives to the character of the teacher, and to his religious and moral training! It is not one of the least difficulties of his work that the children in whose presence he lives, and who will form themselves on his model, have a singular instinct in comprehending their teachers, piercing them with their little eyes through and through."

"Discipline in too many schools is maintained by the aid of corporal punishment. In some its infliction is limited to offences partaking of the nature of moral delinquency. In the great majority the punishment is awarded irrespectively of the nature of the offence."

He gives it as his opinion that the efficiency of a school, judged either as a place of moral training or of secular instruction, is in inverse proportion to the amount of corporal punishment inflicted in it; and for this obvious reason, that the master who dispenses with corporal punishment falls back upon those other resources of discipline which are of a moral character and a more abiding influence. He remarks, too, on the extent to which the habit of inflicting corporal punishment may grow upon the master, and of the callous endurance of it by children, as showing how pernicious it is. The school is ill-managed in which the moving principle is terror of the rod. Its unhealthy moral condition may be disguised from the master, but it is palpable to others. The very faces of the children show it. Sentiments of fear being habitual, a sullen apathy, or the sinister expression of a silent but resolute opposition, is the prevailing condition.

He attributes the prevalence of this mode of punishment either to want of temper or to ignorance of his profession on the part of the master. "The rod or the cane is an obvious and a simple expedient for getting the children's lessons learned, to which a teacher unskilled in the higher resources of his art invariably resorts, with the more energy as he is the more zealous for their welfare, and the more ignorant of the best means of promoting it. The demoralizing influence of a course of discipline like this outweighs any amount of technical knowledge of which it may be the price." "We little appreciate the power in education of patient, enduring, abiding love. Could we but bring to bear upon the work of the teacher the whole power that there is in love—never to be discouraged, wearied, or repulsed,—there is perhaps no obduracy of the heart of a child that would resist it, and no evil that it would not reach and purify. If in a school the spirit of love could remain unbroken from day to day and from year to year, that would constitute the perfection of its discipline. . . Men readily understand the discipline of punishment to secure obedience,—or of reserve; these are easy expedients, in the power of a bad teacher as entirely as a good one; but they do not so easily comprehend the discipline of love. Its fruits are not seen at once. It demands time, patience, perseverance, and is an expedient only within the power of a good teacher."

On the equipment of the teacher, the necessity of professional training, and the principles that should guide teaching, there are many remarks distributed through the reports. A schoolmaster is required to be meet not only for learning, but for dexterity in teaching. He must indeed not only have acquired the knowledge which he has to communicate, but be acquainted with the best methods of communicating it, and thoroughly practised in the use of those methods.

It is in the experience of every teacher, that to embrace a truth one's self, and to be able to present it under the simplest form to another, are essentially different things. It is necessary that teaching as an art should be made the subject of study. Mere practice of this art does not give proficiency. It has principles and rules,* which mustbe the subjects of rational investigation. There must be the habitual study of the best methods, and of the principles on which they are based. It is to be borne in mind that the work of the elementary schoolmaster is one of no ordinary difficulty. That the children who come to him have never been taught to think, have no knowledge which may form the subject of thought, and are without the means of acquiring that knowledge. He has to act on untutored minds, to give them the arts of learning, to teach them to think and understand, and to store their minds with material for thought. This is impossible to those who are not acquainted with teaching as a science as well as practised in it as an art.

"It is the triumph of the art of the teacher to break down the separation interposed between his own and the uneducated mind. From his own ample stores to select those adapted to form the first elements of the knowledge of a child, and so to present them as best to lead the child to reason upon them and to understand them. The principal object of a lesson has been lost in respect to any child on whose mind no impression remains when the lesson is over; and an obstacle has been interposed to its further progress if its reasoning powers have not been exercised, and its intelligence gathered strength from it. The child's mind has been unjustly tasked, and its attention, claimed where it was not due, has been simulated. Thus the efforts of the teacher, which ought to accustom it to apply its thoughts and to reflect on what it has learned, result in giving it the habit of a feigned attention and a wandering mind. "But of all the evils inflicted on a child who is compelled to listen to a lesson which it does not comprehend, the greatest probably is that which is involved in the sacrifice made of its faith in the teacher. 'The child comes into the world,' says Père Girard, 'not only with faculties to learn from others what he is ignorant of, but with a happy tendency to believe them. He is told and he believes. It is thus that the knowledge of others becomes his. Take away faith from the heart of a child, and how can it learn?' When day by day the child is compelled to sit a patient listener to instructions to which it attaches no intelligible meaning, how entirely is this faith sacrificed!" "The deception is carried on to positive falsehood when, in the examination which follows the lesson, the child is made to profess himself to have understood what he did not understand." "The failure of a schoolmaster as a teacher must impair his influence in whatever else, besides teaching, belongs to his office, a proposition the converse of which is also true. Such a teacher is likely to claim of the children that they should understand what he supposes himself to have explained to them, but really has not; and he is likely to be angry with them if they have not understood it. By this injustice he raises up an antagonism in the minds of the children, the more demoralizing that it must be disguised; or if the child remains unconscious that the failure is on the side of the master, and sets it down to his own incapacity to understand what the master has tried to teach him, the injury to the child is none the less by reason of the discouragement which he has experienced, and the distrust which, without foundation, has been created in his mind, of his power to reason and understand."

" Oral instruction is especially an agency by which an uninstructed child may be taught to think and reason; whilst it is the most direct, it is probably the most effectual means of imparting to it that definite amount of knowledge which the master may happen himself to possess. By a most useful reaction it becomes to him moreover a continual process of self-instruction, exercising his faculties of reasoning, and his powers of exposition, prompting him to study the minds of his scholars, and encouraging him to enlarge the boundaries of his knowledge. With this form of instruction it is, however, most important that the use of books should be combined. The child must be made a student. It is not enough that a certain amount of knowledge be imparted to it; if a process of self-instruction be not induced in the process of oral instruction a child is never an independent agent; he neither seeks knowledge for himself, nor unaided encounters any of the difficulties opposed to its acquisition. His mind leans continually on the mind of his teacher; and, unaccustomed to support itself, if some other state be not made to alternate with this, it goes with difficulty alone. It is in the well-balanced union of the two methods of oral instruction by the master, and self-instruction by the child, that the secret of elementary education appears to consist."

In oral lessons there is too often a tendency to travel out of the sphere of the intelligence of the children, and to bring before them subjects in forms unsuited to their years, and foreign to their interest. There is also a want of vivacity and energy in examination. The vagrant thoughts of the children constitute the chief obstacle a master has to contend with in teaching them. This unsettled state of the mind in children, the skilful master, knowing it to be proper to their years, rather seeks to turn to his use than to contend with. To keep alive the interest of the children in the lesson he varies it by frequent examinations; his questions follow in rapid succession ; they tend to a drawing out of the reason rather than the memory, and he shifts continually the point of view in which his subject is presented, giving prominence to those features of it by which it is related to things familiar to the children themselves. All that he does is founded on a careful study of the characteristics of childhood, and a just appreciation of them. He has carefully observed the ways of children, and the efforts they make to reflect, reason, and understand. Of the knowledge he has thus acquired he avails himself to command their attention ; and when this fails he calls the sympathy of numbers to his aid, or throws in the element of emulation. Warming with his task, the interest he feels passes to the children, and the whole group glows with the desire to know. This condition of mind is not transient, the lesson is repeated daily, and it becomes therefore in some degree habitual.

Of defects in oral lessons he observes, "Had the teacher known more of the subject-matter of his lesson, it has been my constant observation that he would have been able to select from it things better adapted to the instruction of children, and to place them in a simpler point of view. That he may be able to present his subject to the minds of the children in its most elementary forms, he himself must have gone to the root of it; and that he may exhaust it of all that it is capable of yielding for the child's instruction, he must have compassed the whole of it." "The cardinal defect of oral lesson in elementary schools is an inadequate knowledge on the part of the teacher of that which he is teaching. If his knowledge of it had covered a larger surface he would have selected matter better adapted to the instruction of the children. If he had comprehended it more fully he would have made it plainer to them. If he had been more familiar with it, he had spoken more to the point. I will endeavour to illustrate this by an example. A teacher proposing to give an oral lesson on coal, for instance, holds a piece of it up before his class, and having secured their attention, he probably asks them to which kingdom it belongs, animal, vegetable, or mineral,—a question in no case of much importance, and to be answered, in the case of coal, doubtfully. Having, however, extracted that answer which he intended to get from the children, he induces them by many ingenious devices, much circumlocution, and an extravagant expenditure of the time of the school, to say that it is a solid, that it is heavy, that it is opaque, that it is back, that it is friable, and that it is combustible. In such a lesson the teacher affords evidence of no other knowledge of the particular thing which is the subject of it than the children might be supposed to possess before the lesson began. He gives it easily, because the form is the same for every lesson; the blanks having only to be differently filled up every time it is repeated. All that it is adapted for is to teach them the meanings of some unusual words, words useless to them because they apply to abstract ideas, and which, as the type of all such lessons is the same, he has probably often taught them before.

"He has shown some knowledge of words, but none ofthings. Of the particular thing called coal as distinguished from any other thing he knows nothing more than the child, but only of certain properties common to it and almost everything else, and of certain words, useless to poor children, which describe those properties. Coal is a common thing to the child, one with which its daily observation is familiar, intimately connected with uses of its life—a substance about which it might be taught many things which would probably be of great use to it in after life, things which it would not be likely ever to know unless it were so taught them. This tendency, from ignorance of things, to teach children words only, runs in a notable manner through almost all of the lessons on physical science which I have listened to."

Other defects are noted. "An earnest teacher, by an excess of earnestness, sometimes becomes minute and interfering, and unconsciously he is unjust, not giving the children credit for being right in their answers when they are right, compelling them to shape such answers precisely in the words which he himself would use,—words not so good, perhaps, as the child's, because not so simple. This tendency is a cardinal defect in teaching, and I believe its influence to be extremely demoralizing." "An examiner ought not to require the answer in a tone of command, authoritatively, but simply as an interrogation, not leading but following the train of thought of the person examined, and, as it follows, guiding it. Some teachers seem to think that all that is required for a good examination is to question rapidly, unhesitatingly. The teacher should specially be upon his guard against an abrupt and over-confident manner in teaching, and a tendency to contradict the children for no other assignable cause than self-assertion when they have answered rightly. His mind should be entirely upon the children, and away from himself."

The plan first suggested by Professor Moseley, of organizing a common elementary school in three divisions, corresponding to the threefold work of such school, bore excellent fruit. The principles which he lays down are admirable. "To educate children, the action of an enlightened teacher upon them is required, with an individual application to each individual mind. There must be the separate contact of the mind of the master with the mind of the child; the separate study of it; the separate ministering to its wants, checking its waywardness, propping up and guiding and encouraging its first efforts, building it up and establishing it. The whole time allowed out of the life of a poor child for its school days is all too short. Nothing can be done unless the most powerful of the resources of the schoolmaster be brought to bear upon every moment of it. If his work be not taken in hand forthwith, not only will he have lost the most favourable season for it, but the whole opportunity. I claim, therefore, as a privilege of the child, and as a paramount duty of the master, that his own individual culture of the child's mind, his own direct and personal labour upon it, should begin from the moment the child first enters the school, and never be interrupted until he leaves it. That the child should not, for instance, be tossed about, as it passes through the school, from hand to hand, from teacher to teacher, beginning at that of the lowest merit, until, if it ever reach the first or second, it comes at length under the master mind of the school, which should have operated upon it throughout. It is not by a process thus broken and disjointed that anything great or permanent will be realized. Many elements of the character of the child, which the master would easily have read in the lowest class of the school, will be disguised from him if he first takes it up in the highest; many evils, which he might have corrected then, will now have become incorrigible : much that he might have built up by a gradual process, growing with the child's growth and strengthening with its strength, will be impracticable to any less sustained and continuous effort."

Accordingly he recommends that each school shall be formed into three groups, and that each group shall pass in turn into a room for oral instruction by the master ; the other groups, being one at preparatory work in classes and drafts, the other at silent exercises in desks. The system thus recommended largely modified the organization of schools. Provision was more extensively made than heretofore for oral teaching by the master, but the system as a whole never made its way, and for obvious reasons. It exacted more from the master than could be given long with safety to his health, and it made no provision for that moral oversight which at least is of as much importance as intellectual culture. The tripartite organization was subsequently adapted by Fletcher to the Borough Road Practising Schools, and in a modified form was extensively adopted in other schools.

This form of organization, modified to meet special circumstances, will probably continue to be employed in village schools. But the Act of 1870, in the powers with which it has invested school boards, has made possible an organization of schools which would go far to solve the problem how to educate to the best advantage the children of our urban population. This would be best done by a system of grade schools, but materially differing from those established by Stow. In his system each school was distinct under its own responsible master, but all the schools in the group were under one roof, with a head master, who was not only responsible for his own school, but for unity of system in all. In lieu of this plan, it would be better to place a group of grade schools in a district of given area, each school easily accessible from all parts of it. Each school in the group, occupying its own separate and distinct building, should have its own curriculum, corresponding to what now constitutes a standard of the Education Department. This should form the minimum of attainment in its own school, and the ability to do it should be the test for admission into the school of the next higher grade. Thus a system of schools would be established, each preparatory to the next in advance; each school would be under a head master, who would be absolutely responsible for its progress within the defined limits, but who would not be restricted to them, during the time the scholars were under his charge. Thus, too, there would be a system of schools which would begin at the very lowest point of elementary attainment, and proceed by easy gradation to the highest point of culture.

SEYMOUR TREMENHEERE was one of the earlier inspectors of schools. The faithfulness of his reports in pointing out defects in schools, and especially those found in British schools, ultimately led to his "promotion" from the inspection of schools to the inspection of mines. Yet he could appreciate and praise good work. "In the boys' school at the village of Illogan the Scriptural and catechetical lessons are made to consist of much more than mere reading and repetition. The due exercise of the understanding seems to be kept very constantly in view. Maps and a few books illustrative of Scripture are used to assist the apprehension, and to awaken greater interest by giving clearer perceptions. Lessons in geography, in the elements of astronomy, on physiology, on metals and minerals, flowers, and other subjects of natural history, tested afterwards, either catechetically or by writing, enlarge the circle of ideas and arouse curiosity. Maps are drawn on the black-board from memory, also on paper. The black-board is used for drawing and illustrating geometrical figures and simple objects of natural history or of art. Grammar is attended to. The arithmetic frame is used for beginners. Some few boys had gone through Bonnycastle's "Mensuration;" others had begun simple equations and "Euclid." None were above thirteen years of age."

In the same report of 1840 he thus incidentally speaks of oral collective lessons :—" The daily oral lesson, as given in the most improved day schools, tested by questions, or by writing its substance, could not fail of its usual result in awakening intelligence and a taste for knowledge. The tendency to fall into mere dogmatical teaching, outrunning in language and subject the intelligence of the children, is natural to those who have not prepared themselves, by previous consideration of each proposed oral lesson, for the difficult and important art of communicating it. The power of mastering any continuous subject, of reducing it to clear, logical order, and of presenting it to the minds of young children in simple terms, in regular gradation from its first steps or simplest element, so as to lead the learner along a clear yet almost insensible path of progression, is far from being of easy acquirement, and yet is amongst the first principles of sound teaching. The skill also by which every answer and every incident is turned to account by an adroit master, for moral or mental discipline, cannot be gained without attention and cultivation."

The oral lesson needs not only careful preparation, and a just appreciation of the several devices to be employed to secure attention and work, but a proper division of the children. "A school of 100" would be divided for this purpose into three large groups, each of which would receive in turn its lesson from the master. Such a lesson is thus described by M. de Gerando,—"In this lesson the teacher instructs and directs a certain number of children together, he addresses to all the same language, the same demonstrations; all execute at once the same things and act in union. He has his eye on all, and all observe and hear him. There is therefore more simplicity and more rapidity in his operations; the strength and time of the instructor are distributed with more economy; imitation and sympathy animate and sustain the children in that common progress which they are making together; the harmony of their labour keeps up a natural discipline.

"It is of the essence of this mode of arrangement and teaching that the children should be divided into large groups, each as nearly as possible equal in age, capacity, and progress. But even under the most careful management this method has its defects, 'as it cannot always happen, when the group is numerous, that all the children should really be of the same degree of capacity and advancement. The weaker therefore remain behind, or the more able are obliged to stop and wait for their comrades.' The mode of simultaneous answering is not an essential part of the simultaneous method of teaching. It is a very questionable practice, as affording a considerable opening for deception. The first words of the answer of the quickest often suggest the whole, is caught with rapidity by the rest, and passes as theirs. A better mode is to desire all who can answer to hold up their hands, and to take a certain number before deciding which is right."

On the function of the school to attend to the education of the whole child he has the following observations:—" The name of Pestalozzi is now so commonly and so exclusively associated with one of the valuable principles on which he insisted—that of making it a primary object of education to draw out and strengthen all the faculties, the physical as well as the intellectual and moral,—that it appears to be overlooked that in enforcing this he was only reviving and giving a more extensive application to what had been the enlightened practice of former times, and the principle of all the most philosophical writers on the subject of education down to his own day." The public and private education of Athens and Rome was eminently one designed to develop all the faculties,—in the language of Milton, "to fit a man to perform justly, skilfully, and magnanimously, all the offices, both private and public, of peace and of war." Fénélon was of opinion that it was of the first consequence "that this should be well heeded." Milton and Locke are of the same mind. Dugald Stewart thus defines the essential objects of education:—"They are, first, to cultivate all the various principles of our nature, both speculative and active, in such a manner as to bring them to the greatest perfection of which they are susceptible; and, secondly, by watching over the impressions and associations which the mind receives in early life, to secure it against the influence of prevailing errors, and, as far as possible, to engage its prepossessions on the side of truth."

That the teacher may rightly fulfil his duty in developing and improving the faculties, and in calling forth and regulating the affections of those committed to his charge, it is essential that he should have some acquaintance with the principles of the human mind. In general, his utmost aim at present, corresponding with the extent of his capacity, is to lead the intellect through some of the lower processes of elementary teaching. Even this branch of duty opens to him a field of usefulness on which he is seldom prepared to enter. Stewart says, "To instruct youth in the languages and in the sciences is, comparatively, of little importance if we are inattentive to the habits they acquire, and are not careful in giving to their different faculties, and all their different principles of action, a proper degree of employment. Abstracting entirely from the culture of their moral powers, how extensive and difficult is the business of conducting their intellectual improvement! To watch over the associations which they form in their tender years; to give them early habits of mental activity; to rouse their curiosity, and to direct it to proper objects; to exercise their ingenuity and invention; to cultivate in their minds a turn for speculation, and at the same time preserve their attention alive to the objects around them; to awaken their sensibilities to the beauties of nature, and to inspire them with a relish for intellectual enjoyment—these form but a part of the business of education; and yet the execution even of this part requires an acquaintance with the general principles of our nature which seldom falls to the share of those to whom the instruction of youth is commonly entrusted."

In the same direction are the following remarks:—
"The power of furnishing the mind, of enlarging and

improving it, can obviously belong only to a master who can command the stores of a well-cultivated mind, and has also learned the art of using them. It is such a one alone who can rise above the mere mechanism of teaching—can call forth all the latent faculties of his pupils, and raise them towards the level of his own. Such a one will see in the world around him some of the most important subjects on which to found his instruction, and will lead the young mind to test, by the true spirit of Christianity, its various acts, responsibilities, and duties. He will not overlook the importance of raising and regulating the character, through a due cultivation and development of the moral sentiments, and a watchful superintendence over the habits and conduct. To this end he will do what, in the generally over-anxious desire to convey a mere knowledge of material facts, is too often omitted—he will open the stores of high and generous examples which history contains, to warm the mind of youth, to raise the thoughts of age, and to invite imitation. The effect of not familiarizing the mind of the young with instances of this kind, inspiring a sympathy with generous natures, awakening admiration for acts of magnanimity and self-sacrifice, and kindling a love of country, is to produce a distrust of the existence of any such motives, and therefore to obstruct and discourage in many ways the cause of public improvement."

"The domain of imagination, through an acquaintance with our best poetry, is far too little cultivated in the ordinary day schools. It is almost entirely neglected. There can be no valid reason for overlooking so powerful an auxiliary in the work of raising the mind and mending the heart. Selected passages of some poetry and of the best prose might be committed to memory in every common school; and the sources of the most refined pleasure thus opened to the mind of youth would most probably yield support and refreshment to a whole life of temptation and toil. A sense of what is beautiful in taste, correct in thought and feeling, and exalted in conduct, might thence be diffused more widely, and the sentiments thus worked into the national mind would result no less in a just appreciation of the literature and institutions of the country than in a proper self-esteem. A schoolmaster who rightly estimates his power of benefiting the community will not throw away this instrument of its welfare. In every common school, passages copied into a book during the school hours might be learnt by heart at home."

He thus describes a class in a school inspected in 1842 :— "Their reading lessons were so conducted as to become a valuable intellectual exercise. If any inaccuracy arises, or any error in pronunciation, accent, or emphasis, the sentence is read again by the boy making the fault until it is corrected. An effort is thence induced to be accurate in the first instance. The meaning of the sentence is then required in their own language; the etymology of every compound word; various derivatives of the same root; the various meanings of the same word; the mode of its use in different senses; the words or clauses in a sentence, in opposition to or in connection with each other; finally, its government and the examples it affords of the rules of grammar and composition. A dozen pages gone through in this manner, slowly and carefully, will have done much towards giving a knowledge of language; while the mental effort required will have raised and strengthened the faculties. The advantage of this kind of training was shown by these boys in their writing exercise." He thus speaks of a class in another school :—" In the second class the first lessons are given on etymology."

INDEX.

ABBOTT; on reproof, 188; on character, 197; moral review, 229.
Æsop's Fables a reading book, 36, 47.
Alphabet; plain card, 45; on teaching the, 51; Bell's plan, 172; kindergarten, 159.
Amateurs and helpers, 262.
Analysis and synthesis, 280.
Apt to teach, 206, 287.
Arnold on chiding hastily. 7.
Aristotle on emulation, 184.
Arithmetic; early lessons, 53, 84; Pestalozzian, 145; Dunning on, 146; Mayo, 148; De Morgan, 148; kindergarten, 159; Lancaster, 193; Grant and *Saturday Review*, 274.
Ascham's schoolmaster, 4.
Attention, 33, 56, 166, 271.
Authority in moral training, 29. 122. 130.

Bell's monitorial system, 162.
Books, 14, 36, 45, 61, 68, 173, 191. 208.
Brougham, Lord, 263.

Caughie, prince of infant teachers, 212.
Caxton, 2.
Cecil on corporal punishment, 5.
Central Society and its work, 264.

Chadwick on Grant, 270.
Character a growth, 197.
Chaucer, 2.
Child-nature, 26, 28, 79, 122, 155, 224, 299.
Child, necessity of exertion, 69, 166, 168.
Children must be employed, 156, 272.
Cicero, 8, 11.
Classical learning and its advantages, 39.
Classification in school, 177, 192, 194.
Colet founds St. Paul's School, 3.
Collective teaching, 261, 290, 298.
Colour and form, 141, 160.
Comenius, 13.
Composition, 38, 47.
Conscience, culture of, 115.
Cornewaile introduces English into schools, 1.
Corporal punishment, 6, 8, 31, 189, 286.
Curiosity, 33.
Currie; action, 221; sympathy of numbers, 235.

Daily News on praise and blame 8
Development in education, 90, 97. 99, 102, 225.
Devices in school work, 170.
Discipline, 6, 18, 29, 62, 80, 120, 182, 196, 220, 286.
Discipline of natural consequences, 32, 62, 128.
Distinction, love of, 201.
Doddridge, pictures in early training, 14.
Drawing, 49, 159.
Dunning, 96, 116, 122

Edgeworths, father and daughter, 48.
Education; according to bias, 28, 40, 123; general, not special, 41, 72, 165; should be religious, 88, 104, 217, 266; principles, 88; should be organic, 89; harmonious, 91; must have unity, 104; essential conditions, 166; golden rule in, 167; relation to citizen, 265.
ducation, tendency to lose ground in, 93; want of faith in, 285.

Educational Department and its work, 276.
Educational systems, tests applied to, 103, 163.
English first taught in schools, 1.
Elementary school, 162; its function moral, 214.
Emulation; a powerful agent, 184; class, 202.
Enthusiasm necessary, 205.
Example stronger than precept, 119.
Experience the starting-point in moral culture, 118.
Exposition of reading lesson, 208, 303.
Evil should never be suggested, 27.

Fear in education, 18, 31, 63, 225.
Feelings, culture of, 113.
Fellenberg on public opinion, 198.
Form and colour, 141; form, 148; kindergarten, 159.
French; on learning, 38, 46.
Fröbel's kindergarten, 154.

Geography, 47.
Gill, Alexander, 4.
Glasgow Educational Society, 213.
God, child's first notions of, 106.
Grade schools; a system of wanted, 297
Graded schools, 238.
Graduation of lessons, 100, 142, 192.
Grammar and composition, 38, 46, 62.
Grant, Horace, 270.
Guessing, ludicrous instances, 257.

History; a home subject, 47; how taught, 61.
Home and Colonial School Society, 93.

Imitation a strong agent, 119.
Infant culture, 48, 83, 100, 135, 148, 273.
Infant school organization, 97.
Infant's schools; Oberlin, 76; Wilderspin, 77; Mayo's, 85;
  Home and Colonial, 93; kindergarten, 154.
Inspectors of schools; their reports, 282.

Intellectual system established, 202.
Interrogation and explanation, 207.
Intuition, 66, 135.
Invention, 50, 158.

Kindergarten system; anticipated, 48; Fröbel's, 154.
Knowledge, first through the senses, 66.
Knox's system, 38.

Lancaster's monitorial system, 189.
Langlande's Piers Plowman, 2.
Langler's phonic method books, 52.
Language; an instrument of culture, 16; pupils' ignorance of, 59; Pestalozzi's practice, 73; ideas before words, 83; object lessons, 136; exposition of, 208; word-getting, 257; Tremenheere on exposition, 203.
Latin, how to be learnt, 12, 45.
Learning; objects of, 7, 33; thorough and familiar, 10, 57, 171; sham leads to immorality, 17; relation to character, 21; not made irksome, 34, 50; not to be a game, 34, 41; no false associations with, 56; definite lessons, 170; relation to teaching, 240.
Learning, revival of, 3.
Lessons; short, 57, 271; on form and colour, 141; on objects, 71, 86, 136; on animals, 139; connection in, 58.
Liberty, not coercion, 90.
Little things in obedience, 201
Locke, John, 19, 83, 221.
Logical faculty, when cultivated, 247.
Long quoted, 183, 232.
Love of approbation, 132.

Managers of schools, how treated, 123.
Master; duties, 180; qualifications, 204.
Mayos, 64, 85, 96, 116, 119, 135, 141.
Memory, 7, 43, 242.

INDEX

Mental faculties, all to be trained, 72, 269, 299.
Method; importance, 42; with young children, 69; of discovery, 241; outlines first, 247; picturing out, 249; training out, 255; induction, 260; in education, 269; synthesis, 277.
Milton's views on education, 14.
Mind, knowledge of, necessary, 204, 265, 271, 298.
Mistakes; how corrected, 8; not to be ridiculed, 33.
Monitorial system; Bell's, 162; Lancaster's, 189.
Monitors; Comenius, 14; Bell, 175; Lancaster, 195.
Moral training; its position, 23; barriers, 25; discipline, 62, 111; chief aim, 80; moral intelligence, 74; nature, 81, 89; moral diseases, 89, 127; practice, not precept, 29; mistakes, 114; emotions of self, 116; moral instruction, 117; conditions, 223; playground and moral review, 228; inseparable from religious, 190, 215.
Moseley's reports, 283.

National system of education first mooted, 275.
Natural consequences of actions, 32, 62, 187.
Necker on a storm of words, 188.
Normal college first established by Stow, 213.

Obedience, 63; in little things, 201.
Object lessons, 71, 86, 136, 292.
Obstinacy, 32, 64, 128, 130.
Offences and offenders, 185.
Ogle on punishments, 125.
Oral teaching, 208, 238, 261, 290, 298.
Order of merit, 201.
Organization; grammar school, 47; infant schools, 97; Bell's plans, 174; Lancaster's, 193; graded school, 238; Battersea, 277; tripartite, 294.
Overwork is pernicious, 272.
Owen on infant training, 76.

Pain, its use in moral training, 30.
Palmerston on good writing, 174.

Penmanship, 37, 174.
Pestalozzi, 14, 16, 48, 54, 56, 64, 86 300.
Phonic method of learning to read, 51, 279.
Physical education, 22, 79.
Pictures; in early training, 49; in books, 14; in religious instruction, 108.
Picturing out, 14, 249.
Pillans' Letters, 203.
Pioneers in education, 1.
Plagiarism prevented, 47.
Plato, 7, 44.
Playground, 80, 82, 228.
Poetry, 62 302.
Practice must be frequent, 195.
Praise, 32, 132, 184.
Precept and practice, 29, 74, 76, 81, 220.
Precept and example, 81.
Principles and plans, 170.
Province of the school, 163, 190.
Public opinion in school, 186, 198, 231.
Punishment; discrimination between offences, 6; depriving of food, 25; seldom in a good school, 124; prevention, 125; spirit of, 127; by natural consequences, 128; design, 186; Moseley on, 286.

Quintilian, 44, 162.

Reading, 18, 34, 36, 44, 61, 161, 172, 192, 203, 208.
Redgrave on colour, 141.
Registers; paidometer, 181; of offences, 186
Reid on public opinion, 233.
Religious education, 75, 104, 106, 163 218, 266, 284.
Repetition, 171.
Reproof, 187.
Restraint, 91, 226.
Rewards, 32, 132.
Reynolds on moral instruction, 119.
Richter on toys, 49.

INDEX. 311

Rote teaching a failure, 203.

Saturday Review quoted, 34, 274.
Sceptical habit formed, 245.
School; work often fruitless, 67; a happy place, 80; a microcosm, 82; method tends to routine, 93; province, 163; moral function, 214.
School-keeping an art, 179.
School life periods, 100, 191.
Schoolmaster, 263.
Scripture prints, 168; instruction, 105; how used, 266.
Self-help, 167.
Senses in education, 66, 68, 83. 88, 135, 268, 273, 278.
Shame, the aim of punishment, 30.
Shuttleworth, 275.
Simple to complex, 70.
Size and weight, 145.
Spectator used in teaching English, 47.
Spelling to follow reading, 73.
Stewart, Dugald, on educating the whole man, 299.
Stow, David, 14, 83, 96, 210.
Sugden on Stow's system, 262.
Syllabification, Bell's plan, 173.
Sympathy; moulds character, 120; easily excited, 129; of numbers, 230.
Synthetic method, 277.

Taylor, Isaac, 134.
Tate's Arithmetic, 56.
Teacher; choice of, 21; confess ignorance, 34; few skilful, 93; weight of character, 125; not slave to routine, 170; influence, 183; qualifications, 204; should teach, 237; example, 280; skilful, 287.
Teaching; method, 83; tests, 167; requires enthusiasm, 190; outlines first, 247; should be studied, 288; inefficient, 292.
Tegetmeier on lessons on animals, 139.
Temptation as a moral agent, 226.
Things before words, 16, 69, 83, 88.

Thorough learning, 171.
Threats, 128.
Training system, 210.
Training and teaching, 213; training out, 254.
Tremenheere's reports, 296.
Trial by jury, 186.
Tripartite organization, 294.

Understanding and memory, 242.
Understanding essential to learning, 10.

Ward anticipated Pestalozzi, 56, 146.
Whitbread attempts to obtain aid to education, 275.
Wilderspin, 77, 96.
Will, training of, 63, 199.
Wits, quick and hard, 9.
Wolsey's instructions to masters, 3.
Wood's Intellectual System, 202.
Words pictured, 251; word-getting, 258.
Writing, 37, 159, 170, 174.
Wykeham's school at Winchester, 2.
Wyse on educational reform, 265.

THE END.

www.ingramcontent.com/pod-product-compliance
Lightning Source LLC
Chambersburg PA
CBHW030755230426
43667CB00007B/972